Land-Use Planning in Oregon

A No-Nonsense Handbook in Plain English

Land-Use Planning in Oregon

A No-Nonsense Handbook in Plain English

Mitch Rohse

Oregon State University Press

Corvallis, Oregon

∞

The paper in this book meets the guidelines for permanence and durability of the Committee on Production Guidelines for Book Longevity of the Council on Library Resources and meets the minimum requirements of the American National Standard for Permanence of Paper for Printed Library Materials Z39.48—1984.

Library of Congress Cataloging-in-Publication Data
Rohse, Mitch, 1943-
    Land-use planning in Oregon.

    Bibliography: p.
    1. Land use—Government policy—Oregon. I. Title.
HD211.07R64   1986   333.73'17'09795   86-12457
ISBN 0-87071-349-3 (alk. paper)
ISBN 0-87071-350-7 (pbk. : alk. paper)

CONTENTS

About This Book   *vi*

About This Author . . . and Those Who Helped Him   *vii*

Chapter 1: The Oregon Program   *1*

Some Reasons for Planning   *1*

Some Myths about Planning   *2*

Oregon Builds a Statewide Program   *3*

After Acknowledgment   *6*

Coordination   *8*

Bringing the Citizens into Planning   *8*

How Much Does the Program Cost?   *9*

Chapter 2: The Permit Process   *11*

Planning Permits   *12*

Building Permits   *16*

Pollution-Control Permits   *17*

Special Permits   *18*

The One-Stop Permit   *20*

Permit Costs   *20*

Is the Permit Process Tougher in Oregon?   *21*

Chapter 3: How To Get A Permit   *23*

Chapter 4: A Glossary of Planning Terms   *38*

Bibliography   *252*

Appendix: Oregon's Statewide Planning Goals   *255*

About This Book

Oregon has the most extensive land-use planning program of any state in this country. Every acre of privately owned land in this state is zoned. Every acre is subject to a comprehensive plan. Planning affects the cost of your home, the distance you drive to work or shop, your property taxes, your schools, your police.

But in spite of the significant effects of land-use planning, many Oregonians don't know much about it. There are several reasons for this. First, Oregon has a relatively new program. Even those who developed it or who administer it are still learning just how it works.

Second, the program is complicated. It combines law, ecology, economics, engineering, and politics. Any one of these fields is difficult to know and understand well. Small wonder, then, that the combination of all five is hard to grasp.

Finally, even though "citizen involvement" is the first among Oregon's planning goals, not much has been written to explain Oregon's planning program to its citizens. Most planners and lawyers have been writing for other planners and lawyers. Their jargon-laden prose isn't comprehensible to those who are not in the field of planning. Come to think of it, some of that prose isn't comprehensible to those of us who are!

The reasons described above have prompted me to write this book. This is a no-nonsense, plain-English guide to land-use planning in Oregon. It is intended mainly for lay persons—for elected officials, real estate salespersons, developers, planning commissioners, students, permit applicants, and the active, involved citizens that are so important to the program. Because so many lay persons have their first encounter with planning when they apply for some kind of permit, the book pays particular attention to the process of applying for permits. It offers many suggestions on how to make that process as painless as possible.

The first chapter provides a brief overview of Oregon's program, that unique combination of state and local planning. The second discusses the permit process that results from that combination. Chapter 3 tells you the "dos" and "don'ts" of getting a permit. The fourth chapter is a glossary of planning terms—a concise encyclopedia with more than 600 entries, from "abate" to "zoning ordinance." The Appendix contains Oregon's statewide planning goals.

As you read the book and encounter unfamiliar terms, turn to the glossary for an explanation. The glossary entries define the terms; many of those entries also discuss key concepts and issues and direct you to related subjects.

I hope you will find this book to be helpful in understanding a program that so strongly affects us all.

About This Author . . .

My career in planning began in the same year that Oregon's legislature adopted a statewide program of land-use planning—in 1973. I worked as a planner with Lane County for two years. Later, I went to Polk County, where I eventually became Director of the Department of Community Development (which encompassed the planning, building, and sanitation divisions). Since 1980, I have been associated with the state Department of Land Conservation and Development in Salem, where I am now the department's information officer. I have taught courses in planning at Oregon State University and Chemeketa Community College. I was appointed to the Board of Directors of the Oregon Chapter of the American Planning Association in 1986.

Before I became a professional planner, I was a Peace Corps volunteer, a weather observer in the Air Force, and a professional student. During seven years at the University of Oregon, I got a Bachelor of Arts degree in political science and a Masters degree in urban and regional planning. I also spent two years in postgraduate work at the University of Hawaii, where I worked as a graduate teaching assistant in geography and was awarded a full scholarship from the East-West Center's Institute for Population Studies.

Although I have been associated with several different agencies in state and local government, this book is strictly my own endeavor. I have received no grants or other formal assistance to produce it. Any errors that you may find are strictly my responsibility.

. . . and Those Who Helped Him

That is not to say that I had no help. Many people have assisted me, providing valuable comments, suggestions, and editing. Many thanks to all of them, particularly those listed here:

- Walter Friday, of the state's Building Codes Division
- Marvin Gloege, Linn County's Planning Director
- the late Paul Gerhardt, Jr., of 1000 Friends of Oregon
- Linda Hilgart, super typist
- Wes Kvarsten, Director of the Bonneville Power Administration's Division of Land Resources
- Gary Messer, of Oregon's Department of Environmental Quality
- Claire Puchy, Director of Portland's Audubon Society
- Elaine Rohse, writer
- Steven Schell, lawyer and former commissioner on LCDC
- David Siegel, planner for the City of Salem
- Daniel Smith, former Administrator of the Oregon Building Codes Division
- Laini Smith, planner and graduate student at Oregon State University

The following persons from the Department of Land Conservation and Development answered many questions and saved me from several blunders: Dale Blanton, Bob Cortright, Ron Eber, Craig Greenleaf, Eldon Hout, Jim Knight, Dick Mathews, Don Oswalt, Mike Rupp and Patty Snow.

Authors rarely have kind words for editors, but I have nothing but good things to say about mine. The OSU Press's Jo Alexander did an excellent job of bringing this book into print, and she was remarkably patient and considerate through it all.

I owe a special debt of thanks to my wife, Louann. She remained cheerful, supportive, and good-humored as my supposedly six-month project went on to take four years.

CHAPTER 1
The Oregon Program

Until the early 1970s, land-use planning in Oregon was pretty much like planning in other states. It was, first of all, almost entirely a local matter. The state passed legislation that enabled planning and zoning to occur; the cities and counties took it from there. And, second, 'planning' wasn't really planning at all; it was the administration of zoning and subdivision ordinances. Most cities and some counties did have 'general plans,' but these were often vague documents that gathered dust on the back shelves of planning departments. Meanwhile, many planners spent most of their time out at the front counter issuing permits. Big questions like "How much land should the city zone for industrial uses?" or "Will that proposed subdivision overextend the municipal water and sewer systems?" often remained unanswered while planners concerned themselves with setbacks and sideyards.

Some Reasons for Planning
Rapid population growth and its accompanying development in the sixties and seventies prompted many Oregonians to become concerned about those larger questions of land use. Underlying their concerns were two basic issues, issues that arise from almost any type of development and land use: environment and economics.

The environmental issues of land use are more tangible and easily understood. A century farm is converted to a subdivision, for example, and 200 acres of prime soils are lost. A shopping center springs up, and nearby streets become congested. A mill locates along a stream, and once-clear waters become polluted. Such problems, particularly the loss of farmland to leapfrog subdivisions, were the principal reason that Oregon's legislature adopted a statewide program for planning land use.

Economics was the other major issue underlying the development of Oregon's planning program. In a state where farming and forestry are the two largest industries, it is obvious that the loss of farm and forest lands could have serious effects on the economy. A less obvious but equally important economic aspect of land use is the cost of public services. A compact city requires fewer streets, shorter sewers, smaller water pipes and fewer police and fire fighters than does its sprawling counterpart. A single industrial park with four firms in it is cheaper and more efficient to serve than are the same four firms scattered about at separate locations.

The relationship between land use and costs of public services sounds obvious in the abstract, but in reality it is hard to evaluate. The principal reason is that the costs of services are disguised in 'average-cost pricing.' Under average-cost pricing, you pay the same rate for service as all the other service users in your district, regardless of how the actual costs to serve you may differ.

Let's illustrate that with an extreme example. The Jones family and the Smith family both live in River City. It isn't a big town, but it sprawls over many square miles. The Joneses live 5 miles from the nearest school, so their children are taken there on a bus; the Smith kids walk to school. The Joneses also are 5 miles from the municipal sewage treatment plant, the water works, the library, the electrical generating plant, the police station, and the fire station; the Smiths are within a block of them all. The costs to River City of providing municipal services to the Joneses clearly are far higher than the costs of serving the Smiths. But the Joneses and the Smiths pay the same rate for those services—rates that have been averged over an entire city, either in user fees (the monthly electricity bill, for example) or taxes (e.g., property taxes for schools). In a very real sense, the Smiths are subsidizing the Joneses.

The example is not meant to be an indictment of average-cost pricing. Such pricing was developed and will continue to be used because it is simple. Imagine the difficulty of establishing true marginal-cost pricing for public services! ("Well, Mr. Jones, your property tax rate will be .023 percent higher than the Smiths' because the police had to drive 2 miles farther than average to patrol your residence, and their cost of travel is 27 cents per mile . . .") But the example serves to show that the use of land has very real effects on the costs of public services, that those effects are not accurately reflected in taxes or service rates, and that the community therefore must find other ways to achieve an efficient distribution of public services. Since average-cost pricing encourages—even subsidizes—an efficient pattern of land uses, the community attacks the problem with other tools: planning and land-use regulations.

Some Myths about Planning

This brings us to a popular myth about planning: "Planning conflicts with free enterprise." That myth derives from a notion that planning is some sort of frivolous environmentalism—that it is quick to sacrifice jobs and profits to save a snail darter or a few barren acres of sagebrush. Those who subscribe to this myth see various proposals for development turned down or regulated by planning and zoning, and they conclude that planning frustrates development and free enterprise.

As with all myths, there is an element of truth in this one. The costs of permits and other forms of planning and regulations certainly add to the costs of development. And some individuals and communities have tried to use planning to stop growth, not to guide it. But for the most part, the myth is false. In fact, economic development *requires* good planning. New businesses must have access to effective public services and facilities. They must be protected from conflicts with other land uses. They may require that certain essential resources, such as timber or water, be available. And they have a strong interest in maintaining a high quality of life in their community. All of those attributes are more likely to be found in the community with effective planning than in the town where anything goes.

As for planning and free enterprise, let us return to the Joneses and the Smiths in River City. That community was reluctant to control land use. In the name of free enterprise it allowed the leapfrog subdivision where the Joneses now reside. A closer look at the situation, however, reveals the very opposite of free enterprise. The developer of that subdivision got a direct subsidy from River City: he got to use cheap land at the city's fringe and did not have to pay for the extra costs of extending sewers, waterlines, streets, fire protection, and law enforcement services to this suburban location. And the Joneses are still getting a subsidy on their property taxes, electricity rates, and so forth, as described above. New developments in River City now will have to face higher costs for public services. Or they may not be able to get them at all if River City has overextended its facilities.

When a firm tries to manage its land, capital, and resources in the most efficient manner, that's called good business. When a community does the same, it's called planning—and one is usually good for the other.

Oregon Builds a Statewide Planning Program

Let's get back to Oregon in the late 1960s and early 1970s, when concerns over growth, the environment, and the costs of public services were sparking an intense interest in planning. In 1969, the legislature established ten statewide planning standards, and it required all local governments to adopt comprehensive plans. That was no small step, but the legislation's effects were dampened by two flaws: the state did not appropriate any money to support the making of all those comprehensive plans, and it did not establish any agency to administer the statewide standards.

In 1973 the legislature set out to resolve those problems by adopting the now famous Senate Bill 100. The new law (later codified as Chapter 197 of the Oregon Revised Statutes) created the Land Conservation and Development Commission (LCDC). LCDC's charge was to "prescribe planning goals and objectives to be applied by state agencies, cities, counties, and special districts throughout the state" (ORS 197.005). The new law also established a state agency, the Department of Land Conservation and Development (DLCD), to administer the statewide goals. Finally, the law appropriated enough money to make the program work.

Bold, new, controversial—all those words describe Oregon's program for statewide land and resource planning. And as might be expected with any such program, it drew, and continues to draw, considerable attention. As a result, many persons see planning in Oregon as nothing more than LCDC and its goals. What tends to be forgotten is that Oregon's 241 cities and 36 counties do the actual planning of land use, and a variety of local, state, and federal agencies conduct programs to manage various types of land, development, and resources. LCDC only sets certain standards and coordinates the programs.

Perhaps it would be useful at this point to clear up a few common misperceptions about the program. First, the state of Oregon does not plan and zone land. State law requires that land be planned and zoned, but it is the cities and counties that carry out that law, not the state. Oregon thus is covered not by one plan, but by a mosaic with 277 pieces.

Second, LCDC and DLCD do not issue permits. Applications for variances, conditional uses, zone changes, partitions, subdivisions, and related planning actions all are filed with and acted on by cities and counties. Some local actions may be subject to review by LCDC, but generally the state of Oregon is not directly involved in the issuance of planning permits. (For a description of other types of permits that are issued by various state agencies, see Chapter 2.)

Third, Oregon's planning program sets no limits on population growth— neither ORS Chapter 197 nor the statewide goals require or even mention restrictions on growth. The notion that the program does aim to slow growth probably arises from the fact that Oregon's governor and some other prominent persons in the early seventies did call for limits on the rapid influx of population that was occurring then. Those sentiments, however, were not transformed into law. In fact, LCDC has routinely approved local plans that contain high projections of growth. It has even ordered some jurisdictions (the small city of Happy Valley, for example) to amend their plans to accommodate greater growth.

Fourth, Oregon's statewide planning standards—the nineteen goals— are not all directed at the conservation of resources. Goal 1 deals with citizen involvement. Goal 7 requires protection against natural hazards. And Goals 8 through 12 all *require* local governments to provide for certain types of development: recreational facilities, commercial and industrial land uses, housing, public utilities and services, and transportation systems.

The form of planning in Oregon, then, is not so much different from that in other states, but the substance is. In most states, the cities and counties may plan and zone; in Oregon they must. In most states, standards for local planning are not uniform from one jurisdiction to another, are not particularly high, and are not enforced by any state agency; in Oregon, general planning standards (the goals) are the same throughout the state, they are high, and they are administered by an agency with clout.

The state of Oregon has clearly identified its interest in and the need for planning. It has not, however, taken over that job. Rather, it has entered into a partnership with local governments to see that the job gets done. The partnership was formed from the following process.

The Land Conservation and Development Commission developed a set of statewide goals for land-use planning in 1974. They were adopted after one hectic year and dozens of hearings throughout the state. The text of the goals is found in the Appendix.

As LCDC adopted statewide goals, its newly created administrative arm, the Department of Land Conservation and Development (DLCD), began to distribute grants to local governments to enable them to bring their plans and ordinances into compliance with the new state standards. Most jurisdictions received several thousand dollars. Some of the larger ones received hundreds of thousands of dollars over a period of several years. Most of that money was spent to hire planning staff and to cover administrative costs of public hearings, mailing, and printing.

With the standards in place and the money flowing, LCDC and DLCD began reviewing local plans. It was originally thought that most cities and counties could bring their comprehensive plans and implementation measures into compliance with the state goals within a year or two. Local governments would submit their plans to LCDC for review. LCDC would specify what changes were needed. The local governments would make the changes, LCDC would aprove the plans, and the bulk of the work would be done by the end of 1976.

These assumptions proved to be highly optimistic. The process took far longer than expected. One full decade after the beginning of the program, a few cities and counties still didn't have their plans approved ('acknowledged' in Oregon's planning jargon).

The failure to complete the review process as rapidly as had been hoped has been one of the biggest sources of disappointment and frustration about the program. Defenders of the state accuse some cities and counties of foot-dragging. Some local officials cite LCDC red tape and 'moving goalposts' as the main problems. The accusations from both sides contain some truth.

It must be remembered, however, that the main objective of Senate Bill 100 was not to get plans acknowledged. Rather, it was to establish effective planning of land and resources throughout the state. What often gets lost in the argument about acknowledgment is that the main objective of SB 100 has been accomplished. Even the cities and counties that got acknowledged late in the process have established planning programs that are far more extensive and effective than those of a decade ago.

Once a local government's plan and land-use regulations have been acknowledged by LCDC, the state's role in local planning decreases greatly. The main difference between the pre-acknowledgment and post-acknowledgment phases is this: before acknowledgment, each land-use decision (a zone change, for example) must be reviewed against the statewide goals. The local government must consider not only the requirements and standards of its own plan and ordinances. It also must weigh and conform to all of the statewide goals. Because there are 19 goals and because they cover a broad range of topics, even a simple land-use action can be a major undertaking prior to acknowledgment. After acknowledgment, the goals for the most part need not be considered. They have been embodied in the local plan. Only if the jurisdiction seeks to amend its comprehensive plan or implementation measures does LCDC get involved.

There are several reasons for a local jurisdiction to seek to get acknowledged. First, state law (ORS 197.250) requires it. Second, there often is a financial incentive: state maintenance grants are given to jurisdictions with acknowledged plans. Third, there is the threat of an enforcement order by LCDC if local progress toward acknowledgment occurs too slowly. Finally, the state may withhold cigarette, liquor, and gas tax revenues from jurisdictions that do not complete their planning in a timely manner. In most cases, however, those reasons remain less important than the procedural one described above: acknowledgment returns a large measure of planning power to a local government and facilitates local decision making.

Acknowledgment does not bring an end to planning. Communities and environments will change, often in unforeseen ways, and plans will have to change accordingly. A plan, after all, is not a prediction but a statement of goals and how to achieve them. A family would adjust its budget after an unexpected raise or paycut. Similarly, a local government must adjust its plan in response to unforeseen population growth, new technology, loss of revenues, and other changes. The law specifies that such adjustments must be consistent with state goals.

After Acknowledgment—
Plan Amendment and Periodic Review

A common problem in land-use planning is that many people focus on the product (the plan) rather than on the process (planning). When the plan is being developed, the planning commission meetings are long and lively. After the document gets adopted, everyone congratulates each other and goes home. The plan gets put on a shelf to gather dust, and the development officials are left to administer permits. (I'm exaggerating somewhat, but the problem is real.)

Planning is an ongoing process, and developing a plan is only one part of the process. Keeping the plan up to date, interpreting it, and applying it are some of the other parts. In the case of Oregon's statewide planning program, the acknowledged plan is the most conspicuous product. The statewide planning program, however, is a process—one that continues after acknowledgment.

Oregon has invested a lot of time and money in acknowledged plans. The state therefore has devised two systems for keeping those plans up to date and off the dusty shelf in a back room. One is the plan amendment process. The other is periodic review.

If you think of Oregon's planning program as something like owning and driving a car, then plan amendments are the irregular and unscheduled repairs you have to make: replacing a worn-out battery, repairing a punctured tire, etc. Periodic review is the scheduled maintenance: a thorough set of checks and adjustments made periodically to keep the car running at its best.

Oregon's laws on plan amendment are set forth in ORS 197.610-.625. They specify that when a local government expects to make some change in its plan or land-use ordinances, it must notify DLCD at least 45 days in advance. DLCD then can comment on whether it finds the proposal to be consistent with the statewide goals. If DLCD finds no problem, the local government can go ahead and adopt the amendment. The local government can still adopt the proposed amendment even if DLCD finds a problem with it, but DLCD is likely to appeal that action to the Land Use Board of Appeals (LUBA). Note that DLCD has no power to stop the local government from acting, and that LCDC is not involved at all.

DLCD reviews several thousand plan amendments every year. It typically participates in about one-third of them, making suggestions to local governments about how to keep the amendments consistent with the goals. DLCD has appealed fewer than 1 percent of the amendments to LUBA.

Oregon's laws on periodic review are found at ORS 197.640-.650. Under these provisions, cities and counties must review their acknowledged plans every three to five years in accordance with a schedule developed by DLCD.

The city or county must review its plan against four periodic review factors. In effect, it must ask four questions. Has there been a "substantial change of circumstances"—rapid and unforeseen growth, for example—since acknowledgment? Have any new goals or state planning policies been adopted? Have any state agencies adopted new programs that affect land use? Are there any tasks that remain uncompleted from acknowledgment?

If the answer to any of these questions is yes, then the city or county will have to amend its plan accordingly. DLCD will review the local government's findings regarding the four factors, and will evaluate the resultant plan amendments (if any) against the goals. If DLCD is satisfied, its director can terminate the review. The process ends there, unless some qualified objector appeals the matter to LCDC. If DLCD is not satisfied, it issues a report to LCDC. LCDC reviews that report and affirms the local government's actions or directs it to take corrective action. In the periodic review process, LCDC gets involved only if DLCD's director or a qualified objector brings the matter before it.

Plan amendment and periodic review share few characteristics with acknowledgment. Acknowledgment was a broad and comprehensive process of building plans; plan amendment and periodic review are narrower processes for maintaining and operating those plans. Acknowledgment was flexible and largely unconstrained by detailed statutory requirements; the two post-acknowledgment processes are defined in great detail in the statutes and thus have little flexibility. LCDC was involved in every acknowledgment; it is not involved in any plan amendments, and it hears only those periodic reviews that get appealed to it.

Coordination

Considerable attention has been focused on the relationship between LCDC and local government. In fact, many perceive planning in Oregon to be largely a two-party process involving a new state agency and the traditional local planning authorities. That view omits a third group very important to the process, namely state and federal governmental agencies and special districts. There are dozens of agencies and thousands of special districts that affect land and resource use in Oregon. Some of them, such as the US Forest Service, own and manage the resources on millions of acres of land. Others, such as the state Department of Environmental Quality, regulate certain types of land use and issue permits. Many of them have long-range plans and management objectives.

Oregon's planning laws and goals do not overlook the great effect that nonlocal governmental agencies and special districts have on land and resource management. ORS Chapter 197 sets forth the responsibilities of state agencies and special districts to coordinate their planning activities with local comprehensive plans and to make their programs consistent with the statewide goals. Goal 2 requires cities and counties to involve affected governmental units in the developing of comprehensive plans. It also requires that the plans and actions of those governmental units be consistent with local acknowledged plans. Finally, OAR (Oregon Administrative Rule) Chapter 660, Divisions 30 and 31, establish various procedures for coordinating the programs of many state agencies.

Bringing the Citizens into Planning

But the group most significant in this state's planning program isn't an agency or government: it is Oregon's citizens. Goal 1 sets forth detailed requirements for the continuing involvement of the public in the development, adoption, and amending of comprehensive plans and land-use regulations. The state's standards for citizen involvement are high, and in most jurisdictions they have been met. At the same time, the courts have also expanded the opportunity for citizen involvement through certain decisions pertaining to notice, remedy, standing, and other aspects of procedural due process.

Many individuals have capitalized on the openness of Oregon's planning program by forming special interest groups. Some of these groups have only a few members and their concerns focus on a single neighborhood. Others, however, are statewide organizations with professional staffs and hundreds or even thousands of members. Interest groups of all kinds have been influential in developing local comprehensive plans, in shaping local and state policies on land use, and in appealing local land-use decisions.

Oregon's encouragement of citizen involvement, particularly the open appeals process, continues to be a lively point of debate. Persons sympathetic to the developer and the permit applicant argue that such extensive involvement destroys the predictability which planning is supposed to bring. If every permit applicant faces the threat of an appeal, how can the process be said to be "predictable"? Other persons argue that the essence of planning lies in the day-to-day decisions made by local governments. Without some citizen participation at that level, the "real" planning gets done by a tight little group of officials and developers. If citizens cannot get involved where it matters most, how can they protect their interests?

How Much Does the Statewide Planning Program Cost?

There is no simple answer to this question. 'The program' is in fact a combination of programs involving local, state, and federal agencies. The Department of Land Conservation and Development, for example, not only administers Oregon's statewide planning program, it also runs the federally supported coastal zone management program for the state. The state's Land Use Board of Appeals (LUBA) was part of LCDC's budget at one time, but is

Table 1.   *LCDC's Budgets for the Decade 1975-85*

Biennium	Type of Costs	State General Fund	Other	Federal	Total
1975-77	Administration	687,563	0	856,660	1,544,223
	Grants	2,200,000	0	2,200,000	4,400,000
	Total	2,887,563	0	3,056,660	5,944,223
1977-79	Administration	1,173,855	0	874,456	2,048,311
	Grants	6,225,977	0	2,000,000	8,225,977
	Total	7,399,832	0	2,874,456	10,274,288
1979-81	Administration	1,521,140	0	1,714,672	3,235,812
	Grants	3,933,555	0	1,928,776	5,862,231
	S. Slough Sanctuary	0	0	122,932	122,932
	Total	5,454,695	0	3,766,380	9,221,075
1981-83	Administration	2,227,514	109,400	874,600	3,211,514
	LUBA	435,120	0	0	435,120
	Grants	2,351,611	0	657,150	3,008,761
	Total	5,014,245	109,400	1,531,750	6,655,395
1983-85	Administration	2,932,696	23,368	635,060	3,591,124
	Grants	1,994,035	0	672,697	2,666,732
	Total	4,926,731	23,368	1,307,757	6,257,856

not now: should LUBA be counted as part of 'the program'? Local governments incur planning costs as a result of state requirements, but they also
get sizable planning grants from LCDC and would have been planning and
zoning even if LCDC had never existed. How, then, does one separate local
costs from costs for statewide planning?

I do not pretend to know the answers to such questions. The best
indicator of costs that I can suggest is LCDC's budgets, from which Table 1
is derived. The figures are from five books: the state Executive Department's
Adopted Budgets for the bienniums (two-year fiscal periods) from 1975 to
1985. All the numbers come from those books' columns of "legislatively
approved budgets," except for the totals in the right-hand column: they are
my calculations.

If all those numbers seem a little overwhelming, the main points are
these:

• The first full decade of the program had a budget of just over $38
million.

• One-third of that was funded by the federal government, for coastal
programs.

• 63 percent of the program was for grants, most of which went to
cities and counties. In other words, three out of every five dollars went into
grants.

The numbers in the table account for far less than 1 percent of the total
state budget. The state's total budget for 1983-85 was over $11 billion.
LCDC's budget for that biennium, including grants and federal dollars,
amounted to well under one-tenth of 1 percent of that figure. In terms of staff,
the Department of Land Conservation and Development is among the smallest of state agencies. Its forty positions in the 1983-85 budget amount to less
than one-tenth of 1 percent of the state's total (41,320 positions).

CHAPTER 2
The Permit Process

We have seen that land-use planning in Oregon rests on a foundation of nineteen goals. Growing out of those goals are the policies and plans of 277 cities and counties. But how are the goals, policies, and plans turned into reality? How can the lofty and abstract objectives of a community or an entire state be made to have some real practical effects?

That question of 'plan implementation' is the most important one in land-use planning. Planners have dealt with it by coming up with quite an array of what they refer to as implementation measures, the tools of the planning process. Differential taxation, capital improvements programming, 'greenbelts,' and transfers of developmental rights are some examples of measures used to put plans into effect. By far the most important planning implementation measure, however, is the direct regulation of land use through various laws, such as zoning and subdivision ordinances. And the way in which governments apply those laws is the permit process.

Let's return to the hypothetical River City of Chapter 1 to show how this system works. Suppose that the citizens of River City decide that one of the policies for their community is to minimize conflicts between residential and other land uses and to provide for adequate air circulation, privacy, sunlight, and fire protection in residential areas. The implementing measure they use to carry out that policy is zoning: they establish residential zones in which no nonresidential structures may be built, where all lots must have at least 6,000 square feet, and where all buildings must be set back at least 10 feet from any property line. Finally, they specify that any person who wants to build a structure or divide land in such a zone must obtain a permit.

That last step is not necessary for every land-use regulation. Many communities have ordinances that restrict the heights of fences, for example, but they do not require that one obtain a 'fence development permit' before building a fence. The law is simple for fence builders to understand and comply with, and the benefits to be derived from having a special permit process for fence building would be far outweighed by the costs to fence builders and the community.

More complex development regulations, however, necessitate a permit process. A government cannot assume that everyone will know about, understand, or honor such regulations. By requiring prospective land developers to get permits, a government accomplishes three things. It gets information about what types of development are happening in the community. It gets an opportunity to convey to the permit applicant information about the community's laws and standards. And it gets an opportunity to turn down or require modifications to those proposals that do not satisfy the laws and standards. It is far more effective to enforce the laws at the planning stage than to take legal action against offending structures after they have already been built.

My example of policy, implementation measure, and permit from River City sounds simple, but the reality of land-use regulation is often complex. Many different governments and agencies have policies on land development, and they use hundreds of laws and standards to implement those policies. The result is a multitude of different types of permits and permit procedures.

Like most states, Oregon has four main categories of development permits: planning, building, pollution-control, and special permits.

Planning Permits

In one sense, almost all land-development permits could be called planning permits, because they are used to implement plans and policies for land use and development. It is far more common usage, however, to apply the phrase to a smaller category of permits: those administered by city and county planners and governed by local zoning and land-division ordinances. The following list describes the land-use actions that commonly are considered to be planning permits:

- Approvals of farm or nonfarm dwellings
- Conditional uses
- Major partitions
- Minor partitions
- Plan amendments
- Planned unit developments
- Subdivisions
- Variances
- Zone changes.

Each of the above terms is discussed under the appropriate entry in the glossary beginning on page 38.

Larger cities and more populous counties have one or more professional planners who administer the planning permits. Smaller jurisdictions use consultants, city managers, city recorders, building inspectors, and other officials to handle applications for planning permits.

Decisions on permit requests are often made by a hearings officer, who may be the planning director of a jurisdiction or an attorney employed in this role. Planning commissions still make some of the day-to-day administrative decisions, but there is a clear trend away from this.

The simplest, most routine types of planning permits (minor partitions, for example) usually involve no public hearings, take a week or two to be issued, and have fees less than $150. The most complicated actions (plan amendments, subdivisions, zone changes) have one or more public hearings, take several months to process, and involve hundreds of dollars for permit fees. Table 2-1 shows the planning permit fees for seven jurisdictions in the Willamette Valley.

Most planning permits involve some form of 'notice,' an official announcement that a permit request is to be reviewed. Such notice is an invitation to persons who might be affected by the land-use decision to participate in its making. Notice may be given in advance of the decision, in which case interested persons can submit written comments to the decision makers and testify at the public hearing (if there is one). Sometimes, official notice is only given immediately after a decision is made. In that case, interested persons can participate in the decision making only by filing an appeal.

Notice about a land-use decision may be given in several ways. The planning department may run an advertisement about a pending land-use decision in the local newspaper two or three weeks before the permit request is to be reviewed. The same department may mail notices to the owners of neighboring properties. Placards describing the permit request and inviting

Table 2. *Permit Fees in Dollars for Seven Jurisdictions in the Mid-Willamette Valley**

	Minor Partition	Major Partition	Conditional Use	Variance	Zone Change
City of Independence	25 per parcel	25 per parcel	85	65	110
City of McMinnville	75	75	150	100	275
City of Monmouth	100	100	100	75	200
City of Salem	231	231	256	101	406
Marion County	175	175	170	100	345
Polk County	140	140	175	125	300
Yamhill County	50	75	150-225	150-225	200-375

* These figures represent the costs for routine permit requests in 1986; fees may be higher for some special actions. The City of Salem charges $750 for a "nonresidential zone change petition," for example.

public participation may be posted on the subject property. Finally, the planning department may send announcements of permit applications to any citizen advisory group that deals with planning in the neighborhood or district where the subject property is located.

Applications for many types of planning permits are reviewed in public hearings. Such hearings usually are fairly informal: witnesses are not sworn in or cross-examined, and participants usually are not represented by attorneys.

Most planning permit actions can be appealed locally, to a hearings officer, the planning commission, or the governing body (that is, the city council or board of county commissioners). Some jurisdictions allow a two- or three-step appeals process through several of these tribunals. That opportunity for appeals is available both to the permit applicant and to those affected or aggrieved by the decision (see **standing** in the glossary). In other words, any applicant whose request for a permit is denied initially probably will get a second or third chance locally. But the applicant whose request is approved may find his or her permit jeopardized because of an appeal from a neighbor.

Because of the appeals process, most planning permits do not take effect at the time they are issued but 10 to 15 days later, at the end of the period in which appeals can be submitted. If an appeal is received within the prescribed period, the permit is 'stayed': that is, it does not take effect until the appeal is resolved.

State law requires that cities and counties take final action on any request for a planning permit within 120 days of the time when the complete application for the permit was received. That schedule includes all local appeals.

After the local appeals have been exhausted, decisions on planning permits can be appealed to the state's Land Use Board of Appeals (LUBA). Beyond that, appeals go to Oregon's Court of Appeals and then to the state Supreme Court.

Most local planning departments do not have code enforcement officials to inspect development sites and enforce ordinance requirements after planning permits have been issued. Instead, the planners often rely on the building inspectors to do that job.

Suppose, for example, that a local planning regulation specifies that all buildings must be set back at least 100 feet from a certain scenic river. An applicant for a permit to build a house near that river is advised by the planners about the setback requirement and then goes on to get a building permit. It is not the local planner who later goes to the building site to see whether the house is at least 100 feet from the river; the building inspector is charged with that task.

Some building officials are uncomfortable with that dual role. They feel that they have their hands full just administering building code requirements, and they sometimes do not have much appreciation for or understanding of planning requirements. Planners, on the other hand, argue that the building

Figure 1. The appeals process is very much like a ladder. Appellants must start at the lowest step. If they want to go on, they must ascend one step at a time. The number of lower rungs and the names on them vary from place to place, but the top three rungs are the same throughout the state.

inspector must go to the site anyway to inspect construction, and they argue against the creation of yet another layer of bureaucracy, i.e., the 'planning inspector.'

Regardless of which opinion is right, it is often the case that planning permits are not monitored or enforced as closely as other types of permits. That will probably continue to be true as long as local planning departments do not have their own field staff.

Building Permits

Construction of almost all types of buildings and large structures through-out Oregon is subject to state regulations (ORS 456.775). The entire set of regulations is called the state building code. "The code" is really a collection of more than a dozen specialty codes, each of which deals with some specialized topic: structure, plumbing, mechanical systems, electrical wiring, boilers, elevators, etc. The most extensive of these specialty codes is the *Structural Specialty Code and Fire and Life Safety Regulation* (Building Codes Division 1986). It is based on the Uniform Building Code of the International Confer-ence of Building Officials (ICBO). For that reason, some persons refer to Oregon's structural specialty code as "the Uniform Building Code" or "the UBC." Some persons are referring only to the structural specialty code when they say "the building code."

In 1986 the Building Codes Division of the state's Department of Com-merce produced a code for one- and two-family dwellings. That document was intended to be a simplified code for homebuilders. It is made up mainly of excerpts from the broader *Structural Specialty Code.*

Anyone who intends to build any type of structure that is subject to the state codes must have his or her plans reviewed against the applicable codes and must get a building permit—*before* beginning construction.

Most large cities and counties employ local officials to administer the main state codes. In such places, the applicant for a building permit can get plans for structures, wiring, and plumbing all reviewed and approved at the city hall or courthouse. Some smaller cities do not have their own building officials but instead contract with the county for such permit services. Finally, many less populous cities and counties do not employ any building officials or have service contracts. In such places, applicants have to seek permits from state building inspectors at the nearest regional office.

The review of detailed construction drawings and specifications is a time-consuming process. For the simplest project, it may take only a few days, but occasionally several weeks may be needed. Building officials often face a sudden rush of applications for building permits in the spring, causing delays and frustration for would-be carpenters inspired by the first sunshine of the year.

After a building permit is issued, building officials will inspect the project at various stages of its construction to ensure that the approved plans and the applicable requirements are being followed. This necessitates continuing coordi-nation between the permit applicant, the builder, and the officials. For example, the electrical inspector usually must inspect the wiring in a house before insulation or sheetrock is put on the walls. If the inspector is busy or if the construction site is far from the inspector's office, the inspection process may delay construction.

The maximum fees for permits governed by state codes are set by the state. Most involve a sliding scale: the cost of the permit depends on the value of the project. The fee for a building permit, for example, is calculated according to a scale of values set forth in Table 3-A of the state's structural code. The permit and plan-checking fees for a $50,000 home in 1986 added up to $466.95.

Building permits differ from planning permits in that the former are **ministerial,** while most of the latter are **quasi-judicial.** (See the glossary for discussion of these terms.) Ministerial actions do not involve notice to surrounding property owners, public hearings, or other procedures that are required for quasi-judicial actions.

Building permits also differ from planning permits in another way: the applications for planning permits usually are not subject to a local appeals process. If an applicant for a building permit encounters undue delays or other administrative problems with a building official who is employed by local government, the applicant should deal with the local department head or elected officials. There may be a 'structural code review board' or some similar local body that the applicant can turn to. Problems with the provisions of a state code or the way in which they are applied, however, often must be directed to the appropriate *state* body—the Structural Code Advisory Board, for example.

Pollution-Control Permits

Oregon's Department of Environmental Quality (DEQ) administers programs to control air pollution, water pollution, noise, and solid waste disposal. Six main types of permits are associated with those programs:

- Subsurface sewage disposal
- Air contaminant discharge
- Waste discharge
- Indirect source contamination
- Water pollution control facility
- Solid waste disposal site.

As with building permits, the programs for all of the above are administered primarily by the state, but counties can contract with the state to provide local permit services. Local pollution-control officials are known as sanitarians. Most of the more populous counties employ one or more sanitarians, primarily to handle the numerous requests for subsurface sewage disposal system (septic tank) permits. In the less populous counties, applicants for a septic tank permit (or any other pollution-control permit) must deal with the nearest DEQ regional office, in Astoria, Bend, Coos Bay, Medford, Pendleton, Roseburg, or Salem. The DEQ's headquarters is in Portland.

Most of the pollution-control permits listed above apply only to large commercial developments or to very specialized projects such as a municipal sewage treatment plant. The subsurface sewage disposal permit program, however, affects many amateur builders and small projects. Roughly 30 percent of Oregon's homes use septic systems (Department of Environmental

Quality 1981). Almost any builder of a rural residence will have to rely on such a disposal system—and get the permit for it.

The first step in getting a subsurface disposal system approved is to have the proposed site evaluated by an sanitarian. He or she will test the soils at several different places on the property, find the best location for the system, and determine what kind of system is needed.

A few sites just are not suitable for any of the fifteen subsurface systems approved by the DEQ. In most cases, however, one or more of the approved systems will work. The main problem with difficult sites is that the exotic systems needed to serve them are much more expensive than the standard system.

An approved site evaluation is an assurance from the DEQ that a construction and installation permit for a specific system can be issued at some point in the future—after one buys the property or gets a loan to build a home, for example.

The state's fee in 1986 for a site evaluation for a new dwelling is $150. The fee for a construction and installation permit for a standard septic system is $120; for a special system, the permit may be as high as $280. The permit fee may be reduced by $60 under certain conditions if the permit is sought within six months of having a site evaluation. Note that these fees are what the DEQ charges. Counties with their own sanitarians may opt to charge less than the state does; they cannot charge more unless authorized to do so by the DEQ.

Subsurface sewage disposal permits are ministerial actions. No notice is given to adjoining property owners; no public hearings are held.

Some DEQ officials known as variance officers have the authority to modify the standards for subsurface sewage disposal systems under certain conditions. Applicants for septic system permits who do not receive approval initially may seek a variance from such an officer, or they can request a denial review from regional DEQ officials.

Special Permits

In addition to the planning, building, and pollution-control permits described above, there is a very long list of regulations and permits that apply only to certain specialized structures, land uses, and activities. Some of those permits derive from local ordinances. It is not uncommon for cities to have special permit procedures for tree cutting, placement of signs, design review of certain commercial structures, and solar access, for example. Other special permit procedures grow out of federal laws. See, for instance, the discussion of federal regulation of interstate land sales under **subdivision** in the glossary. Most of the special permits are associated with state programs.

Some of the activities, structures, or types of development that typically need special permits or would be subject to special regulations are listed below:

- Airports
- Altering, demolishing, or moving a historical structure
- Appropriation of groundwater
- Billboards
- Building a road across a railroad
- Building a structure near an airport
- Building in a floodplain
- Community water supplies
- Condominiums
- Construction along a beach
- Converting an apartment building into a condominium
- Dams
- Demolition of a building
- Drilling for geothermal energy, oil, or gas
- Field burning
- Fill and removal (of soil, rock, sand, etc.)
- Fuel storage facilities
- Mobile homes
- Mobile home parks
- Power-generating plants
- Recreational vehicle parks
- Taking access onto a public road
- Salmon hatcheries.

Construction in or near the following types of areas also may be subject to special permits or regulations:

- Agricultural lands
- Beaches and dunes
- Estuaries
- Forest lands
- Hazardous building sites (steep slopes or unstable soils, for example)
- Natural areas
- State trail routes
- Waterways
- Wetlands
- Wildlife habitats
- The Willamette River Greenway.

It is not feasible to describe special permits at length here. Most of them are associated with less common forms of development and thus are of little interest to the reader who only seeks to find out what is involved in getting permits for, say, a new home. Beware, however! 'Special' permits can become very much a part of what appears to be a routine project. The applicant who seeks to build a home on farmland, for example, may find the project anything but routine if the building site is in a floodplain, access to the home must come off a state highway and across a railroad track, and there is already one dwelling on the farm. The application for such a project would involve half a dozen agencies, as many permits, and months of processing, and it could be denied for any number of reasons.

The One-Stop Permit

That example of the nonroutine farmhouse in the floodplain highlights a problem that is common to many development proposals: they involve several permits, different sets of regulations, and a variety of agencies.

Development officials are well aware that permit applicants often face a bewildering array of regulations and redtape. They have made many attempts to ease that problem and to streamline and consolidate permit procedures. A few years ago, most cities and counties in Oregon had separate planning, building, and sanitation divisions, often housed in separate offices or buildings and under different managers. Today, many cities and counties have established 'departments of community development' (or some similar title) that bring all those divisions together under one roof and one manager. Indeed, state law requires them to develop 'consolidated' systems (ORS 215.416(2) for counties; ORS 227.175(2) for cities).

Many applicants today can get a 'one-stop permit' for routine development projects. Permits generally are processed faster and more efficiently than they were a decade ago. But the one-stop permit is by no means universal, and it never will be.

Regardless of the obvious benefits of the one-stop system, regardless of the well-intentioned law and the real progress that has been made, many applicants for development permits still face a multi-stop, multi-agency process. That is one of the costs of having a federal system with strong state governments and considerable local control over development procedures. The only way to have a real one-stop permit process would be to have one superagency at the state or federal level administer all controls on development. After reflecting on the alternatives, most people probably would prefer local control over greater centralization.

Permit Costs

In the preceding sections I cited several examples of permit fees. A very general rule of thumb for such fees is this:

• Fees for one simple ministerial action typically run $50 to $150.

• For the combination of permits typically required for construction of a rural home (partition, septic tank, and building permits, for example), expect to pay $500-$1,000.

• Fees for big or complex projects will cost more than $1,000—perhaps much more.

Two other types of expenses related to permits add greatly to the 'front-end costs' facing a developer: service charges and fees for professional services.

Service Charges. Most local governments require applicants for certain types of permits to pay costs incurred by the government in extending services such as sewers and water lines to the new developments. These 'hook-up fees' typically cost several hundred dollars for an urban dwelling.

In the last decade many local governments have turned to systems development charges (SDCs, also known as impact fees) to finance public facilities and services. Anyone new to development should be aware that SDCs can add greatly to the front-end costs of development. An SDC for a single dwelling could run into thousands of dollars. For a large industrial plant, the charge might be tens or even hundreds of thousands of dollars.

The SDC differs from the hook-up charge in that the latter is limited to the immediate costs incurred by the city or other service provider in connecting the new building with existing services, mainly sewers and water lines. The SDC, on the other hand, is designed to recoup some of the costs to the community likely to be generated over several years by the development—costs from the generation of traffic or large volumes of effluent into sewers, for example.

Cities and counties also may require applicants for certain types of permits, particularly subdivisions, to dedicate land to the local government for streets, parks, and schools. Applicants may also be required to pay cash in lieu of land for those same purposes. (See **exactions** in the glossary.)

Fees for Professional Services. Fees for technical advice and professional services are not charged by the permitting agencies, but they often are incurred because of permit requirements. An example is surveying. The applicant for a partition may be charged only $50 by a county for the permit to divide land. But he or she may be required to survey the property before it can be divided, and a survey of rural property could cost several thousand of dollars. Permit applicants often incur significant costs for the professional services of attorneys, engineers, hydrologists, architects, planners, surveyors, or draftsmen. The need for such services depends of course on the type and complexity of the development that is being proposed.

Is the Permit Process Tougher in Oregon?

Since Oregon has the most extensive planning program in the country, it might be assumed that permit applicants face a tougher challenge in Oregon than in other states. That conclusion is supported by several facts.

First, because the planning program is so extensive, some persons must obtain permits for activities that are not regulated in other states. Rural land in some states is not zoned, for example; in Oregon all private urban and rural lands are zoned.

Second, the standards for approving permits in Oregon are high. Permit applicants often must satisfy stringent requirements that are rooted in state laws and goals.

Finally, Oregon's emphasis on citizen involvement in land-use planning has fostered extensive citizen participation. Many citizens and interest groups are well informed about and actively involved in community planning, and development proposals that do not satisfy all applicable standards are perhaps more likely to get appealed in Oregon than elsewhere.

However, Oregon's planning program also brings some real benefits to the permit applicant. First, it establishes a process that is predictable. Every community has a plan that specifies where and how development should occur. The rules of the game are for the most part clear and objective. That protects the permit applicant from spurious appeals and from any meddling bureaucrats who might otherwise be inclined to make up their own rules.

Second, the restrictions in Oregon's program are balanced by some incentives. The developer of an industrial plant knows quite well that his plant cannot be built on farmland, for instance, but will find in every community's plan a clear description of where such a plant can be located. In effect, that developer has a promise from the community that the plant can be built in certain areas that are protected from conflicting land uses and that will get suitable public services.

Finally, Oregon has taken steps to streamline its permit process. It has set time limits on the length of time for processing permits. It has passed laws requiring consolidated permit administration, and it has created a special court to deal exclusively with matters of land use.

CHAPTER 3
How To Get A Permit

In the preceding chapter I described a complex system of permits, regulations, and agencies—and probably scared some readers who had been thinking about applying for some type of permit. Please keep reading. You need not rush out to hire an attorney or a planning consultant. A great many development permits are obtained by amateurs who have had little or no experience with the permit process. You too can be a successful applicant, particularly if you take a few minutes to learn the most basic rules of the game. That is the purpose of this chapter: to explain those rules and to provide some suggestions for the person who is seeking a development permit for the first time.

Reading this chapter is not guaranteed to make the permit process fun, nor can I promise that your application will be approved. I do believe that the following suggestions will lessen frustration, make the process faster and easier, and greatly increase the odds of getting the permit you seek.

I am a planner and this is a book about planning, so my comments here are focused on the proper steps to obtain a planning permit—a variance, conditional use, zone change, partition, or subdivision. Most of the suggestions, however, are equally valid for other kinds of permits. Certainly the first rule is.

1. Assume that you will have to get a permit.

If you intend to divide land, build any structure larger than a doghouse, do a major remodeling, or change the use within a building (convert your home to a florist shop, for example), assume that the activity is regulated by government. Assume that you do not know all the applicable regulations. And assume that you will need to obtain some type of permit.

A few types of development are not regulated by government, but the great majority are. Play it safe: ask about permits before you begin pounding nails. If your inquiry reveals that no permit is necessary, then you will only have wasted a little time. If you assume no permit is needed but discover midway through your project that your assumption was wrong, the costs may be very great indeed.

The corollary to the above rule is this: assume that several permits may be needed. See Chapter 2 for a description of the many agencies that regulate land development and the different kinds of permits they require.

2. Get the required permits before you commit yourself to a project.

One fine summer day a few years ago, a cheerful middle-aged woman walked into the county planning office where I worked and asked me about putting a mobile home on a rural parcel of land that she owned. I checked the zoning and found that mobile homes were listed as a conditional use in the zone that applied to her land.

"I don't anticipate much problem," I told her. "The planning commission will review your application in a public hearing, and you will have to meet certain requirements for parking, storage, and skirting around the mobile home. I can't promise you how the commission will decide on the request, but if you meet those requirements, I think it's safe to say that the odds of getting the permit approved are quite high."

"When will the planning commission be able to hear my request?" the woman asked. Her smile had disappeared.

"Their next meeting is in four weeks," I replied. "If we get your application filed immediately, we should be able to send out our notice and get you on the agenda."

With that, the woman burst into tears. "Four weeks!" she exclaimed. "I have already put money down on my mobile home. They are going to deliver it to my property tomorrow!"

This particular story had a happy ending. The county issued a 30-day permit to store the mobile home on her land without hooking it up to a septic tank or water system. Four weeks later the planning commission reviewed the permit request and routinely approved it. But what if they had not?

The moral of the story is this: make sure that you know what kinds of permits are needed, and get them *before* you put money down, sign a contract, or even get too engrossed in dreams about your project.

Yes, some people beat the system. Ignorant or contemptuous of the law, they add on a room or divide their land illegally and never get caught. That was particularly true before the 1970s. The advent of statewide planning in Oregon, however, has generated considerable interest in and knowledge about land-use planning. Local officials and your neighbors are much more aware of the planning laws and are much more inclined to insist on their enforcement.

If you do go ahead without the required permits, you risk some or all of the following consequences:

• The local building official may slap a stop-work order on your project, and demand that you get the appropriate permit. Even if your project qualifies for the permit, you may lose several weeks of construction time. If you have to modify your plans to satisfy the permit requirements, you may have to spend much more money than you had expected.

• Local officials may get a court order calling for you to abate (dismantle or remove) your project.

• You could be fined or even wind up in jail. Some jurisdictions do specify criminal penalties for violations of land-use laws.
  • You could wind up in court—or in a whole series of courts.
  • You could have some very stressful encounters with your neighbors.

3. *Make your first inquiries at city hall or at the county courthouse.*

Although the state sets many of the rules and regulations for land development, the administration of development permits is carried out primarily by local officials. Almost all planning permits are handled by local planners, and even the permits for state building and sanitation programs are most often issued by local building officials and sanitarians.

If you will be dealing with property inside city limits, your first step should be to contact city hall. For areas outside a city's corporate limits, contact county officials at the courthouse. A special situation arises if the property lies outside city limits but inside the city's urban growth boundary. Land in such urban growth areas usually is regulated by the county, but some counties and cities enter into agreements whereby the city exercises control over permits there. If you are uncertain who has jurisdiction, try the county first.

There is considerable variety in the ways that planning, building, and sanitation programs are managed, so you may have some difficulty finding the name of the appropriate office. Larger cities and counties often combine all three programs under a department labeled 'Community Development' or 'Environmental Management.' Other jurisdictions may have three separate departments. And the less populous cities and counties may not have any local planning, building, or sanitation staff: rather, they administer their programs through some combination of private consultants, attorneys, state officials, and staff on contract from other local governments. Regardless of that variety of systems, a call to your city or county will get you started toward the right office.

4. *Allocate adequate time to obtain the necessary permits.*

The amount of time needed to get a permit depends mostly on four things: the complexity of the permit being sought; the efficiency of the agency processing it; the extent of opposition to the permit; and appeals. The simplest of permit actions can be processed in less than a week. An unusually complicated zone change that gets dragged through the courts in a series of appeals might take years. A simple permit involving a persistent applicant and a determined appellant also can get caught up in a lengthy series of appeals— from planning commission to city council to LUBA to the Court of Appeals and perhaps even to the state's Supreme Court.

Sometimes, a permit application gets caught in a series of remands. Consider a request to partition some farmland, for example. The county approves the request initially, but a group dedicated to the preservation of farmland appeals that decision to the Land Use Board of Appeals. LUBA can affirm, reverse, or remand the county's decision. (See **remand** in the glossary.) LUBA remands, declaring that the county's decision was not supported by adequate findings. Such a remand does not say that the county's decision was wrong; it only says that the decision was not properly documented. The county is left with three choices: it can reconsider the case and deny the permit application; it can appeal the remand to the state's Court of Appeals; it can bolster its findings and reissue the permit. If the county chooses that third option (as is often the case), the matter may very well get taken to LUBA again.

State laws specify that local permit processing, including local appeals, must be completed in 120 days (ORS 215.428 for counties; ORS 227.178 for cities). The amount of time that the Land Use Board of Appeals can take to decide its cases also is limited by state law (ORS 197.830). Likewise, appeals from LUBA to the state's Court of Appeals must be acted on within time limits set by ORS 197.855.

You can help reduce the amount of time needed to process your permit. First, make sure that your application is complete, has all the necessary signatures, and is accompanied by all the required materials (more about that later). Second, plan your project far enough ahead to avoid the busy season: an application that would be processed in one month in January may take three or four months if it is submitted in May.

5. Allocate adequate money for permit fees.

Fees are charged for processing applications for almost every type of permit. They will constitute a significant part of the total expenses for most projects. See Chapter 2 for some examples.

The next sentence will prevent a lot of misunderstandings, so please read it carefully. *Permit fees are not refundable even if your request for a permit is denied.* A few jurisdictions will refund the money paid for an appeal if the appellant prevails, but the general rule still holds: there is no money-back guarantee on permit applications.

Fees for state-run programs are for the most part similar throughout Oregon. Fees for planning permits vary from one place to another. Low fees are not necessarily evidence of more efficient management. More often, they reflect differences in the viewpoints of the governing bodies. Some cities and counties set their permit fees strictly on the basis of actual costs. If it costs $200 in staff time, gasoline for trips to the building site, postage, and paper to review an application for a partition, then the fee for a partition is set at $200. Other jurisdictions set their fees at prices lower than the actual costs of administration. Such cities and counties are, in effect, subsidizing permit applicants with money from their general funds.

Some jurisdictions consolidate their fees for multiple permit applications. If you apply for a variance and a partition at the same time, for example, you would be charged only for the higher of the two, not for both. Do not expect such special rates for all combinations of permits. If a city is charging $200 for a variance and $600 for an associated building permit, for example, the $600 is to administer requirements from the building code, not from the city's zoning ordinance. Rest assured that the city's planning department will not give up its $200 just because a permit required by the building code is going to cost you another $600.

6. Discuss your plans and proposals with development officials before you apply for any permits.

Some applicants for permits are in a hurry. They dash into the planning department, accost the nearest secretary, and say something like, "Give me an application for a variance." Only later do they discover that it was a conditional use permit that they needed. Great haste in the beginning is likely to cause confusion, mistakes, and lost time later in the process. A far more effective approach is to make a preliminary visit to the development officials. Explain to them what you want to do, not what kind of permit you think you need. Find out what regulations will apply to your project and how the permit process works.

Many planning departments have formalized such initial discussions. They require a preapplication conference before they will accept an application for a permit.

7. Find out who will be involved in the decision-making process.

The simplest of permit applications involve only two people: the applicant and the administrator. A more complicated permit might involve the planning director and the planning commission. At the worst extreme (one involving a quasi-judicial or legislative action that gets appealed), the application might go through these levels: planning staff, development review committee, neighborhood advisory group, hearings officer, planning commission, city council, state Land Use Board of Appeals, the Court of Appeals, and the state Supreme Court. Few applications get that complicated, but it is wise to know all the possible players before you get into the game.

Applications for planning permits may involve some organizations that the applicant has never heard of. These special committees and advisory groups usually have no formal power to deny or approve a permit request, but their recommendations may be quite influential. Check with the local planner to see whether your application will be reviewed by any of the following groups:

• *Neighborhood Advisory Groups* (also known as citizen advisory committees, planning advisory committees, neighborhood planning organizations, etc.): Almost all cities and counties have such organizations, but only some jurisdictions send permit applications to those groups for their comments. A few groups are active, well-informed, and dynamic forces in permit review, but many are not.

If you seek a permit that involves some controversy and if your application will be referred to a neighborhood group, it is very much to your advantage to attend their meetings. By being there to answer questions, you defend yourself against the possibility of the group recommending against your application simply because they lack information or have misconceptions about it. Your presence also will make it more difficult for the group to recommend denial: it's harder to say no to a real person than to a piece of paper.

• *Special Advisory Committees:* Many jurisdictions have special bodies that advise the local government on matters such as parks or roads. A request for approval of a subdivision, for example, might be routed through a parks committee for a recommendation on the land to be dedicated for parks, and through a roads committee for comments on road layout and construction.

• *Design Review Board:* Certain types of permits may be subject to review by a special committee that has considerable power over matters such as offstreet parking, building setbacks, signs, landscaping, and building design. The design review process is used most often in downtown commercial districts where harmony of design is considered to be important in attracting customers.

• *Development Review Committee:* Most cities and counties routinely send permit applications through several offices to coordinate all the different regulatory activities. The building official sends an application for a building permit to the planners to see whether the proposed structure is a permitted use at its intended site, for example. Some jurisdictions expand on that by bringing together development officials every week or two to discuss the permit applications they have received. A typical county development review committee would be made up of the directors or senior staff from the planning, building, sanitation, public works, and surveyor's offices. Such committees usually do not issue formal recommendations or make reports, and their meetings are not intended to be public hearings or conferences with applicants.

• *Committee for Citizen Involvement (CCI):* State law requires each city and county to have a CCI that monitors citizen involvement. In some jurisdictions the planning commission has taken over that function. CCIs usually do not review permit applications, but they might become involved if an application generates problems with notice, standing, or some other aspect of citizen involvement.

8. Beware of oral permits.

An oral permit is one that results from a telephone call or a casual inquiry to development officials. Suppose, for example, that you want to start a bookkeeping service in your home, which is in an R-1 zone. You intend to convert the entire first floor of your house to an office, provide four new parking spaces, put up a sign, and employ a full-time assistant from outside the family. You call the local planning department and say something like this: "I want to open up a little bookkeeping service in my home; is a home occupation like that permitted in an R-1 zone?" A voice at the other end says yes, and you proceed to set up your business.

Weeks later, a neighbor complains to the planning officials. They declare that you will have to reduce the size of your office, get rid of the parking area, and quit bringing in outside help: none of those are permitted under the provisions of the R-1 zone or in the regulations on home occupations.

"But your department approved it!" you cry.

"That seems unlikely," the planning director replies. "The zoning ordinance specifically limits home occupations to activities that don't use more than 50 percent of the floor area on any one level of a dwelling, don't have designated parking areas, and don't bring in outside employees."

Without a letter or some record of that oral permit that you got on the telephone weeks ago, you have nothing with which to document your claim. Even if the planner who took the call remembers that conversation, he or she may point out that you said a "little office," not half a house, and you didn't mention a parking lot or an outside employee. The planner assumed that when you said "home occupation," you were using the term as it is defined and limited in the zoning ordinance. Perhaps that planner can be faulted for having assumed so much, but it is you who will pay the price—a price that could have been avoided if you had checked more carefully and had requested a written statement of what would be permitted.

9. Ask to see the applicable ordinances and policies.

If you seek to establish a home occupation, for example, ask the planner to show you the relevant sections of the zoning ordinance and the comprehensive plan's policies on home occupations. There are four reasons for that suggestion.

First, you will avoid misunderstandings such as those in the preceding paragraphs.

Second, you will see exactly what standards your permit application will be reviewed against. You can provide written and oral comments that address those standards, and you will not waste your time or anyone else's by dwelling on irrelevancies.

Third, by examining the regulations, you have a chance to interpret them for yourself. Laws often can be interpreted in more than one way. Read the ordinance for yourself and see whether you share the planner's understanding of it. Reading the local ordinances is rarely a big chore, incidentally: the provisions that apply to any one situation may not amount to more than a few paragraphs.

Finally, becoming familiar with applicable regulations protects you from mistakes by the development officials. This will draw upon me some wrath from my fellow planners, but the plain fact is that the staff working the counter sometimes do not have a very thorough knowledge of their own ordinances. I know—I was once one of those staff. No amount of college will enable the person working the counter to provide accurate advice about the details of the local ordinances. Only thorough study or intensive on-the-job training will do that, and some staff have not had either.

There are two causes for that problem. First, many planners and other development officials do not like to work the counter. It is a stressful job that demands skill in human relations as well as technical knowledge, and it does not get the pay or prestige associated with "higher" positions. Second, many cities and counties have no organized training. They simply throw the poor novice into the breach and hope that he or she will learn quickly. Those that survive the process come to be highly valued personnel because of their intensive frontline experience. But just in case you do not get such a veteran, make sure that you get to see the actual policies and laws.

10. Know the odds.

Before you invest a lot of time, energy, and money in a development proposal, you should estimate the odds on getting your permit. Each permit involves a unique set of conditions, but in terms of the odds for their approval, three main categories of permits can be described: the sure thing, the probable, and the doubtful.

Most ministerial actions lie in the first category. A building permit is an example. Your application will be approved if you conform to the applicable standards—if you use 2-by-10 joists where the code says you should, and so forth. The standards are clear and objective: all you have to do to get your permit is follow them.

Most applications for quasi-judicial permits (variances and conditional uses, for example) are 'probables.' They involve some uncertainty. The standards for approving them are sometimes neither entirely objective nor entirely clear, and the process relies heavily on the judgment of one or more decision makers. The odds are in your favor, but you should not count on approval until you actually have the permit in hand.

My third category is the 'doubtful.' You will know your application fits this category when the planner raises his or her eyebrows at your description of the project and says, "Well, you can apply for that if you want to, but . . . ." The main characteristic of the 'doubtful' category is that it seeks permission to do something that the comprehensive plan and its implementing measures specifically discourage—putting a furniture store in a farm zone, to use an extreme example. The applicant for such a permit is in effect asking the entire community to change its policies (or is asking the decision makers to ignore them). The applicant can expect the odds against approval of such requests to be very high. He or she should not be surprised if the request gets turned down. Some types of development in some locations *should be* turned down: a basic principle of zoning, after all, is to keep incompatible or inefficient forms of development out of certain areas.

11. File a complete application.

Different application forms are used for different types of permits, and forms and filing procedures vary among the regulatory agencies. Almost all permit processes have these two things in common, however. First, an incomplete or improperly prepared application will cause delays or denial. Second, the application will have to have the following information and attachments:

- Appropriate signatures
- Township, range, section, and tax lot number of the subject property
- Plot plan
- Assessor's map of the subject property
- Legal description
- Names and addresses of nearby landowners
- A statement of what is being proposed or requested
- A check for the permit fee.

Signatures. The question of what signatures are necessary on a permit application is not always as simple to answer as one would suppose. Can an agent acting on behalf of a property owner sign the application? Is the signature of a contract purchaser sufficient, or is the signature of the property's titleholder needed as well? Is one spouse's signature enough or must both sign the application? The answers to those questions vary with the situation. Just make sure that you are aware of what signatures are required for your permit and that you get them all.

Township, Range, Section and Tax Lot Number. This long string of numbers can be found on your property tax statement. You will need it because planning departments have zoning maps that are based on tax assessor's data. Each parcel and lot is identified by a tax-lot number from the assessor's numbering system. The zoning maps do not show street numbers, so a street address often is not adequate to pinpoint the location of a particular lot.

Plot Plan. You do not have to be a trained cartographer to draw a suitable plot plan. Just use a black pen (blue lines do not photocopy well) and a straightedge to sketch the following:

- Boundaries of the lot or parcel that is the subject of the application.
- Property lines of all lots and parcels in the notification area. The administrator will tell you how large that area is; 250 feet from the subject property is typical.
- Public rights of way (for roads, alleys, railroads, etc.).
- Locations of all main buildings on adjacent properties.
- Locations of all main buildings, land uses, accessory buildings, wells, utility lines, easements, septic tanks and drainfields on the subject property.
- Significant natural features.
- Locations of new structures or new property lines proposed in the application.
- The scale of the plot plan (one inch equals 100 feet, for instance).
- Orientation (north at the top of the page is the conventional practice).
- Your name, address, telephone number, and relationship to the property (contract purchaser, agent, etc.).

In many cases you can draw all of the above on a standard 8½- by 11-inch sheet of paper. You can save yourself some work and get a more accurate map, however, by getting a copy of the tax assessor's map of the property and using it as a base for your map. Such maps usually can be obtained at the office of the county tax assessor, county surveyor, or city recorder for a nominal fee.

If you have aerial photos, topographic maps, or other maps relevant to your property, bring them along. Even if they are largely unintelligible to you, maps and photos are useful because the planners know and love them. The planners will understand your proposal much more quickly if you can present it to them in the medium they know best.

Assessor's Map. Most permit agencies will insist on getting a recent copy of the official tax assessor's map, regardless of whether you have used one as the base map for your plot plan. The officials use the unmarked assessor's map as the base from which to prepare the maps used in legal notices and for notices mailed to property owners.

Legal Description. The legal description will appear on the deed or in the contract for the subject property. Such descriptions have three main forms: metes-and-bounds; township, range and section number; lot and block numbers. See the glossary for discussions of each. If you are unable to find such a description in your own records, you probably can find one recorded at the county clerk's office. There will be a small charge for a copy of that document.

Names and Addresses. Cities and counties mail notices of proposed permit actions or of appealable decisions to property owners within specified distances of the permit property. The responsibility for preparing the list of names and addresses for such notification often rests with the permit applicant. Some jurisdictions require that the applicant hire a title company to make a certified list of all the properties within 250 feet (or whatever distance is specified) of the subject property. Others allow the applicant to prepare his or her own list, using information shown on the county tax assessor's maps. The assessor's maps are easy to find and use, so preparation of such a list is not a big job unless you are dealing with a very large property that has dozens of lots along its perimeter. Do not rely on your memory or knowledge of your neighbors' names and addresses to prepare any list!

Note that it is usually a list of names and addresses that is required, not a petition bearing the signatures of adjacent property owners. Only for certain types of zone changes is an applicant expected to solicit signatures from neighbors.

Statement of the Proposal. This should be a brief summary of what you are proposing that requires a permit and the type of permit being sought. Note: Do not confuse such a summary with *findings,* the supportive material on which the permit decision will be based. See Section 12, immediately below.

Checkbook. Painful though it may be, you should bring your checkbook: you will have to pay some sort of fee when you apply for your permit. Cash may be suitable, but it suffers from the drawback that some planning departments do not have much money on hand with which to make change. Besides, a cancelled check provides a useful record.

12. *Help to build strong findings.*

Most of the decisions by planning officials regarding permit applications must be based on findings. In other words, the officials cannot approve your request for a permit with a simple "yes." They must say, "We approve this permit *because* . . . ," and then explain in writing all the facts, reasons, and conclusions that underlie their decision. The details of what should go into a set of findings and why findings are required are discussed at some length in the glossary entry, **finding.**

The findings are what your case is built upon. If someone appeals that case, your permit will live or die by the quality of those findings. Even if the decision to issue the permit seems absolutely correct to everyone other than the appellant, it will get remanded if it is not supported by proper findings.

You may feel that, as the permit applicant, you have no responsibility to worry about findings. After all, isn't it up to the permit officials to take care of such matters? In theory, the answer to that question may be yes. In practice, however, the answer is less clear-cut. Those officials may not have enough time to gather the information that really is needed. They may not have anyone on their staff with the expertise to deal with specialized matters such as hydrology or geology. They may not have access to information that you do. And it is not they who have the most invested in the permit decision. It is you. The type and amount of information needed to build good findings for your permit is something you should discuss with the permit officials. It may not be necessary for you to provide anything beyond what is asked for in the application. If your application is complicated, however, be prepared to do some homework. You may even want to hire one or more consultants.

If technical information on population growth, soils, groundwater, or some such topic is needed, don't jump to the conclusion that you must hire a consultant. And don't be intimidated by an appellant who is armed with a dazzling array of facts and figures. An enormous amount of information is available to you, and much of it is free. Dozens of public agencies deal with specialized topics like soils, water, pollution, transportation, historical places, farming, forestry, population, economics, and so on. Your tax dollars are helping to pay for them, so you might as well avail yourself of their services.

The first place to start looking for technical information is in the local comprehensive plan's background document or factual base. You may be surprised how much material you will find there. If you do not find what you want, talk to the local planners. They should be able to direct you to an appropriate agency.

When a committee of planners and a lawyer reviewed the draft of this book, they suggested that I add some material on information sources. I thought that was a good idea, until I realized that one could write a complete book on that topic alone. In fact, someone has. Oregon's Intergovernmental Relations Division periodically publishes the *Handbook of State Programs for Local Governments.* In it you will find descriptions of over two hundred programs and the names, addresses, and telephone numbers of the agencies that run them.

Another useful publication to direct you to the right sources is the Oregon *Blue Book,* which is published by the Secretary of State. Finally, there is a state agency that collects information, publishes low-cost pamphlets, and maintains a library on matters pertaining to planning and local government: the Bureau of Governmental Research and Service, P.O. Box 3177, Eugene, Oregon 97403. The bureau's telephone number is 686-5232.

13. Participate effectively in the public hearing.

If your application is to be considered in a public hearing (either initially or on appeal), by all means go to that hearing. If no one appears on behalf of your permit request, the decision makers may postpone action on it. Your absence may be interpreted as a lack of interest, or it may keep the decision makers from getting the oral testimony that would enable them to approve the request.

Do not be intimidated by the idea of speaking at a public hearing. Planning commission meetings and the like are not trials. They are relatively informal meetings intended to allow everyday people to explain their requests in their own words. The majority of permit applicants at local hearings are not represented by attorneys or consultants.

Your main purpose in speaking at the hearing should be to provide the decision makers the information they need to approve your request. That may sound obvious, but far too many speakers at such hearings wander off on tangents. Some speakers use the meeting as a forum in which to espouse political beliefs or to harangue the decision makers about permits, planning, big government, and all manner of injustice. That may be therapeutic for the speaker, but it is not an effective way to get a permit approved.

Some themes you should always avoid, because they are irrelevant and often insulting, are these:

The regulations that require me to get this permit are bad. That may even be true, but the decision makers are holding the hearing to determine how the existing laws should be applied, not whether those laws should be repealed. The decision makers have taken oaths to uphold those laws, not to scuttle them.

The review process isn't democratic. It is not supposed to be. The democratic process was used to develop the comprehensive plan, the zoning ordinance, and other development regulations. Those are the statements of how the community wants its land to be used. The planning commissioners (or whoever is hearing your permit request) are not supposed to ignore those statements, even when an entire roomful of friends and neighbors of the applicant express opinions to the contrary.

I really want or need the permit. Remember that the hearings officials are acting on behalf of the community. They know that you want the permit. What they need to be shown is that your project will serve the community's wants and needs as they are expressed in the plan and regulations.

So-and-so got an application just like this approved over in River City. Each piece of land is different from all the others. Each applicant's proposal is different from any other. And the laws of River City probably are not the same as those that govern your request. For all those reasons, anecdotes are not likely to provide substantial evidence on which the hearings officials can base their decision.

The public hearings process has some fundamental rules and objectives that grow out of the famous case, *Fasano v. Washington County.* For a summary of them, see **Fasano** in the glossary, particularly the quoted material on procedural issues.

14. *Inquire about the appeals process.*

The appeals process is important to you for two reasons. If your application gets denied initially, you may have one more chance or several to get it approved. If it gets approved initially, other parties may have a right to challenge that decision.

Ask what the appeals period following the initial decision will be. Ten days is a typical period. If your permit application gets approved, do not begin your project until those ten days have passed. If the initial decision goes against you and you decide to appeal, make sure that you do so promptly. An appeal submitted even one day after the deadline will not be accepted.

Almost any type of permit decision can be appealed. See Chapter 2 for a description of the appeal processes for the main types of permits.

You should also ask your local development officials about the local requirements on 'standing'—that is, who could appeal your permit application if it gets approved. Local governments have some authority to limit standing, but not many do. In the absence of any clear limitations on standing, you should assume that any person who can show that he or she is "aggrieved or has interests adversely affected by the decision" (ORS 197.830) would be able to appeal it.

15. *Relax.*

Most of us have learned to deal with certain types of officials and red tape since our teens. We pay a clerk to renew a motor vehicle license. We stand in line at the courthouse to buy a dog license. We spend hours each spring deciphering complicated instructions about how to give money to the IRS. These are all activities that none of us enjoys but that most of us accept. We plan for them rationally and effectively, allocating adequate time and money, because we are familiar with them.

Development controls are not so familiar or routine. Many persons have not encountered planners, building inspectors, or sanitarians. Such persons are not familiar with planning requirements or permit fees. They have allocated neither time nor money for such things, and they are startled to learn that a permit may cost hundreds of dollars, take weeks to process, and then could still be denied.

Many persons unfamiliar with development regulations also have invested large amounts of emotion (and sometimes money) in long-held dreams about a home in the country, a big profit from land sales, or a family store. It is little wonder, then, that the first encounter with the permit officials can be a frustrating or even devastating experience.

Even for those who have not made a premature emotional investment in some project, the regulations, permits, fees, waiting, and restrictions on what you can do with your land are likely to be unpleasant. That unpleasantness may be lessened by the following thoughts.

First, many of those rules and regulations that are new to you have been on the books for a long time. Development controls are more extensive than they used to be, but they certainly are not new. Many have existed for decades.

Second, the good reasons that underlie the development controls may not be readily apparent, but they do exist. It may seem absurd, for example, that building code requirements for western Oregon call for roofs to carry heavier snow loads than those in central and eastern Oregon. "Ridiculous," the impatient builder from Salem mutters. "They get ten times as much snow in Bend as they do here!" What he is overlooking is that the snow in the Willamette Valley is usually wetter and therefore far heavier; milder winds clear less snow from the roofs than do the stronger winds in Bend. Development officials cannot be expected to explain or even to know such nuances for every regulation they administer.

Third, development regulations are, like all tools, imperfect. The field of planning in particular has been dogged by a lack of effective implementing measures. The most lofty goals to preserve or achieve certain qualities in the community often must be implemented with regulations that seem to have little relation to those goals. For example, few people will argue with a policy to preserve agricultural lands, but many will argue with a law that seeks to implement that policy by preventing the creation of any parcel of farmland smaller than 40 acres. Such a minimum discriminates against the new farmer. It denies opportunity to the 'hobby farmer.' It is a fixed standard that lacks flexibility. All of these criticisms are accurate, but they only affirm what is almost a truism: any regulation invariably falls short of the goals it was designed to implement. Permit officials are quite aware of that problem, which I call the implementation gap. You will be able to deal with those officials more effectively if you recognize that gap, too, and resign yourself to it as much as possible.

Fourth, remember that the permit official that you deal with at the counter only administers the regulations and policies; he or she did not create them. It is elected officials who devise most of those regulations. The "duty planner" probably does not have much latitude in dealing with your application for a permit. If you become angry or frustrated, save it for the policy makers. You are better off to view the staff planner or building official as an ally. Blowing up at him or her won't help your application get approved, and it isn't fair to blame that official for what you find to be a stupid law.

Finally, remember that an absence of development controls would also restrict your freedom to use your property as you would like. As economists are always saying, there is no such thing as a free lunch. It was problems with fire, conflict among land uses, pollution, high costs of public services, excessive 'nuisance' litigation, and other ills that caused development controls to be adopted in the first place. When you are applying for a permit, it is tempting to wish that all those regulations would go away. But if that wish came true, you might face some much bigger problems in using and developing your land.

Enough philosophy! Good luck in getting your permit.

CHAPTER 4

A Glossary of Planning Terms

The following glossary contains approximately 650 words and phrases that you might read in a comprehensive plan, see in a zoning ordinance, or hear from a planner. It includes some terms from ecology, statistics, geography, demography, engineering, law, real estate, and planning. Obviously, no single book can do justice to even one of those fields. Therefore, I offer four cautions to the users of this glossary.

First, many of the brief discussions of terms only scratch the surface of some very deep topics. **Taking,** for example, has been the subject of numerous books, and it continues to be debated by many lawyers.

Second, this book is written for the lay reader—the nonprofessional. It is not a law book. For one who seeks a complicated permit or is involved in a lawsuit, the services of an attorney or planning consultant are recommended.

Third, land use is regulated by literally hundreds of governments and agencies. Their definitions and understandings of terms will vary. Terms such as 'home occupation' may be defined in very different ways from one place to the next. This glossary provides only a general description of how most planners view a particular term.

Finally, some of the terms in the glossary are quoted directly from Oregon's statutes, goals, or administrative rules. This has been done only to indicate how certain state agencies or bodies interpret such terms. It does not imply that the quoted definitions must be or are used throughout the state. Indeed, it is not at all uncommon to find one term that is defined in different ways in different chapters of the statutes.

A

Abate. To remove, eliminate, or destroy a structure or land use that is in violation of a land-use regulation. Abatement of an offending use is one of several means of enforcing such regulations. If, for example, a person were found by a court to be guilty of violating a zoning ordinance by building a house on land where that is not permitted, the court could order the house to be removed. *See* ORS 215.185.

Access. The relation between a lot and the public road or street system nearest it. A lot having several hundred feet of frontage along a public highway and the legal right of entry to that highway would be considered to have good access. A lot with no frontage and no other means of access, such as an easement, to a public way is said to be landlocked.

Most jurisdictions ensure that all newly created lots and parcels have adequate access by establishing minimum requirements for frontage: a typical urban residential lot is required to have at least 50 feet, although that requirement is reduced for pie-shaped lots that front on the turning bulb of a cul-de-sac.

Accessory use; accessory building. A use or structure associated with and incidental to the main use on a lot. Typical examples include private garages, fences, decks, patio covers, pergolas, tool sheds, ramadas, and dog houses. Zoning ordinances usually permit such uses outright in almost all zones, and often exempt them from setback, building height, and yard requirements. The same ordinances also carefully define and limit such uses to ensure that larger, incompatible buildings are not constructed under the guise of accessory uses. Accessory uses are also known as secondary or ancillary uses.

Acknowledgment. Official recognition by LCDC that a local government's plan and implementing ordinances conform to the statewide goals. The complete phrase is "acknowledgment of compliance."

Acknowledgment review. The review by LCDC of a local government's comprehensive plan to determine whether that plan complies with the statewide planning goals. When a local government has adopted its comprehensive plan, it sends copies of the relevant material to the Department of Land Conservation and Development (DLCD). DLCD schedules a hearing for acknowledgment review before the Land Conservation and Development Commission (LCDC), and invites comments on and objections to the plan from interested parties, including many state agencies. DLCD then reviews the plan (and the comments and objections it has received), prepares a report, and distributes it to LCDC and all interested parties. At the scheduled hearing, LCDC reviews the report, hears testimony, and then decides whether the plan complies with all of the applicable statewide goals. If the plan does not comply, the local government must revise it as directed by LCDC. If it does comply, it is said to be acknowledged.

Acre. The most common measure of land area used in American planning and surveying. One acre contains 43,560 square feet. A perfectly square lot containing 1 acre would measure 208.7 feet on each side. There are 640 acres in one square mile.

Activities of statewide significance. Significant public land development or land uses, such as highways, sewage-treatment plants, solid-waste disposal sites, and schools. Senate Bill 100 originally gave to LCDC the authority to designate those activities that it found to have statewide significance and to regulate them directly through a state permit process. LCDC did not designate or regulate any such activities, and the provisions enabling it to do so were removed from the statutes by the 1981 legislature.

ADT. Average daily traffic. See *traffic flow* and *trip.*

Adverse possession. A process by which one who occupies real property may acquire title to that property as the result of his occupation of it. Suppose, for example, that the owner of a farm builds a barn on land that he understands to be part of his farm. Many years later, however, a survey reveals that his barn stands on his neighbor's land. The farmer does have some basis to claim title to the ground on which the barn stands. He is said to have a 'color of right.'

The legal tests for adverse possession generally are that it must involve "*(1)* actual possession which has been *(2)* open and notorious, *(3)* hostile, *(4)* exclusive, *(5)* continuous and *(6)* for the period of the statute, *(7)* under color of title or claim of right" (Oregon State Bar 1982, pp. 60-1, 60-2). 'Hostile' in this case does not mean aggressive or violent. It means something more like 'assertive.' In our example, the farmer asserted his right to the land by building a barn there. Had he sought permission, his claim would be greatly weakened. The period of the statute referred to above is 10 years or more.

Affected area. The area that is affected by some existing land use or that one could expect to be affected by some proposed land use. How this area is defined determines, in part, who will get notice of pending land-use decisions and who will have standing during the making of such decisions. Some have argued that any significant land-use decision will have effects throughout the community. The contrasting view is that only the properties adjacent to a proposed land use can be considered to be affected. See **standing.**

Agricultural land.
> . . . in western Oregon is land of predominantly Class I, II, III and IV soils and in eastern Oregon is land of predominantly Class I, II, III, IV, V and VI soils as identified in the Soil Capability Classification system of the United States Soil Conservation Service, and other lands which are suitable for farm use taking into consideration soil fertility, suitabilty for grazing, climatic conditions, existing and future availability of water for farm irrigation purposes, existing land use patterns, technological and energy inputs required, or accepted farming practices. Lands in other classes which are necessary to permit farm practices to be undertaken on adjacent or nearby lands, shall be included as agricultural land in any event. (Goal 3, "Agricultural Lands")

This is probably the single most important definition from the statewide goals. It has been the subject of numerous court cases, policy papers, and actions by LUBA and LCDC. Two main points deserve mention here. First, the word 'predominantly' is important. Goal 3 requires that agricultural land, as defined above, be preserved and maintained. If you own a 100-acre farm in western Oregon and it has 70 acres of Class II and 30 acres of Class V soils, don't jump to the conclusion that you can partition the 30 acres and sell them for homesites. Your 100-acre parcel is 'predominantly' Class II soils and therefore is to be maintained as a unit of agricultural land.

Second, the definition has three parts: the Soil Conservation Service (SCS) rating, 'other lands suitable,' and 'other lands necessary.' Many people overlook the last two. They check the SCS ratings for their land, find that those ratings are not Class I-IV, and assume that their land therefore is not covered by the definition. It may, however, be 'other lands' suitable or necessary for agriculture.

Airport zoning. Special zoning applied to airports and their environs to reduce or resolve certain problems associated with aircraft operations. These problems include the following: *(1)* the threat of aircraft accidents to adjacent land uses, particularly those where groups of people might assemble; *(2)* hazards to aircraft from tall structures, smoke, glare, bright lights, radio interference, and birds that gather at landfills, ponds, etc.; *(3)* the effects of noise on persons who live or work near the airport; and *(4)* encroachment of urban uses around an airport, eventually forcing its closure.

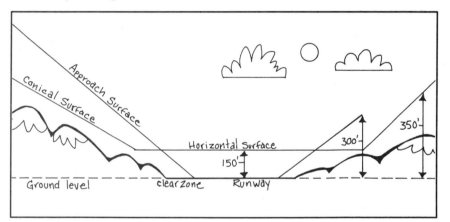

Figure 2. The imaginary surfaces above airports. Federal regulations specify the dimensions of such surfaces for each public airport. Local land-use ordinances limit the heights of structures so that they will not penetrate any of those surfaces, and they restrict the types of land uses permitted near the airport, particularly in the clear and approach zones. Source: Aeronautics Division 1981.

Airport zoning usually involves two levels of protection. The airfield itself and the lands owned by the airfield's manager often have a base zone, such as "Airport Operations," that addresses many of the concerns described above. Land adjacent to the airfield usually is controlled with an airport overlay zone. Limitations on the heights of structures are common in such zones. The standards for such regulations derive from the Federal Aviation Regulations, Part 77 ("FAR-77"), which establishes a group of imaginary surfaces that should not be penetrated by any structure. For a description of these surfaces, see *Airport Compatibility Guidelines* (Aeronautics Division 1981: pp. 19-25).

Air rights. The rights to use the space above a piece of land. Air rights can be sold or leased. The owner of an urban parking lot, for example, might sell the air rights for that lot to a developer. The developer then could build a platform for shops, apartments, etc., above the parking area.

Alteration. 1. A change or modification made to some structure. Minor repairs, routine maintenance, painting, and minor changes that do not involve structural members usually are not subject to building and zoning codes. Other alterations, such as the addition of a room, almost certainly will be subject to building code requirements and may be governed by zoning regulations as well.
2. "Any man-caused change in the environment, including physical, topographic, hydraulic, biological, or other similar environmental changes, or changes which affect water quality." This definition is from OAR 660-17-005, "Classifying Oregon Estuaries." Its use is largely limited to those rule provisions that deal with estuaries.

American Planning Association (APA). A national organization of professional city and regional planners and lay persons involved in planning. It was formed by the merger of the American Institute of Planners (AIP) and the American Society of Planning Officials (ASPO) in 1979.

Amicus curiae. A Latin phrase that means 'friend of the court.' The phrase refers to a party who has no legal standing in a particular case but who is allowed to introduce information or evidence to assist the court in rendering a decision. The plural form is *amici curiae.*

The term is to be contrasted with 'intervenor,' who likewise is not one of the principal parties in a legal case but who is allowed to enter into it in order to protect or further his or her own interests. The intervenor has some ax to grind; the *amicus* presumably does not.

Amortize. To do away with or eliminate a structure eventually. Some zoning ordinances contain amortization provisions for nonconforming uses. These provisions give a local government the power to require that a pre-existing nonconforming use be destroyed or made to conform to zoning within a specified time. A junkyard that existed in a residential area at the time the area became zoned residential, for example, would be 'grandfathered in,' as most nonconforming uses are. It could continue to operate legally, but only for a limited period, such as two or three years. This procedure is sometimes called time zoning.

Animal unit. An index that provides a basis for comparing the effects of different species of animals on land. Many zoning ordinances restrict the number of animals that can be kept in certain zones. This is done to ensure that rangeland will not be overgrazed or to limit conflicts between animals and other uses, such as surburban residences. Rather than listing all of the different numbers and types of animals that are permitted in each zone, the ordinances simplify matters by specifying how many animal units can occur per acre in each zone.

The Bureau of Land Management provides a definition that is most commonly used: "A standardized unit of measurement for range livestock which is equivalent to one cow = one horse = five sheep = five goats = four reindeer all over 6 months of age" (Bureau of Land Management 1980: p. 179). Some local ordinances expand that to include specified numbers of poultry and rabbits. Very few of them mention reindeer!

A-95 review. Review by state, regional, and local agencies of proposals for projects involving federal funding. The purpose of such review is to enable the jurisdictions most directly affected by a federal project to have a voice in how the project is conducted. The federal policy to require such reviews was initiated in the Intergovernmental Cooperation Act of 1968. Circular No. A-95 of the federal Office of Management and Budget (OMB) established the specific procedures for such review in 1969—hence the term, 'A-95 review.'

The phrase is obsolete. The OMB's Circular No. A-95 was repealed by President Reagan's Executive Order 12372 on 14 July 1982. The local review of federally supported projects still is carried on, however. And A-95 review is such a well-established term that it still is used frequently to describe that process.

Annexation. An extension of the boundaries of a city or special district. Annexations by cities are governed by ORS Chapter 222; those done by service districts generally are addressed in ORS 198.850-198.867. Both types of annexations are subject to the state-wide planning goals (ORS 197.175). In the Portland and Eugene metropolitan areas annexations are also subject to review by boundary commissions. See **health-hazard annexation.**

AOC. *Association of Oregon Counties.*

APA. *American Planning Association.*

Apartment. 1. A room or combination of rooms designed for use as a dwelling, and located in a building with other such units.
2. The building that contains such units. This second usage is less common. Usually 'apartment' means the individual dwelling unit, while 'apartment house' or 'multifamily dwelling' denotes the entire building. The state's building code (Section 402) declares an apartment house to be "any building or portion thereof which contains three or more dwelling units and, for the purposes of this code, includes residential condominiums."

Appeal. The taking of a decision by some agency or court to a higher level of authority for review of that decision. See *remedy* and *standing.*

Appraisal. An estimate of the value of property, as made by the tax assessor, for example. All real property is appraised by the county tax assessor, and the information from such appraisal is available to the public in the assessment roll. Appraisals by the tax assessor, however, often do not reflect the current market value of a property. The tax assessor is often several years behind in appraising. Oregon law requires only that real property be appraised by the tax assessor "at least once every six years" (ORS 308.234). In the meantime, the assessor adjusts valuations of property not recently appraised through a process known as indexing or trending. See *market value* and *property tax.*

Appreciate. To increase in value. Real property gains in value as the result of three types of change: improvements or additions made to the property itself; improvements in the roads, parks, schools, and other public facilities and services that serve the property; and the general growth of the community, regional, or national economy. Appreciation usually refers only to the gains that occur as the result of the last two types of changes. Since landowners benefit from the actions of society and not through any efforts of their own, the amount that the land appreciates beyond what was paid for it is sometimes called a windfall or unearned increment. Some economists and planners have argued strongly for "increment taxes" that would capture some of that gain.

Area of critical state concern. A place that is found by the Land Conservation and Development Commission to require special state control or regulation and that has been designated an area of critical state concern pursuant to ORS 197.405. The legislature must approve any such designation. In the decade since this statute went into effect, LCDC has not designated any areas of critical state concern.

Arterial. A major road that has as its primary function the efficient movement of traffic and that provides little or no direct access to adjoining properties. See **road.**

Assemblage. The buying of several contiguous lots in order to create a single lot for some large development. See **plottage.**

Assessment. See **property tax.**

Association of Oregon Counties (AOC). An organization to provide for the exchange of information, ideas, and technical assistance among Oregon's 36 county governments. The AOC was formed at a meeting of county judges and commissioners in 1936. Today, it is directed by an executive committee made up of county officials representing all sections of the state. It has standing committees on eleven topics of concern to county governments, including land use, agriculture, and urban affairs. The AOC has maintained an office and staff in Salem since 1959.

Association of unit owners. See **homeowners' association.**

Avigation and hazard easement. There is no 'n' missing here: the word 'avigation' means 'aerial navigation.' The Oregon Department of Transportation's Aeronautics Division defines this type of easement as one "which provides right of flight at any altitude above the approach surface, prevents any obstruction above the approach surface, provides a right to cause noise vibrations, prohibits the creation of electrical interferences, and grants right-of-way entry to remove trees, or structures above the approach surface" (Aeronautics Division 1981: p. 192).

B

Baker conflict. A situation in which the zoning of an area allows uses more intensive than those permitted by the plan map's designation for the same area. For example, the zoning of a city block for apartments when the plan designation for that block calls for single-family dwellings creates a Baker conflict. The name derives from the 1975 Oregon Supreme Court case, *Baker v. City of Milwaukee*. The court held that the comprehensive plan is the controlling land-use instrument and that such conflicts are therefore not permissible.

Bancrofting. A slang term for the formation and financing of local improvement districts (LIDs) under the provisions of Oregon's Bancroft Bonding Act (ORS 223.205-223.295).

Base flood. See *flood.*

Baseline. A parallel; one of the lines of reference used in the ***township-and-range survey system.***

Base zone. A zone that has had an overlay zone placed upon it. For example, an area zoned R-1 Residential may have a Floodplain (FP) Overlay Zone placed on it. Such an area would be subject to the provisions of the R-1 Zone (the base zone) and to the additional requirements of the FP Zone (the overlay zone). Base zones are occasionally referred to as parent or underlying zones.

Beltway. An arterial that passes partly or entirely around the edge of a city. It enables local traffic to move quickly from one side of the city to the other, while avoiding the congested core, and it allows through traffic to avoid the city completely. The beltway also can provide an effective barrier to urban sprawl, but only if access to it is limited and effective land-use controls are in place. Also known as a 'beltline road' or 'ring road'.

Benefit-cost analysis. A method for comparing the costs and benefits of various alternatives in order to find which is the most efficient. The results of such analysis are usually presented as benefit-cost ratios. A benefit-cost ratio lower than one indicates a project whose costs will exceed its benefits. The greatest theoretical limitation of such analysis is that it requires quantification of all components. The analyst thus may be faced with the prodigious task of placing a dollar value on a scenic view, a human life, or the benefit of some project at a point fifty years in the future. The analysts have been equal to the task, however: such intangibles are routinely quantified.

Betterment. 1. An improvement to real property that goes beyond mere repair or maintenance; a modification that would increase the value of real property (particularly as seen through the eyes of the tax assessor).
2. An increase in the value of real property that occurs not as the result of improvements made by the owner but as the result of improvements in the streets, sewers, parks, and other public facilities that serve the property. This is chiefly a British usage, but it is not uncommon in American writings on planning. See *appreciate.*

Bikeway; bicycle trail. A path for bicyclists. Such paths are usually paved, and may be designed exclusively for bicycles or for pedestrians and joggers as well. ORS 366.514 defines 'bicycle trail' as "a publicly owned and maintained lane or way designated and signed for use as a bicycle route."

Bikeways are classified by Oregon's Department of Transportation as follows. Class I bikeways are 'independent' paths; they are separated from roads and streets, and may have their own rights-of-way. Class II bikeways adjoin roads and streets, but are protected from vehicles by some barrier, usually a low concrete curb. Class III bikeways share the roadways with motor vehicles, but special lanes are designated with a painted stripe.

ORS 366.514 requires that footpaths and bicycle trails be built to accompany new, reconstructed, or relocated state highways, roads, and streets. With certain exceptions, no less than 1 percent of each year's revenue from the state highway fund is to be used for such paths and trails.

Billboard. A large sign placed near a highway or street and used to advertise goods or services sold or provided at some other location. Many local zoning ordinances specify that such signs are to be permitted only in commercial or industrial zones, or impose other restrictions on them. The state restricts their use along highways. Oregon's statutes do not specifically define 'billboard,' but speak rather of "outdoor advertising signs." That term is defined in ORS 377.710(25).

Block. A parcel of land bounded by intersecting streets. The dimensions of blocks are controlled in most subdivision ordinances. Blocks that are too short (i.e., 200-300 feet or less) require an excessive number of streets, thus increasing costs to the developer and the public. Blocks that are too long (i.e., a thousand or more feet) often contain lots that cannot be served effectively by streets and utilities.

Boarding house. A house at which board, or board and lodging, may be obtained for payment. This is typically considered to be a commercial activity not permitted in single-family residential zones. Some ordinances, however, list small boarding houses as conditional uses in such zones. They usually limit the number of boarders to four or five. See **lodging house.**

Boundary commission. A lay body of seven members appointed by the governor to review and recommend upon annexations and the expansion of service districts and privately owned community water and sewer systems. Three commissions were established initially, but only two continue to operate, one for the Portland metropolitan area, the other in Lane County. The third, the Marion-Polk Boundary Commission, was dissolved in November 1980. The responsibilities of the boundary commissions are set forth in ORS 199.410-199.519.

Buffer; buffer zone; buffer strip. A strip of land that separates two land uses and protects one from the smoke, noise, lights, vibration, odors, or unsightliness of the other. Buffers are commonly required where commercial or industrial uses abut residential areas.

Buildable lands. "Lands in urban and urbanizable areas that are suitable, available and necessary for residential use" (Goal 10). In 1981 the same definition was made a part of ORS Chapter 197 by Senate Bill 419. See ORS 197.295(1).

Buildable lands inventory. An inventory of land suitable, available and necessary for residential use. Every city is required by Goal 10 to have such an inventory. It generally must include a map or other information to specify the location of buildable lands; an explanation of the types and densities of housing that can occur in specific areas; a description of the physical constraints on and public services available to housing in each area; and a description of the acreage designated on the plan map and zoned for different types and densities of housing.

Building. "Any structure used or intended for supporting or sheltering any use or occupancy" (State Structural Code, Section 403). Note that building and structure are not synonyms: a fence is a structure but it is not a building.

Building area. The area covered by the buildings on a lot. The term is somewhat narrower than 'lot coverage,' which is sometimes defined to include paved parking areas, patios, etc., in addition to the areas covered by buildings.

Building code. A set of regulations that govern the construction of buildings and other structures. Oregon has adopted a building code that, with occasional local modifications, applies throughout the state (ORS 456.775). The state building code is made up of more than a dozen specialty codes, such as the *Structural Specialty Code and Fire and Life Safety Regulations.* See Chapter Two's section on building permits (pages 16-17) and the glossary entry for *Uniform Building Code.*

Building inspector. A local or state official who examines the construction of buildings for compliance with the state building code. See *building code* and *building official.*

Building line. An imaginary line beyond which a building cannot be located or constructed. The lot line of a property defines the outer boundary of the yard; the building line defines the inner boundary.

Building official. The official who administers the building code and issues building permits, and who often is also the local zoning enforcement officer. Although this official commonly is called 'the building inspector,' such usage may not be correct: the building official often is the head of a department that includes several plan examiners (or 'plan checkers') and building inspectors.

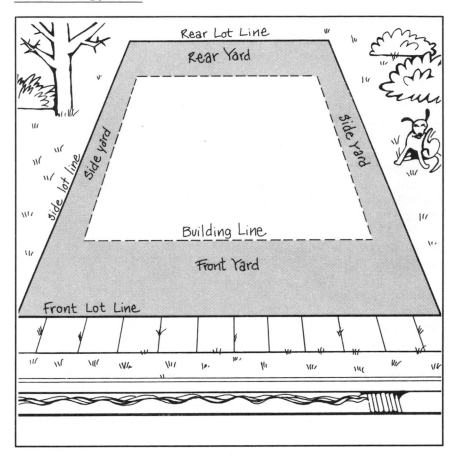

Figure 3. The building line defines the area where buildings can be erected. In the shaded area, buildings are prohibited by setback and yard requirements from the zoning and building codes.

Building permit. Authorization from the local building official to build, alter, or place structures on real property in accordance with the provisions of the state's building code and other applicable regulations.

The maximum fees charged for a building permit are set by state law. See Table No. 3-A of the State Structural Code. The fees vary according to the value of the proposed building. The fee for a $50,000 home in 1986 was $283, for example. In addition to the permit fee, a plan-checking fee equal to 65 percent of the permit fee is required for most buildings. Local governments can elect to charge less than the maximums set by the state; they can charge more only if such fees have been approved by the Director of the Department of Commerce. See ORS 456.760.

Built or committed. Planning jargon to describe rural land that has been built on or otherwise divided, improved, and developed to such an extent that it cannot be used for farming or forestry. See **committed lands.**

Built out. A slang term to describe an area of once-vacant land that has been developed to the maximum extent practicable or permitted by law. A subdivision with twenty lots, for example, would be 'built out' when the twentieth house had been built there. An oddity of planning jargon is that once an area experiences sufficient 'infill' it becomes 'built out.'

Built-up area. A vague, informal usage meaning land that is developed or used intensively. It sometimes means the land within a city's corporate limits plus that in the urban fringe. In other cases it refers only to the urban fringe, excluding adjacent lands in the city proper. Finally, it also is used simply to contrast rural developed land with that which has not been built on.

Bulk regulations. Regulations to limit the height, density, lot coverages, and location of structures. Such regulations are usually objective, numerical standards: e.g., "No structure in the RS Zone shall exceed a height of 35 feet or $2\frac{1}{2}$ stories, whichever may be less."

Bulk regulations generally are intended to ensure that dwellings receive adequate light, air, access, fire protection, and open space. Such regulations are sometimes referred to as dimensional standards.

Bulk variance. A variance of the bulk regulations in a zoning ordinance, as opposed to a use variance. See ***variance.***

"Bundle of rights." See ***property.***

Bureau of Governmental Research and Service (BGRS). A research agency established by the state in 1933. The bureau's purpose is to aid state and local governmental agencies by providing information, statistics, model ordinances, and technical consultation. It is located in Eugene, on the University of Oregon campus.

C

Cadastral map. 1. A cadastre is a public record of the location, extent, value, and ownership of land for purposes of taxation. Maps such as those maintained by each county's tax assessor, then, are known as cadastral maps.
2. Any map that shows the property lines of individual lots and parcels.

Camping vehicle. "Either a vacation trailer or a self-propelled vehicle or structure equipped with wheels for highway use and which is intended for human occupancy and is being used for vacation and recreational purposes, but not for residential purposes, and is equipped with plumbing, sink or toilet" (ORS 446.003(4)).

When does a camping vehicle become a mobile home and thus become subject to land-use regulations? That knotty problem is addressed in different ways (or not at all) in different ordinances. A common approach is to define 'residential' in terms of time (e.g., a camping vehicle occupied on the same lot for more than 30 days would be considered a residential use) or in terms of utility connections. For example, a camping vehicle would be considered a mobile home if it were connected to a public sewer, water system, electrical lines, etc. See **mobile home** and **recreational vehicle.**

Capital improvement. A public service facility, structure, or system: sewers, roads, water systems, libraries, fire stations, etc.

Capital improvements program (CIP). A plan to describe how some or all of a community's capital improvements are to be developed. A CIP covers a relatively short period of time, typically five to ten years. It contains detailed information on technical items such as sizes and capacities of pipes as well as information on projected costs and methods of financing. Many cities and counties do not have such programs, and LCDC does not construe the goals to require them.

The 1983 legislature, however, amended the statutes to declare, "A city or county shall develop and adopt a public facility plan for areas within an urban growth boundary containing a population greater than 2,500 persons" (ORS 197.712(2)(e)). See *public facility plan.*

Carrying capacity. "Level of use which can be accommodated and continued without irreversible impairment of natural resources productivity, the ecosystem and the quality of air, land and water resources" (LCDC Goals).

The concept underlying carrying capacity—that natural systems have limits—is fundamental to planning and resource management. The term is often used, however, in a glib manner that disguises its complexity. When one encounters the words 'carrying capacity,' it is always helpful to pause and ask these questions: capacity as defined by whom, measured how, and with respect to what?

Case law. The body of law based on administrative or judicial decisions rather than statutes. This Anglo-American system relies on the legal doctrine of *stare decisis,* a Latin phrase which means that principles and precedents established by previous court decisions can be accepted as the law in later cases of a similar type. Oregon's *Fasano* case provides a notable example of how case law works. As a result of this 1973 decision, which went to Oregon's Supreme Court, many types of land-use decisions that once were considered legislative are now held to be quasi-judicial. This important change has led to the development of so-called Fasano rules of procedure to be used by local governments in deciding land-use cases. These rules have come to be law not because Oregon's legislature wrote a statute on the topic but because a significant court case set the precedent for them. And the precedent has already been modified by subsequent cases: law changes and evolves continually as new cases are decided.

CBD. Central business district.

CCI. Committee for Citizen Involvement.

CCRs. Conditions, covenants, and restrictions. See *covenant.*

Census. An official counting of an entire population. The population of a place can be estimated by sample surveys, registration of vital events such as births and deaths, and by other techniques. The term 'census,' however, is properly applied only to an actual count, or enumeration, of the population.

Censuses may be *de jure,* counting persons according to their legal residence, or *de facto,* counting persons according to where they actually are on the date of the census. The US Census uses a compromise between the two: one's 'usual residence' (i.e., the place where one usually sleeps) is the basis for the federal enumeration. Regarding Oregon's laws pertaining to the census, see ***population estimates.***

Census tract.
. . . small, relatively permanent areas into which large cities and adjacent areas are divided for the purpose of providing comparable small-area statistics. Tract boundaries are determined by a local committee and approved by the Census Bureau; they conform to county lines. Tracts are originally designed to be relatively homogeneous with respect to population characteristics, economic status and living conditions; the average tract has about 4,000 residents. From time to time, changes may be made in tract boundaries; they are not necessarily comparable from census to census. (Bureau of the Census 1970: p. 86)

Central business district (CBD). The part of a city where the greatest concentration and variety of retail commercial activity is found. The CBD contains the peak value intersection, the point of highest land cost in a city. The Bureau of the Census defines the CBD as "an area of very high land valuation . . . characterized by a high concentration of retail businesses, offices, theaters, hotels, and service businesses . . . and high traffic flow."

Central city. 1. A city that is the main market and service center for some larger trade area; a central place.
2. An informal synonym for the 'downtown' or central business district.
3. A term used by the federal Bureau of the Census to describe the major city or cities in a standard metropolitan statistical area (SMSA).

Certificate of occupancy (occupancy permit). Official authorization by the building official that a public building is suitable for use or occupancy. Section 307 of the state's structural code requires that "no building or structure shall be used or occupied, and no change in the existing occupancy classification of a building or structure or portion thereof shall be made until the building official has issued a Certificate of Occupancy therefor." Dwellings and accessory buildings are exempt from that requirement.

Certification. Official approval by LCDC of a state agency's rules and programs. Just as local governments must submit their plans to LCDC, so also must state agencies submit their programs. If LCDC finds such a program to be consistent with the statewide planning goals and with acknowledged local plans, the program is said to be certified. 'Certification' thus is to state agency programs what 'acknowledgment' is to local comprehensive plans.

Several federal programs also use the word 'certification' in special ways. The Coastal Zone Management Act of 1972, for example, establishes a process for 'consistency certification.' See **consistency review.**

Change of use. 1. A change in the manner in which a building or structure is used—converting an old house to a florist shop, for example. Certain land-use permits may be required for changes of use, even when no structural alterations are involved. And some changes of use are simply prohibited. The old house could not be converted to a florist shop in most residential zones, even if no changes to the building were to be made. The state building code requires that a certificate of occupancy be obtained whenever a change of use occurs in a commercial or industrial building (State Structural Code, Section 307).
2. As it relates to the Willamette River Greenway, "making a different use of the land or water than that which existed on December 6, 1975" (Goal 15, Section K(1)). Further explanation is provided in Goal 15 and in OAR Chapter 660, Division 20.

CIP. Capital improvements program. Among planners in Oregon, this abbreviation also is sometimes used for citizen involvement program.

Citizen advisory committee (CAC). A group of citizens organized to help develop and maintain a comprehensive plan and its land-use regulations. Local governments usually establish one such group for each neighborhood in a city or each district in a county. The groups typically meet monthly. Their advice and concerns are given to the planning commission or governing body. CAC meetings are quite informal, and are open to all, without dues or formalities of membership. CAC meetings are often attended by members of the local planning department, who can answer technical questions or keep a record of the comments.

Citizen Involvement Advisory Committee (CIAC). A standing committee appointed by the Land Conservation and Development Commission to advise that commission on matters of citizen involvement, to promote "public participation in the adoption and amendment of the goals and guidelines," and "to assure widespread citizen involvement in all phases of the planning process." The quoted passages are from ORS 197.160, the statute that sets forth the need for and duties of the CIAC. Note: there is only one CIAC. It is a state committee, formally defined by statute. By contrast, see *Committee for Citizen Involvement.*

Citizen involvement program (CIP). A program established by a city or county to ensure the extensive, ongoing involvement of local citizens in planning. Such programs are required by Goal 1, "Citizen Involvement." They must contain or address six 'components' set forth in Goal 1. CIPs are reviewed by LCDC and by CIAC, the state Citizen Involvement Advisory Committee. Changes to approved programs also must be reviewed by LCDC and CIAC.

City planning. The planning and regulation of land use in urban areas; urban planning. A few planners consider 'city planning' to involve only those areas within municipal corporate limits and 'urban planning' to encompass the urban fringes as well as the city proper. That fine distinction, however, is not widely maintained. See *comprehensive plan.*

Class "A" permits. " . . . state permits affecting land use that require public notice and public hearing at the agency's discretion prior to permit approval . . . ." (OAR 660-31-010(3)). A fill and removal permit from the Division of State Lands is one example.

Many state agencies administer permits for activities that affect land use. Oregon's planning laws specify that those agencies can issue such permits only when the proposed activities would satisfy two conditions. First, they must comply with the statewide planning goals. Second, they must be compatible with local land-use plans that have been acknowledged by LCDC.

The process of ensuring compliance with the goals and compatibility with local plans is called state agency coordination. The distinction between Class A and Class B permits grows out of the administrative rules that govern such coordination. In general terms, Class A permits involve larger, more complex activities; the state agency must hold a public hearing to determine whether the proposed activity would be consistent with applicable goals and acknowledged plans. Class B permits are smaller, more routine actions; the state agency relies on findings made by local officials, and it need not hold a public hearing.

Class "B" permits. " . . . those state permits affecting land use which do not require public notice or an opportunity for public hearing before permit issuance . . ." (OAR 660-31-010(4)). A subsurface sewage disposal permit from the Department of Environmental Quality is an example of a Class B permit.

Cluster development. The concentration of structures on one part of a lot to preserve the remainder of the property for open space. It is considered to be a progressive and innovative alternative to the conventional grid-plan subdivision. A 10-acre parcel developed with traditional subdivision techniques at a density of five units per acre, for example, would create fifty rectangular lots with small, inefficient yards. With clustering, fifty units of townhouses or garden apartments could be placed on 4 acres, leaving the remaining 6 acres for private yards and courts and landscaping, gardens, tennis courts, a playground, etc.

Cluster development usually is permitted only under planned unit development procedures. Some zoning ordinances do not provide for such alternatives. Those that do usually permit clustering only on parcels or collections of contiguous lots with a minimum area, typically 5 acres. The clustering provisions of most ordinances require a professional design team of architects and engineers. This may increase the costs of cluster development. Clustering offers the potential for savings in other areas, however: the sewer and water lines and streets needed to serve a cluster may be much shorter than those necessary for a traditional subdivision of comparable density.

Coastal goals. Statewide planning goals 16-19, all of which were adopted on 18 December, 1976. Goal 16 is "Estuarine Resources." Goal 17 is "Coastal Shorelands." Goal 18 is "Beaches and Dunes," and 19 is "Ocean Resources." (See Appendix). These goals apply to the western part of the state defined as the coastal zone.

Coastal shorelands. "Those areas immediately adjacent to the ocean, all estuaries and associated wetlands, and all coastal lakes" (LCDC Goals). Goal 17 delimits these areas. Generally, they comprise the lands west of the Oregon Coast Highway, within 1,000 feet of any estuary, or within 500 feet of a coastal lake. See Goal 17 for a more precise description.

Coastal zone.
   The area lying between the Washington border on the north to the California border on the south, bounded on the west by the extent of the state's jurisdiction, and in the east by the crest of the coastal mountain range, with the exception of: *(a)* The Umpqua River basin, where the coastal zone shall extend to Scottsburg; *(b)* The Rogue River basin, where the coastal zone shall extend to Agness; *(c)* The Columbia River basin, where the coastal zone shall extend to the downstream end of Puget Island." (LCDC Goals)

Coastal zone management (CZM). The management of land and water resources in coastal areas in accordance with a program adopted pursuant to the Coastal Zone Management Act of 1972 (PL 92-583). Oregon's coastal management program is administered by the Department of Land Conservation and Development (DLCD). The program was approved by the federal Office of Ocean and Coastal Resource Management in 1977. Oregon's program was the second in the country to be so approved (after Washington).The core of Oregon's program is the four statewide planning goals that deal with coastal resources. See ***coastal goals.***

Code. A book containing standards and regulations. Planners, for example, often refer to the zoning ordinance as 'the zone code' and to the regulations on subdivisions and partitions as 'the subdivision code.' To nonplanners, 'the code' usually means the state's building code. See ***building code*** and ***Uniform Building Code.***

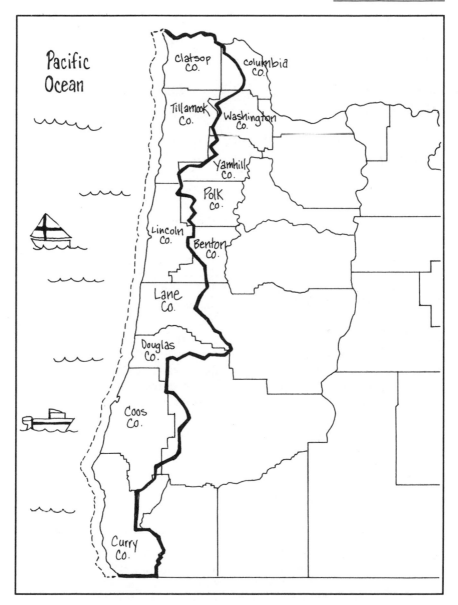

Figure 4. Oregon's coastal zone encompasses all or part of a dozen counties, 35 cities, and the state's 'territorial sea' (the waters up to 3 nautical miles from shore).

Code administration. Planning jargon for the administration of the zoning and subdivision ordinances. Code administration is also called current planning in some departments.

COG. Council of governments. See *voluntary association of governments.*

Collector. A road or street designed to collect traffic from local streets and funnel it onto arterials, where it can move rapidly and efficiently to its destination. A collector combines two functions, providing access to property and facilitating movement of traffic. See *road.*

Combining zone. A synonym for *overlay zone.*

Commercial. As used by planners, an adjective to describe business activities that do not involve manufacturing. A grocery store, for example, is a commercial land use. A mill, however, is not; it would be considered an industrial land use. See *industry.*

Commercial acre. What is left of an acre of land in a new subdivision after the area devoted to streets, sidewalks, utilities, and other public uses has been subtracted. Such public areas typically take up 20 percent of the land in a subdivision: a commercial acre then would be approximately 35,000 square feet. See *density.*

Commercial agricultural enterprise. This key phrase from Goal 3 is expanded on in OAR 660-05-005(2) as follows:

"Commercial agricultural enterprise" consists of farm operations which will:

(a) Contribute in a substantial way to the area's existing agricultural economy; and

(b) Help maintain agricultural processors and established farm markets.

(c) When determining whether a farm is part of the commercial agricultural enterprise, not only what is produced, but how much and how it is marketed shall be considered. These are important factors because of the intent of Goal 3 to maintain the agricultural economy of the state.

This phrase comes from an important sentence in Goal 3 about agricultural land: "Such minimum lot sizes as are utilized for any farm use zones shall be appropriate for the continuation of the existing commercial agricultural enterprise within the area." Some people might argue that a 5-acre farm that grosses $500 per year is a "commercial agricultural enterprise." Others would argue that the threshold is much higher. The rule language quoted above is an attempt to clarify LCDC's view of just what those crucial three words mean. LCDC has consistently rejected the notion that hobby farms, martini farms, ranchettes, etc., can be considered to be commercial agricultural enterprises. The legislature reinforces that with its general policy to hold commercial farmland in large blocks (ORS 215.243).

Commercial forest land. "Forest land that is capable of producing crops in industrial wood, generally in excess of 20 cubic feet per acre of annual growth; land that is not totally withdrawn from timber use but may have limited timber production capacity because of use restrictions, stocking levels, technical or economic limitations, etc." (Oregon Department of Forestry 1977: p. 149). Note: This definition is not used in Oregon's forestry statutes or in statewide planning Goal 4, "Forest Lands," which makes no distinction between 'commercial' and any other type of forest land.

Committed lands. Rural lands on which it is "impracticable" to carry out farming or forest management because they are "irrevocably committed" to nonfarm uses. The commitment must result from physical factors that hinder resource management. Past zoning, previous land divisions, and other "paper" factors do not in themselves establish such a commitment. For example, a 20-acre parcel of farmland surrounded by rural residences on 1-acre lots could be considered committed; a similar parcel surrounded by small platted lots with neither houses nor services would not be. The official standards for determining commitment are found in OAR 660-04-028, Goal 2, and ORS 197.732.

Committee for citizen involvement (CCI). A local group appointed by a governing body for the purposes of "assisting the governing body with the development of a program that promotes and enhances citizen involvement in land-use planning, assisting in the implementation of the citizen involvement program and evaluating the process being used for citizen involvement." The quoted material is from Goal 1, which requires local governments to establish such committees. In some cases, a local government may choose to have itself or its planning commission serve as the CCI, an arrangement that must be approved by LCDC.

CCIs are often confused with citizen advisory committees, but the two types of organization have much different purposes. The former advises the local government only on matters pertaining to citizen involvement and Goal 1. The latter advises the local governing body on a wide range of planning topics relating to all of the goals. Each city and county has only one CCI, but they may have several citizen advisory committees.

Common wall. A wall shared by two buildings and that lies along the property line between them; a party wall. Common-wall construction has been used for commercial and industrial buildings for many years. It enables a developer to reduce construction costs and to use all of the land on the lot. Common-wall construction for dwellings has seen little use in the US in all but the largest cities. Many zoning ordinances have in effect prohibited it by requiring side yards of 5 to 15 feet in residential zones. Great increases in the cost of constructing conventional houses in the last few years have led to a greater demand for other forms of dwellings. Some jurisdictions therefore have eliminated sideyard requirements or established 'zero lot line' provisions that allow the construction of rowhouses, townhouses, and other types of common-wall dwellings.

Community plan. A detailed plan containing information and policies regarding a particular geographic area within a city or county. The community plan may also be referred to as a neighborhood, district, unit, area, or subarea plan. The community plan usually is intended to complement and add detail to a framework plan for the entire jurisdiction. A comprehensive plan may be made up of a framework plan and several community and functional plans.

Completion bond. See *performance bond.*

Compliance. The act or state of conforming to the statewide planning goals. A local comprehensive plan and its implementing ordinances are said to be 'in compliance' if they have been reviewed by the state's

Land Conservation and Development Commission and have been acknowledged in accordance with the provisions of ORS 197.251. Compliance is required for all cities and counties by ORS 197.250.

Comprehensive plan. An official document adopted by a local government in which are set forth the general, long-range policies on how the community's future development should occur. Comprehensive plans vary widely in their terminology and from one place to the next, but the following points are generally true of such plans in Oregon.

First, the terms 'general plan,' 'master plan,' and 'comprehensive plan' are largely interchangeable. The last is by far the most common because it has become the official usage: Oregon's statutes and statewide goals use it and do not mention the other two. See further discussion under **master plan.**

Second, comprehensive plans are usually adopted by ordinance. Their policies are mandatory and have the force and effect of law. This has not always been the case in Oregon's past, and is still not true of most other states. The decade of legislation and case law in Oregon in the seventies, however, gave teeth to the plan, and made it the instrument that controls zoning and subdivision ordinances.

Third, comprehensive plans are—well, comprehensive. At a minimum they address all the topics in the statewide planning goals, and they often address other topics of local concern as well.

Fourth, most comprehensive plans cover the period from the late 1970s to the year 2000. That planning period is not set by law, and as we approach the turn of the century, plans to the year 2010 or 2020 have begun to appear.

Fifth, a comprehensive plan comprises several parts, among which are the following:

• An inventory, which may be incorporated in the plan and adopted with it or kept separate and simply referred to in the plan.

• A policy element, which contains the official statements of the community's policies on future development. This is the heart of the plan, and indeed is sometimes referred to as 'the plan.' If the community has adopted community plans or functional plans, this overriding city- or county-wide document often is described as the 'framework plan.'

• Community plans, which contain special information and policies regarding neighborhoods or districts within the city or county.

• Functional plans, which deal with individual public services and facilities such as parks, transportation, sewers, and water. Such plans also may be called elements, as in 'the transportation element of the comprehensive plan.'

• A plan map, which specifies what parts of the planning area are subject to what policies by assigning a plan designation to each part. Areas designated Residential thus are subject to the plan's policies on housing, those designated Industrial are subject to the corresponding policies on industrial development, and so on.

• Implementation measures, such as zoning ordinances, capital improvement programs, etc. Technically, implementing ordinances

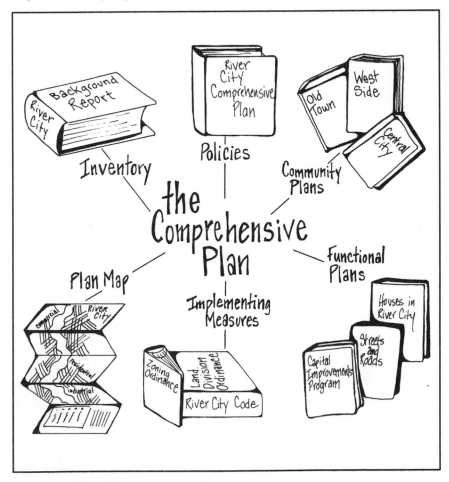

Figure 5. The comprehensive plan.

are not properly part of the plan even though they are vital to it, but many persons mean to include the zoning and subdivision ordinance when they speak of 'the comprehensive plan.'

Oregon's statutes on planning define the term as follows (from ORS 197.015(5)):

> "Comprehensive plan" means a generalized, coordinated land use map and policy statement of the governing body of a local government that interrelates all functional and natural systems and activities relating to the use of lands, including, but not limited to, sewer and water systems, transportation systems, educational facilities, recreational facilities, and natural resources and air and water quality management programs. "Comprehensive" means all-inclusive, both in terms of the geographic area covered and functional and natural activities and systems occurring in the area covered by the plan. "General nature" means a summary of policies and proposals in broad categories and does not necessarily indicate specific locations of any area, activity or use. A plan is "coordinated" when the needs of all levels of governments, semipublic and private agencies and the citizens of Oregon have been considered and accommodated as much as possible. "Land" includes water, both surface and subsurface, and the air.

Condemnation. **1.** The forcing of a sale of real property to the government under the government's powers of eminent domain. Property may be taken without the owner's consent if it is to' be used for a public purpose, but the seller must be given just compensation. The appropriate amount is determined by a court. Condemnation typically occurs in order for the government to acquire land for roads, public buildings, and other public uses. See *eminent domain* and *taking.*
2. The closure and demolition of an unsafe structure by some governmental agency. With this type of condemnation, the government does not acquire the property and it need not pay compensation.

Conditional use. Zoning ordinances specify three types of uses for each zone: uses that are permitted outright, those that are prohibited, and those that may be permitted after review and approval by the local government. Those in the last category are described as conditional uses.

The list of conditional uses for each zone typically includes activities and land uses for which there is no specific zone and which may require special restrictions. Schools, for example, are often listed as conditional uses in residential zones.

The term 'conditional use' continues to be ambiguous, and hence has been the subject of several court cases. In *Anderson* v. *Peden,* 284 OR 313 (1978), Oregon's Supreme Court stated:

> Standing alone, the term "conditional use" can convey quite different meanings. It could mean that the specified use is a permitted use whenever certain conditions exist or are satisfied. Or, second, it may mean that the use will be permitted subject to special conditions attached to the individual permit. Third, "conditional use" historically has often been employed simply as a device to permit discretionary decisions on certain uses, without much attention to the meaning of conditional.

The courts and LCDC have held that the discretionary process cannot be used to discriminate against a needed housing type (such as mobile homes) in cities. That case law was put into the statutes by the 1981 legislature (ORS 197.295-197.307). When needed housing types are listed as conditional uses, they must be subject to clear and objective standards, not to discretionary review. For other types of conditional uses, however, local governments still may use any or all of the three approaches described by the Supreme Court.

Condominium. A system of ownership under which one may own an individual unit in an apartment or other building complex and share in the ownership of common elements such as the land. The word is also widely used to mean the buildings that are owned under such a system. It is sometimes used incorrectly as a synonym for apartment. Condominiums in Oregon are regulated under the provisions of ORS Chapter 94. Some types of condominiums with many units are subject to the provisions of the federal Interstate Land Sales Full Disclosure Act. See **subdivision.**

Conflict of interest. A situation in which personal bias or the prospect of personal gain prevents a member of some public body from carrying out the purposes of that body in a fair and objective fashion. It might be expected, for example, that a planning commissioner could not vote fairly and objectively on the rezoning of his or her mother's property if the rezoning would cause a $20,000 increase in the value of her land: there would be a clear conflict of interest. Oregon law requires that a planning commissioner not take part in a decision in which he or she might have such a conflict. ORS 215.035 is the statute that governs conflicts of interest on county planning commissions; ORS 227.035 covers the same topic for cities.

Conservation easement. A contractual limitation on the use of land so as to preserve natural, scenic, recreational, cultural, or historical features on that land. The conservation easement enables a governmental body or nonprofit organization to preserve an important landmark at less cost than would be required to buy the landmark outright.

Although most easements involve the purchase of rights from a landowner to use the land for certain activities, a conservation easement usually is a restriction on how the *landowner* may use the property. For example, a society to preserve historical places might pay the owner of a historical building a certain fee for the right to place a restriction on his or her deed. The restriction would prevent the alteration or demolition of the historical building. Title to the building would remain with the landowner, but the conservation easement would limit the manner in which the building could be used. When such an easement is given to a governmental body, compensation to the landowner usually comes through reduced taxes. State laws governing conservation easements are found in ORS Chapters 271, 273, and 390.

Conservation estuaries. "Estuaries lacking maintenance jetties or channels, but which are within or adjacent to urban areas which have altered shorelines adjacent to the estuary" (OAR 660-17-010(2)).

Oregon has 22 major estuaries. The following six have been classified in OAR 660-17-015(2) as conservation estuaries: Necanicum River, Netarts Bay, Nestucca River, Siletz Bay, Alsea Bay, and Winchuck River. Of the other sixteen, five have been classified as natural estuaries, eight as shallow-draft development estuaries, and three as deep-draft development estuaries. See Goal 16 in the Appendix.

Consistency review. 1. A process established by OAR Chapter 660, Division 31, to ensure that the permits required and approved by state agencies are consistent with the statewide planning goals and with local acknowledged comprehensive plans.
2. The process of determining whether certain types of development proposals in coastal zones are consistent with the federally approved

state coastal management plan. The Coastal Zone Management Act of 1972 requires that "each Federal agency conducting or supporting activities directly affecting the coastal zone shall conduct or support those activities in a manner which is, to the maximum extent practicable, consistent with approved state management programs" (Section 307(c), 16 USC 1456(c)).

Consultant. One who gives professional or expert advice. Most larger cities in Oregon have one or more planning consultants or consulting firms. Their clients comprise two main groups: private individuals and firms, and local governments. Consultants can help private parties to obtain various planning permits and to plan developments. They help local governments by preparing technical documents, writing plans and ordinances, and doing research and special studies on land use.

Planning consultants usually are found in the yellow pages of the telephone directory under the title City and Regional Planners. They are often associated with architectural, surveying, engineering, or law firms.

There are no state or national requirements or standards for planning consultants. To put it bluntly, all you have to do to be a planner is to call yourself one. The American Planning Association (APA) does accredit planners. Its standards for allowing a planner to place the initials AICP (American Institute of Certified Planners) after his or her name include a test and an evaluation of education and experience. Note that membership in the APA does not imply accreditation or formal recognition as a planner by that organization. It simply means one has paid his or her membership fee.

Continuance. An order by LCDC declaring that it has reviewed a local government's comprehensive plan and found some parts of it to be inconsistent with the statewide planning goals and specifying a period of time within which these inconsistencies are to be corrected. LCDC may grant, deny, or continue a local jurisdiction's request for acknowledgment. The continuance has been by far the most common action. Typically it is granted for a period of 150 days, during which time the local government is supposed to revise its plan and land-use regulations in accordance with directives issued by LCDC in its continuance order.

Contour map. A map that shows the topography or relief of an area through a pattern of lines (contours) that connect all points of equal elevation. Elevations are described in reference to some datum plane, usually mean sea level. The vertical distances between contours (contour intervals) are fixed. On small-scale maps, the contour interval is large, perhaps 50 or 100 feet. On large-scale maps, such as those for a subdivision or plot plan, the contour interval is usually small, often 2 feet. Comprehending a contour map takes some practice, but in a

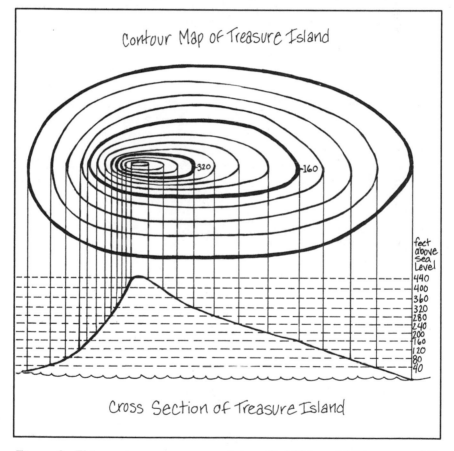

Figure 6. This contour map uses an interval of 40 feet. Making every fifth line (the 'indicator contours') heavier and numbering them is a standard system that makes the map much easier to decipher.

little time one can learn the useful art of perceiving three dimensions from a two-dimensional map. As can be seen in Figure 6, steep slopes are indicated by a pattern of closely packed contours, while shallower inclines are shown with widely spaced lines.

A path perpendicular to contours represents the steepest route that can be chosen. A road built on such a route is said to run "against the contours" and is not an efficient alternative. A road or development that is blended into the topography with shallow grades and little need for cut and fill is said to work 'with the contours,' and is considered to have a more efficient design. Note: contour lines cannot cross. To draw a map with, say, the 10- and the 20-foot contours crossing would be to say that the point where they intersect is at once 10 and 20 feet above sea level.

Conversion. A change in the type of land use that occurs in a building or on a unit of land. Some conversions involve remodeling, but the term also applies to changes of use that involve no alterations of a structure. For example, a farmer might be able to open a welding shop in a barn without remodeling the barn. Such a conversion from an agricultural use to a commercial or industrial use would be prohibited in most agricultural zones even though the barn's structure remains unchanged.

Planners also use the word 'conversion' to describe the following special types of changes:

(1) The division of a single-family dwelling into duplexes or multifamily dwelling units. This type of conversion is common in areas where the demand for housing is high and the supply limited. Frequently it is done in spite of zoning that prohibits it. Such illegal conversion is hard to detect and difficult to prosecute, so zoning officials are often inclined to ignore it.

(2) The changing of an apartment building into a condominium. This may involve no alteration of the building itself but only a change in its ownership. This type of conversion is becoming popular in urban areas where the high cost of housing has driven those who want to own their own home to seek something more affordable than the conventional detached single-family unit. It may impose a burden on those who rent in that it reduces the supply and increases the cost of rental units.

(3) The development or urbanization of rural lands, as when a farm is transformed into a subdivision.

Cooperative. An apartment building or other multifamily dwelling owned by its residents, each of whom owns a share of the building and land. The difference between a cooperative and a condominium is that in the latter, the individual dwelling units are owned by their occupants while the halls, stairways, parking areas, and land are maintained in common ownership. In the cooperative everything is held in common; one buys or sells a share of the entire cooperative, not an individual dwelling unit.

Coordination. As it occurs in the Oregon statutes and planning literature, this word means specifically the coordination that occurs among local governments and other agencies (federal, state, and local bodies and special districts). ORS 197.015(5) declares that a plan is coordinated "when the needs of all levels of governments, semipublic and private agencies and the citizens of Oregon have been considered and accommodated as much as possible." Goal 1 states, "Federal, state and regional agencies and special purpose districts shall coordinate their planning efforts with the affected governing bodies and make use of existing local citizen involvement programs established by counties and cities." Goal 2 requires that "each plan and related implementation measure shall be coordinated with the plans of affected governmental units."

There are two main components in all this coordination. One is state agency coordination (SAC), a program administered by the Department of Land Conservation and Development. DLCD reviews the rules and programs of certain other state agencies to ensure that they are "in compliance with the goals and compatible with acknowledged comprehensive plans" (ORS 197.180(7)). Formal approval by LCDC of such rules and programs is called certification.

The other component is local coordination among cities, counties, and special districts. The main responsibility for that type of coordination lies with the counties. ORS 197.190(1) states, "Each county . . . shall be responsible for coordinating all planning activities affecting land uses within the county, including planning activities of the county, cities, special districts and state agencies, to assure an integrated comprehensive plan for the entire area of the county." The same statute provides that coordination responsibilities can be given to a regional planning agency formed by the county and city governments of an area.

The above discussion focuses on Oregon's requirements for coordination. Several federal laws and programs also have provisions for various forms of agency coordination. See, for example, **consistency review,** 2.

Coordinator. A local official employed by a county or council of governments to coordinate the planning efforts of the local governments in the area. The coordinator's aim is to ensure that the area's city and county comprehensive plans are consistent with each other and with the statewide planning goals. The coordinator's salary usually is paid from 'coordination grants' issued by the state's Department of Land Conservation and Development. As local plans have been acknowledged and coordination grants have stopped, the number of coordinators has declined.

Corner cutback. See **vision clearance.**

Cost-benefit analysis. See **benefit-cost analysis.**

Council of governments (COG). A regional planning agency. See **voluntary association of governments.**

County road. See **local access road** and **road.**

Covenant. A private contractual agreement to limit the use of real property; a deed restriction. The term often is used as part of the phrase, 'conditions, covenants, and restrictions' ('CCRs'). CCRs are used to protect property values and to control conflicts among land uses.

CCRs are quite common in residential subdivisions. A typical set of CCRs might declare that all dwellings in a subdivision must have shake roofs, at least 1,500 square feet of floor area, and no home occupations. Although CCRs are often thought of as devices to protect residential property, their use with commercial and industrial lands is by no means uncommon.

In some states, an extensive system of CCRs substitutes for zoning. Houston, Texas, is the most commonly cited example of such "private zoning."

Criterion. A standard on which a judgment or decision (regarding a permit application, for example) may be based. See **standard.** Note that *criterion* is the singular form, and *criteria* is plural.

Cubic-foot site class. A system with which to express the productive capacity of a forest site in terms of the volume of growth in cubic feet per acre per year for some typical commercial forest species, such as Douglas-fir. The most productive forest lands will have a cubic-foot site class of 1 and the least productive a rating of 7.

   There are other systems for expressing the productive capacity of forest lands: site index, site class, etc. Cubic-foot site class is significant because it is the system that has been used by most Oregon counties and cities to classify forest lands. For the most part, LCDC has required counties to use it. Cities have been permitted to use other systems in some cases.

Cul-de-sac. A local street, usually only a few hundred feet in length and closed at one end, designed to serve the interior of a subdivision or large tract of land. A cul-de-sac usually has a circular area, a so-called turning bulb, at its end to allow vehicles (including fire trucks and service vehicles) to turn around. In some cases, a cul-de-sac may have a pair of short opposed driveways at its terminus, in which case it is referred to as a hammerhead street.

   Note that a cul-de-sac is designed from the outset to be a dead-end street. A dead-end street that is intended to be developed and extended as a through street in the future is called a stub street.

   A cul-de-sac may be the only way to provide access to interior lots in an irregularly shaped subdivision. It also is sometimes cheaper (at least at the outset) to use one or more culs-de-sac rather than through streets. But culs-de-sac may present problems to the community. If they are used often, they impede circulation and frustrate the stranger to the neighborhood who is looking for some unfamiliar address. In addition, fire trucks and other large service vehicles sometimes cannot turn around in a cul-de-sac's turning bulb. Most communities restrict the length of culs-de-sac, typically to 400 or 500 feet, and set a minimum radius for the bulbs. A few cities have policies not to permit culs-de-sac at all.

Cumulative zoning. See *Euclidean zoning* and *exclusive zoning*.

Current planning. Planning jargon for the administration of zoning and subdivision ordinances. This odd-sounding phrase evolved because planning departments usually have two main functions: the development of comprehensive plans, which came to be called 'long-range planning,' and the administration of the land-use ordinances, which was contrasted with the long-range section by being labeled 'current planning.' It also is known as 'code administration.'

Curtilage. The area occupied by a dwelling, its outbuildings, and the yard associated with them. This legal term is not often seen in the planning literature, but it could serve a useful purpose. Planners often must distinguish the developed part of a lot from the unused area, the farm house and yard from the surrounding fields, etc. For such situations this legal term is more precise than the ambiguous words that are commonly used: homesite, homestead, building area, etc.

Cut and fill. See *fill.*

CZMP. Coastal zone management program (as specified in Section 305 of the federal Coastal Zone Management Act of 1972). See **coastal zone management.**

D

Dedicate. To give private property to the public. This verb is most commonly used in reference to subdivisions, where the developer often is required to dedicate land to the local government for parks, schools, or street rights-of-way. In such cases the fee simple ownership of the land actually passes from the developer to the public at large as represented by the local government. The term is to be contrasted with 'reservation' and 'easement,' neither of which involves change in ownership. See *exactions.*

Deed. A document that describes a transfer of real property from one person to another. There are different types of deeds (e.g., quitclaim, bargain and sale, warranty), and detailed discussion of them exceeds the scope of this book. One important point with regard to planning should be noted, however: the terms of a deed do not override planning and zoning laws. Just because your deed grants to you the rights to build, say, a glue factory on your lot does not mean that you can ignore the zoning ordinance's provisions to the contrary. To make that point more widely known, the 1985 legislature required that the following statement be placed on any "instrument transferring or contracting to transfer fee title to real property":

> This instrument will not allow use of the property described in this instrument in violation of applicable land use laws and regulations. Before signing or accepting this instrument, the person acquiring fee title to the property should check with the appropriate city or county planning department to verify approved uses.

Deep-draft development estuaries. "Estuaries with maintained jetties and a main channel maintained by dredging at deeper than 22 feet" (OAR 660-17-010(4)). OAR 660-17-015(4) identifies three deep-draft development estuaries: Columbia River, Yaquina Bay, and Coos Bay. Oregon's other estuaries are classified as shallow-draft development, natural, and conservation. See Goal 16 in the Appendix.

Deflation plain. "The broad interdune area which is wind scoured to the level of the summer water table" (LCDC Goals).

Demolition permit. A permit to tear down a building. The state's building code requires that such a permit be obtained prior to the demolition of most types of structures (State Structural Code, Section 301). The property owner usually is required to fill any excavations, cap sewer and water pipes, and take any other measures necessary to leave the demolition site safe.

Despite what the law says, demolitions frequently occur without the required permits, particularly in rural areas. Many people are unaware that such permits are required, and counties are hard-pressed to monitor demolitions or enforce the permit procedures for them.

Demolition rate. The rate at which dwellings are removed from a city's total supply of housing through demolition. It is usually expressed as a percentage per year. A rate of 1 percent is a common rule of thumb, but major variations from it are common.

Denial. Generally, an action by a decision-making body to disapprove some request, as in "the hearings officer's denial of the application for a variance." In Oregon the term also has a special meaning related to the acknowledgment process. In that sense, the word means an order from LCDC declaring that a local comprehensive plan has numerous deficiencies and conflicts with the statewide planning goals, and that those problems are likely to take a "substantial period" to resolve. LCDC has used the denial order sparingly. It has denied requests for acknowledgment only in those cases where a local jurisdiction's plan and land-use regulations were far from complying with the statewide goals. It has been equally sparing in acknowledging submittals the first time they are presented. In the great majority of cases, it has issued a continuance order. See *acknowledgment review* and *continuance.*

Density. The measure of intensity of residential development on a particular piece of land. It is usually expressed in numbers of dwellings per acre. Typical rural densities range from one dwelling unit per several hundred acres to one unit per 1 or 2 acres. A typical low-density suburban subdivision has three to four units per acre. Medium-density development usually is considered to range from six to twelve units per acre, numbers characteristic of duplex subdivisions, mobile-home parks, and clusters of townhouses. High-density development covers a broad range from one dozen to several dozen units per acre, as would be found in high-rise apartments.

Density may be described as 'gross' or 'net.' Gross density, the more common of the two, refers to the number of dwelling units for each acre of land, including areas devoted to streets, parks, sidewalks, and other public rights-of-way. Such publicly owned lands commonly require 15-25 percent of a neighborhood's land. Gross density sometimes is defined also to include land for the shopping facilities necessary to serve the residences.

Net density is the number of dwelling units for each acre of land devoted to residential uses, i.e., excluding the public rights-of-way. When net and gross densities are calculated for the same neighborhood, the net density will always be the higher. Example: a subdivision with 6,000-square-foot lots and 20 percent of its land in public ways will have a gross density of 5.8 dwelling units per acre; its net density will be 7.3 dwelling units per acre. See *commercial acre.*

Density bonus. An increase in the number of dwelling units per acre permitted in a planned unit development, cluster development, or subdivision. This special increase beyond the density normally allowed by the zoning or subdivision ordinance is given as an incentive for exceptionally good design or for amenities such as parks and landscaping.

Department of Energy. An agency created in 1975 by Oregon's legislature to carry out research on and planning for energy conservation and use. This department is often informally abbreviated DOE, but that acronym also is used for the Department of Education.

Department of Environmental Quality (DEQ). The state agency that administers programs and regulations to reduce or minimize pollution of the air, water, and land. Solid waste, chemical wastes, wastewater, air contaminants, and noise are the main targets of this department's activities. Several of its programs impinge directly on land-use planning, most notably the permit program for subsurface sewage disposal (that is, septic tank systems). Many of the DEQ's activities are carried out in accordance with the standards and policies of the federal Environmental Protection Agency (EPA).

The DEQ was formed in 1969. The policy-making body that directs its operation is the Environmental Quality Commission (EQC).

Department of the Interior. The federal agency responsible for the management of most of this country's publicly owned lands and natural resources. The Department of the Interior has several agencies within it, including the Bureau of Land Management (BLM), the Fish and Wildlife Service, and the National Park Service. Nationally, the Department of the Interior owns over half a billion acres of land. In Oregon, its various divisions own 16,554,365 acres (Bureau of Land Management 1980: pp. 19-22).

Department of Land Conservation and Development (DLCD). The state agency responsible for administering Oregon's statewide planning goals and statutes. Its policy-making body is the Land Conservation and Development Commission (LCDC). DLCD and LCDC were established in 1973 by Senate Bill 100, the Oregon Land Use Act. DLCD has a staff of about forty, with its central office in Salem and field representatives in Newport, Medford, Bend, and Portland.

Department of Revenue (DOR). This state department's main significance to land use and planning is that it oversees the application of the property tax by county assessors and local budget officials. The state occurs in order for the government to acquire land for roads, public buildings, and other public uses. See *eminent domain* and *taking.*
2. The closure and demolition of an unsafe structure by some governmental agency. With this type of condemnation, the government does not acquire the property and it need not pay compensation.

Department of Transportation (ODOT). The state agency that adminsters Oregon's transportation system. Many of the divisions and programs of this agency affect land use. The Aeronautics Division, for example, owns and operates 37 airports and administers a statewide Aviation System Plan. The Parks and Recreation Division runs programs for preservation of historical places, recreational trails, scenic waterways, and state parks.

Design review. The review of certain types of development proposals to ensure that they conform to community standards for design and aesthetics. A typical design-review ordinance would give a planning commission the power to review all proposals for commercial buildings in a city's central business district. Unlike most other land-use controls, such ordinances specifically deal with aesthetics, and may give considerable discretion to a planning commission to regulate building materials, style, and even colors of proposed buildings.

Destination resort. A large, self-contained recreational development. The state's recreational goal (Goal 8) offers an extended definition of the term. Development proposals that conform to that definition are allowed on farm or forest land without having to take exceptions to the farm- or forest-land goals. Smaller resorts may be permitted on resource land, but they must get exceptions. Some examples of destination resorts in Oregon: Sunriver, Black Butte (both near Bend), and Salishan (on the central coast).

Development. "The act, process or result of developing" (LCDC Goals, "Definitions"). This definition is too broad to be of much use. It includes the division of land, the installation of sewer and water lines, the cutting of trees, and the growing of crops. In common usage the word applies to a narrower range of activities. Many persons, for example, would not consider the subdivision of land to be development, but would use that word for the installation of sewers, sidewalks, waterlines, etc. Others would classify neither the subdivision of land nor the installation of utilities as development, but would save that for the actual building of houses. It is common practice to distinguish 'subdivider' (one who only divides, but does not build) from 'developer' (one who builds).

Because of the vagueness of this widely used word, it is carefully defined in many statutes, administrative rules, and local ordinances. Those definitions often differ considerably.

Development rights. The rights to build on or otherwise alter real property, as contrasted with mineral rights, water rights, air rights, and others from the 'bundle of rights' associated with property.

Differential assessment. The special assessment of land at a value different than its market value, to encourage conservation, development of blighted areas, or some other specified purpose. This policy tool, like zoning and other implementation measures, is a means of influencing or controlling land use. It is used most often to conserve farmland. It works by giving the landowner a lower tax bill, which acts as an incentive to him or her to hold the land in large blocks and continue farming it. See *exclusive farm use zone* and *farm tax deferral.*

Dimensional standards. See *bulk regulations.*

District. 1. A zone or use district—that is, a section of a city or county that has been zoned so as to permit certain uses and exclude others. A residential area subject to the provisions of the R-1 zone, for example, is described as an R-1 district. This usage derives from an attempt to relieve the double duty that has been thrust upon the word 'zone,' which means both a set of ordinance provisions that apply to certain lands, and an area to which those provisions have been applied. If 'zone' were always used for the ordinance provisions, and 'district' for the area, a useful distinction could be maintained. The R-1 zone then would be a set of requirements in the zoning ordinance, while an R-1 district would be an area so zoned. That nuance has been lost, however; district and zone are now used interchangeably.
2. A specific area to be served by one or more public services, such as a fire-protection district. See **special district.**

Division of State Lands (DSL). The administrative agency for Oregon's State Land Board. The Board and DSL are responsible for the management of the Common School Trust Fund and the lands that generate income for that fund. Those state-owned properties include 600,000 acres of rangeland, 132,000 acres of timber land, 800,000 acres of offshore lands, various coastal estuarine tidelands, and the submerged and submersible lands of navigable waterways (*Oregon Blue Book*, 1985-86, p. 107).

DLC. Donation land claim.

DLCD. Department of Land Conservation and Development.

Dominant tenement. See **easement.**

Donation land claim (DLC). A tract of land given free to an Oregon settler during the mid-1800s under the provisions of the Donation Act of 1850. The amount of land given ranged from 160 to 640 acres. Most of the original DLCs have since been divided many times, but their irregular pattern still appears in the cadastral maps of western Oregon, where most of the claims were made.

Double-frontage lot. See **through lot.**

Downzone. To change the zoning of a property so as to require lower density or less intense use; a change from rural residential zoning with a minimum lot size of 5 acres to agricultural zoning that requires 40-acre lots, for example. The reverse process, of course, is upzoning.

DSL. Division of State Lands.

Dwelling. In its most general sense this word simply means any residential structure. Some plans and land-use regulations use the term as a synonym for single-family dwelling. Others use it more broadly, to include duplexes and mobile homes. Like 'residence,' the word is imprecise. If it is to be used in plans, ordinances, applications for permits, or other official papers, it should be defined at the outset. The State Structural Code, Section 405, offers this definition: " . . . any building or portion thereof which contains not more than two dwelling units."

Dwelling unit. " . . . Any building or portion thereof which contains living facilities, including provisions for sleeping, eating, cooking and sanitation, as required by this code, for not more than one family" (State Structural Code, Section 405).

The way in which dwelling units are designed or arranged provides the basis for distinguishing among many different housing types: single-family dwelling, multifamily dwelling, duplex, apartment, efficiency, studio apartment, boarding house, guest house, etc. The number of dwelling units per acre provides a convenient index for describing the intensity of residential development. See **density.**

E

Easement. A right to use, for a specified purpose, a particular piece of land owned by another. A parcel that does not have road frontage, for example, may gain access through an easement that allows the construction of a driveway across the intervening land. The most common forms of easements are for access and for utilities.

Many easements are 'affirmative'; that is, they give the holder of the easement the right to use land for some purpose. For example, affirmative easements enable utility companies to extend gas lines, power lines, and other service facilities across properties they do not own. Easements may also be 'negative,' however, in which case they limit the ways that land may be used. See *conservation easement.*

The estate against which the easement is held is called the servient tenement; the estate that gains the easement is the dominant tenement. In the case of a small landlocked parcel that obtains access by an easement across a neighboring farm, the landlocked parcel is the dominant, and the farm the servient, tenement.

Easement of necessity. See *way of necessity.*

Economic life. The length of time that a structure can be used profitably and efficiently. The term is to be contrasted with the 'physical life' of a structure, which may be much longer. A mill, for example, may be profitable to run only for a period of thirty years, until its design and equipment are rendered obsolete. The structure itself can be expected to stand, however, for many more years, unless it is revamped or destroyed.

Economies of scale. Increases in efficiency that come about as the result of increases in size. The concept is important in planning particularly as it relates to public facilities and services. Some public facilities (sewage treatment and water systems, for example) seem to experience economies of scale for populations into the millions. In other

84

words, the larger the population to be served, the cheaper will be the per capita costs of sewage treatment and water service. For other services, however, such as fire protection, economists have not observed any clear economies of scale. Finally, for some services, there may be diseconomies of scale. That is, they may become more expensive per capita as the population to be served increases.

The difference in the size of population at which economies of scale for different services occur is one of the major flaws in the argument of those who assert that there is some optimal size for cities—50,000 people, for example. What is an optimal size for one public service may very well be less than optimal for another.

Efficiency dwelling unit. " . . . a dwelling unit containing only one habitable room" (State Structural Code, Section 406). Also, an "efficiency." The term "studio apartment" is similar, but usually one distinction is maintained: the efficiency unit does not have a separate kitchen or kitchenette, while the studio apartment does.

Effluent. That which flows out or emanates; the liquid discharged by sewage-treatment plants, or the waste liquids and gases emitted by industrial plants. The term can encompass gases, but in common usage refers only to liquids. It is the basis for the cynic's pun about the United States being "the effluent society." It should be noted, however, that not all effluents are serious pollutants. Those that have been treated carefully, as with tertiary sewage treatment, may add little pollution to their environments.

EFU zone. Exclusive farm use zone.

EIS. Environmental impact statement.

Element. A part of a comprehensive plan. The word is used most often to refer to a particular functional plan, e.g., "the transportation element of the comprehensive plan."

Eminent domain. A government's power to take private property for public uses if it pays "just compensation." The quoted phrase comes from the Fifth Amendment to the Constitution, which ends with the clause, "nor shall private property be taken for public use, without just compensation." That 'taking clause' is repeated almost verbatim in

Article I, Section 18, of Oregon's Constitution. The meaning of the word 'taking' continues to be the basis of a lively debate among scholars of constitutional law and those who deal with land. See *inverse condemnation, police power,* and *taking.*

Enabling legislation. The federal constitution gives plenary powers—the general powers to legislate and regulate—to the states. Local governments do not have such broad powers: they derive their powers from the states. One means with which the state delegates authority to cities and counties is through enabling legislation. Such legislation gives a local government powers pertaining to some specified matter. ORS Chapter 227, for example, is the legislation that enables cities to zone land. ORS Chapter 215 gives to counties a similar power.

Endangered species. "Any species which is in danger of extinction throughout all or a significant portion of its range other than a species of the Class Insecta determined by the Secretary to constitute a pest whose protection under the provisions of this Act would present an overwhelming and overriding risk to man" (Federal Endangered Species Act of 1973). The term "species" includes both plants and animals. The word "Secretary" means the Secretary of the appropriate federal department: Interior, Commerce, or Agriculture.

A related term from the same federal act is "threatened species." Other terms pertaining to this general topic, but not standardized or as widely accepted, include rare, unique, disjunct, peripheral, and endemic species.

Endangered Species Act of 1973. A federal law that provides for the conservation of habitats for endangered and threatened species. It replaced the Endangered Species Conservation Act of 1969.

Energy recovery. The extraction from solid waste of materials that can be used to generate heat or other forms of energy. See *resource recovery.*

Enforcement. The act or process of enforcing laws. In the case of land-use regulations, enforcement is often weak or ineffective for four reasons. First, many jurisdictions lack the staff to monitor violations of the land-use codes: the violations cannot be corrected or prosecuted if they are not even seen by the planning authorities. Many jurisdictions rely on the local building official to do such monitoring. The building official and his staff, however, often have many other higher-priority tasks and also may not have a complete understanding of the zoning and subdivision ordinances. Their bailiwick is, after all, the building code.

Second, prosecution of and convictions for violations of land-use laws are difficult to obtain. Many district attorneys and judges view such cases as trivial in comparison to criminal cases.

Third, the sanctions for such violations often are not commensurate with the crime. If a house is built 2 feet closer to a property line than the zoning ordinance allows, abatement of the dwelling (i.e., tearing it down) or imprisonment of its builder is far too severe a penalty. If no suitable penalty is provided for in the code, charges against the violator may simply be dropped. As a result of this problem more jurisdictions have come to abandon criminal sanctions, such as imprisonment, and call for civil penalties in land-use matters. A typical civil sanction is a fine of up to $500 per day for each day the violation occurs.

Fourth, although Oregon has set statewide standards for planning and zoning, the state has no system to monitor or enforce the day-to-day administration of those standards. If a violation of a state goal or an acknowledged local plan occurs, the state is unlikely to learn of it. And even if it does, DLCD and LCDC have little power to take corrective action. The state relies almost wholly on local governments, interest groups, and concerned citizens to monitor and enforce the administration of the statewide planning program.

Despite the problems described above, violation of land-use regulations is not as rampant as might be expected. A large amount of 'enforcement' does occur through complaints from interest groups or the neighbors of those who violate land-use ordinances. With the great increase in citizens' awareness of and involvement with planning over the past decade, such informal monitoring and enforcement can be expected to increase. To those who view planning laws as an extreme infringement of personal liberty, it may come as a surprise to hear that local planning officials often receive more calls from neighbors who want those laws toughened than they receive from persons offended by the existing laws.

ORS 215.185, "Remedies for Unlawful Structures or Land Use," sets forth the actions that may be taken to enforce land-use requirements in counties. The list includes injunctions, mandamus, abatement, and "other remedies provided by law." ORS 227.280, "Enforcement of Development Regulations," is the equivalent legislation for cities. It simply declares that city councils "may provide for enforcement" of development regulations.

Enforcement order. An order issued by the Land Conservation and Development Commission to a local government to compel it to take special action toward complying with one or more of the statewide planning goals. ORS 197.320 sets forth seven situations that require the issuance of such an order. Generally, an enforcement order is issued only when a jurisdiction has fallen far short in its progress toward developing a comprehensive plan and implementing ordinances that comply with the goals, or has engaged in a pattern of land-use decisions that flout the goals. Enforcement orders typically require the local government to cease all land divisions or the issuance of building permits or both until the problem is resolved. They may apply to the entire land area in the jurisdiction or only to certain places (e.g., the agricultural land of a county).

Environmental impact statement (EIS). A report concerning effects on the environment that can be expected to occur as the result of some major federal action, such as the construction of a dam. An EIS is required under the provisions of the National Environmental Policy Act of 1969. An EIS comprises two parts, a draft statement (DES) and a final statement (FES). The draft contains technical information and analyses; the final statement is a draft that has been revised to address comments from citizens and agencies.

Erosion. A group of processes by which rock or soil is transported or worn away by the action of wind, water, glaciers, waves, etc. Erosion that occurs at a more rapid rate as a result of human activities— plowing, for example—is sometimes described as 'accelerated,' in contrast to 'normal,' 'natural,' or 'geologic' erosion.

There are many different kinds of erosion. 'Sheet erosion' or 'laminar flow' is the transport of soil particles by a thin film of moving water. 'Rainsplash' erosion is the displacement of particles from the impact of falling raindrops. 'Rill erosion' causes small channels, or rills, to be cut into the soil. 'Gully erosion' occurs when a large volume of rapidly flowing water carves large channels into the soil.

Oregon's statutes provide for the control of erosion through the formation of local improvement districts known as soil and water conservation districts (SWCDs) (ORS 568.210 to 568.890). The formation of such districts is optional. The statewide planning goals do not require erosion-control measures, and most local land-use ordinances do not directly regulate this significant land-use problem. Some jurisdictions, however, have recognized the significance of erosion, and have adopted cut-and-fill regulations, ordinances to limit development on slopes, and other erosion-control measures. Chapter 70 of the state's building code contains standards for excavation and grading. It is an *optional* section of the code: local governments may adopt it at their discretion.

ESEE consequences. Economic, social, environmental, and energy consequences of some land-use decision. Five of the statewide planning goals (numbers 2, 3, 5, 12, and 14) require that these four types of consequences be considered in certain types of planning.

A detailed analysis of these four types of consequences could require months of work and reams of reports. In fact, the standard for judging such analyses has been low: LCDC has not used this goal language to require full-blown environmental impact statements in situations where ESEE consequences must be evaluated.

Estate. The type, extent, or degree of interest held in real property. The different types of interest are defined according to the number of parties who hold interests in a particular piece of property, their relationship to each other, the quantity or types of interests held, and the length of time the interests are enjoyed. There thus are many different types of estates. See *fee simple estate* and *property.*

Estate zoning. See *large-lot zoning.*

Estuary.
A body of water semi-enclosed by land, connected with the open ocean, and within which salt water is usually diluted by freshwater derived from the land. The estuary includes estuarine water, tidelands, tidal marshes, and submerged lands. Estuaries extend upstream to the head of tidewater, except for the Columbia River Estuary, which by definition is considered to extend to the western edge of Puget Island.

This definition occurs in the goals and in OAR 660-17-005(6), "Classifying Oregon Estuaries." OAR 660-17-010 defines four types of estuaries: natural, conservation, shallow-draft development, and deep-draft development. Those definitions and lists of the estuaries that have been classified in each are found in this book under the appropriate alphabetical listings (**conservation estuary, natural estuary,** etc.).

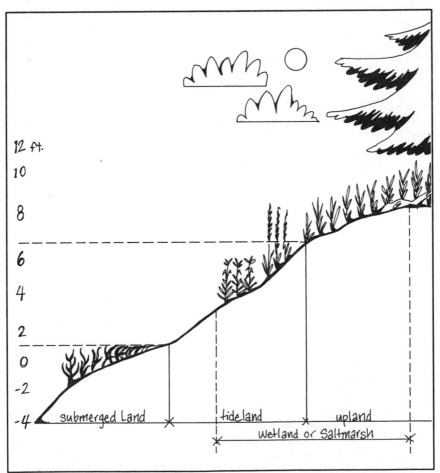

Figure 7. The profile of a typical estuary. Adapted from Thompson and Snow 1974.

Euclidean zoning. The type of zoning affirmed by the US Supreme Court in its 1926 decision, *Village of Euclid v. Ambler Realty Company.* The village of Euclid's system, like those adopted in many communities in the early 1900s, was to divide the town into "use districts" of three different types: industrial, commercial, and residential. Residential zones were considered the highest and industrial zones the lowest in the three-part hierarchy. Lower commercial and industrial uses were not permitted in the highest (i.e., residential) districts, but higher uses could locate in lower zones. That is, a glue factory could not be built in a residential zone, but a home or a store could be built in an industrial zone. This system of allowing higher uses in lower zones is often called cumulative zoning. Although it was popular in the early days of zoning, the cumulative approach is used less today. In its place most communities have adopted 'exclusive zoning'; now there are dozens of zones instead of three, and 'high' uses such as housing are not permitted in the 'low' industrial districts.

A few planners use the term 'Euclidean zoning' quite narrowly, to reflect its origins in the village of Euclid. They apply the term only to zoning that is cumulative and that has a few basic zones. (See, for example, the discussion in Hagman 1971: p. 71.) Most people, however, use the term in a broader way. They mean any land-use ordinance, in Oregon or elsewhere, that divides land into distinct zones where some uses are allowed and others prohibited.

Exactions. The charges, conditions, and dedications demanded from a developer by a local government in return for approval of some proposal for development (usually a subdivision). Example: a city approves an application for a subdivision on the condition that the subdivider dedicate 6 percent of the subdivision's land to the city for a park.

The rationale for exactions is this: new developments generate costs to the community, so those who profit from the development should help the community pay those costs. A new subdivision will generate additional traffic, for example, so the subdivider should dedicate land and pay money for the streets needed to accommodate that traffic.

Exactions for roads, parks, school sites, and infrastructure are common. Requirements for them can be found in most subdivision ordinances. The courts have found the general practice to be acceptable. At some point, however, exaction becomes extortion, and the courts have said no to communities that ask too much. The question of how much is too much is the subject of much litigation. Generally, there must be some reasonable linkage between the exactions sought and the impacts of the proposed development on the community.

Typical exactions include the following:

- Dedication of land for roads, sidewalks, schools, parks, and fire stations. The amount of land to be dedicated may be specified by a formula in the subdivision ordinance.
- Payment of money in lieu of land for the above facilities.
- Payment for costs to the community stemming from the development. See **systems development charge.**
- Installation of improvements such as streets, sidewalks, sewers, water mains, culverts, traffic signals, storm drains, street lights, and fire hydrants.

Exception. 1. The waiving of a statewide planning goal in accordance with procedures set forth in Part II, Goal 2, "Land-Use Planning." The formal definition (from Goal 2) is this:

. . . a comprehensive plan provision, including an amendment to an acknowledged comprehensive plan, that:

(*a*) Is applicable to specific properties or situations and does not establish a planning or zoning policy of general applicability;

(*b*) Does not comply with some or all goal requirements applicable to the subject properties or situations; and

(*c*) Complies with standards for an exception.

The standards set forth in Goal 2 (as amended in 1983) and in ORS 197.732 allow for three types of exceptions. First, land may be exempted from certain goals if it is physically developed. A crossroads community with one store, a gas station, and several homes can be excepted from the requirements of Goal 3, "Agricultural Lands," for example, even if it sits on prime farm land. In that example, the exception just ratifies the obvious: you can't grow crops on the land if it is already built on.

Second, exceptions may be taken for land that is "irrevocably committed" to nonresource uses. In our example of the crossroads community, there might be several vacant lots that cannot be farmed because they are small, irregularly shaped, and surrounded by residences: they are not actually developed, but they are committed to nonfarm uses.

Finally, exceptions may be taken in certain cases when "reasons justify why the state policy embodied in the applicable goals should not apply" (Goal 2, Part II (c)). Several standards must be met for this type of exception: there's more to it than just saying "Goal 3 shouldn't apply because I want to build a house here." This third type of exception is used most often for unusual activities that need to locate on resource land for some special reason—a dam, its reservoir, and a commercial power-generating plant on forest land, for example. An exception is not a device through which a local government can exempt itself from a goal with which it disagrees.

2. The word also refers to a dissent from a DLCD staff report on a request for acknowledgment. ORS 197.251(3) provides that the local government and parties who have objected to or commented on an acknowledgment request shall be given "a reasonable opportunity to file written exceptions to the report."

3. A synonym for variance. This usage is not common in Oregon. It is just as well, given the extensive use to which the word has already been put.

Exclusionary zoning. The use of land-use regulations to keep certain social, economic, or ethnic groups from moving into a community. The use of large-lot zoning in residential areas, for example, may keep low-income persons from buying or even renting homes in such areas.

Exclusive farm use (EFU) zone. Zoning that protects agricultural lands in accordance with the provisions of ORS Chapter 215.203 to 215.293. Not every zone with the word 'farm' or 'agriculture' in its title is a bona fide EFU zone: only those that comply with the statutes can be counted as such. The statutes are quite detailed. They define farm use (ORS 215.203(2)(a)), list the uses that may be permitted outright in an EFU zone (ORS 215.283(1)), specify what conditional uses may occur (ORS 215.283(2)), and establish procedures for land divisions (ORS 215.263). They also specify procedures by which nonfarm dwellings may be located in an EFU zone (ORS 215.283(3)).

Land in a bona fide EFU zone is automatically subject to farm tax deferral (i.e., a landowner need not make a request to the tax assessor to get the deferral). The state Department of Revenue determines which zones qualify as EFU zones.

Consistency with ORS 215's provisions for EFU zones is also necessary for counties to achieve compliance with the statewide goals. Review for such consistency is done by LCDC.

Exclusive zoning. A modern form of zoning that greatly limits and clearly specifies what types of uses are permitted in each district. Unlike the older Euclidean zoning, exclusive zoning is not cumulative; that is, the 'lower' commercial and industrial zones do not allow all of the uses permitted in the 'higher' residential zones. This term should not be confused with exclusionary zoning, the use of land-use regulations to keep certain social, economic, or ethnic groups out of a community.

Ex parte. A Latin phrase meaning 'from or in the interests of one party only.' In planning, it is most commonly used in the expression "ex parte contacts." The expression refers to private meetings or discussions between a member of a reviewing body (e.g., a planning commission) and a person who has some interest in a case to be heard by that body.

Some types of ex parte contacts are frowned on because they may cause hearings officials to be unduly or unfairly influenced by special interests. An example: a developer wines and dines a planning commissioner a few days before the commission is to hear that developer's application for a subdivision. Oregon law doesn't necessarily forbid such contacts. It just requires that decision makers disclose them publicly. The statute applicable to county hearings officials is ORS 215.422. For cities, the pertinent statute is ORS 227.180.

Externality. That which is outside or external to a situation or system; a side effect. The word is often used to describe costs or benefits from a transaction that accrue to some party not involved in it. Such costs and benefits are not reflected in the price of the goods sold in the transaction. Acrid smoke from a widget factory is the classic example of an externality. The smoke represents a cost to those downwind of the factory, but that cost is not reflected in the price of the widgets. The demand for widgets thus is higher than it would be if the total costs of widget making, including pollution, were represented in their price. Externalities typically provide a windfall to some and an uncompensated loss to others. In the widget example, the maker and the buyers get the windfall—an 'external economy' or 'external benefit.' And the persons downwind of the factory get the loss—an 'external diseconomy,' 'external cost,' or 'social cost.'

Exurb. A small community, usually unincorporated, located beyond the suburbs of a city.

Exurbanite. A person who lives in a small community beyond the city and its suburbs, but who earns his or her living in the city. The term is sometimes derogatory, connoting one who is caught up in and acutely conscious of upper-middle-class values and conceits.

Exurbia. An outlying suburban area characterized by opulent homes, rural low densities, and upper-class residents who commute to the city. The word is often use in a derogatory sense to connote snobbery and exclusivity.

F

Factual base. See *inventory.*

Fair market value. See *market value.*

Fair share. As it relates to housing and Goal 10, the concept that each community has a responsibility to provide for its proportion of regional housing needs. In other words, a city cannot ban types of housing that some of its residents perceive to be undesirable. If there is a need for those types of housing in the region, the city must plan and zone land for such housing.

   The concept has been made into an administrative rule for the Portland metropolitan area. OAR 660, Division 7, specifies the types and densities of housing that individual communities in that region must plan in order to do their share in meeting the region's need for housing.

Family. As it is described in the federal census, a family is:
> two or more persons living in the same household who are related by blood, marriage, or adoption. (No families are recognized in group quarters.) All persons living in a household related to each other are regarded as one family. For instance, a son of the head and his wife living in the household are treated as part of the head's family.

The census also differentiates among "primary families," "subfamilies," "husband-wife families," "other families with male head," and "other families with female head."

   The State Structural Code, Section 407, defines family as follows: " . . . an individual or two or more persons related by blood or marriage or a group of not more than five persons (excluding servants) who need not be related by blood or marriage living together in a dwelling unit."

The word family often is carefully defined in land-use regulations so that certain provisions can be administered precisely and objectively. A single-family dwelling, for example, is permitted outright in many residential zones, but a boarding house is not. A distinction between the two can only be made if the ordinance specifies what a single family is. Unrelated 'groupers' are often regarded as a problem in resort, college, or military towns, where they drive up housing costs by bidding up rents to levels that families cannot afford.

FAR. Floor-area ratio.

Farm. A piece of land, often with a dwelling and outbuildings, on which crops or animals are raised. The word is perfectly concise and self-sufficient and it is defined in the state's structural code, but many planners find that it needs embellishment. One almost never sees it used alone in the planning literature. Rather, it is modified or replaced with clumsy phrases such as 'agricultural enterprise,' 'agricultural activity,' 'farming activity,' or 'farm operation.'

Farm dwelling. A residence associated with a farm and occupied by persons who work that farm. ORS 215.283(1)(e) and (f) provide that the following types of dwellings may be permitted outright in an exclusive farm use (EFU) zone:

    (e) A dwelling on real property used for farm use if the dwelling is:

        (A) Located on the same lot or parcel, as those terms are defined in ORS 92.010, as the dwelling of the farm operator and

        (B) Occupied by a relative, which means grandparent, grandchild, parent, child, brother or sister of the farm operator or the farm operator's spouse, whose assistance in the management of the farm use is or will be required by the farm operator.

    (f) The dwellings and other buildings customarily provided in conjunction with farm use.

    A residence that is to be built in an EFU zone and that does not satisfy the above criteria is called (informally) a nonfarm dwelling. Such dwellings are permitted in EFU zones only if they meet certain criteria set forth in ORS 215.283(3).

Farm tax deferral. A tax incentive for farmers to continue farming their land rather than dividing and selling it for development. Many states presently have such programs for 'farm-use taxation.' Oregon's program has been in effect since 1961. It lessens the property tax burden of the farmer by assessing his or her farm only at its value for farm use.

Most real property is assessed at its market value. That value includes the potential of the land for future division and development. In assessing a farm only at its value for farm use, the tax assessor ignores that potential. The farmer's acreage is valued at, say, $1,000 per acre rather than the several thousand it might bring for homesites. This process of differential-assessment is intended to hold the farmer's taxes at a manageable level and thus keep the farm intact. See **property tax.**

In order to ensure that the owner of farm acreage does not reap the benefits of this tax subsidy for several years and then divide and develop the property, the program has a 'rollback' penalty. If the owner of land on farm deferral initiates some action to divide and develop the property (a rezoning, for example), that owner must pay the extra taxes that would have been required if the property had been assessed at its full market value. The higher tax assessment is 'rolled back' for a period of up to ten years.

As set forth in ORS 308.370 to ORS 308.406, Oregon's program has two parts. One provides an automatic deferral for the owners of land in exclusive farm use (EFU) zones. The other, for owners of farm land not under EFU zoning, must be applied for by the land owner, who must meet certain standards regarding his or her gross income derived from farming. For example, the owner of a parcel with an area of 5 to 20 acres must demonstrate that during three or more of the preceding five years he or she has made at least $100 "gross income" per acre from that land.

The income standards for obtaining a farm tax deferral for lands not zoned EFU are quite liberal. It is not uncommon to hear an applicant for a partition declare in a planning commission meeting that the land is totally unsuited for farming and is only useful for homesites. On being asked the question, "Are you on a farm tax deferral?" the answer often is, "Well, yes, but . . . ."

Farm use. Oregon's statutes (ORS 215.203(2)(a)) define this term as follows:

. . . the current employment of land for the primary purpose
of obtaining a profit in money by raising, harvesting and selling
crops or by the feeding, breeding, management and sale of, or
the produce of, livestock, poultry, fur-bearing animals or honey-
bees or for dairying and the sale of dairy products or any
other agricultural or horticultural use or animal husbandry or
any combination thereof. 'Farm use' includes the preparation
and storage of the products raised on such land for human use
and animal use and disposal by marketing or otherwise. It does
not include the use of land subject to the provisions of ORS
chapter 321, except land used exclusively for growing cultured
Christmas trees as defined in subsection (3) of this section.

FAR Part 77. Federal Aviation Regulations, Part 77; the federal
standards regarding obstructions in the airspace around airports. See
airport zoning.

Fasano. The most well known of Oregon's court cases on planning
law, and deservedly so. In 1971, a developer sought a zone change
from Washington County that would enable him to build a mobile-
home park. The county's board of commissioners approved his request,
largely without making findings or showing that the zone change was
consistent with the comprehensive plan. Such a failure was hardly
unusual in those days: small-tract zone changes and similar land-use
actions were considered to be legislative actions and thus exempt from
such procedural falderol. Legislative actions then and now have
'presumptive validity' in court. That is, any court reviewing such a
decision must presume it to be valid, unless an appellant can show that
the action violates the constitution.

But Oregon's courts declared that the *Fasano* zone change was not
a legislative decision: the Washington County board was not *making*
law when they approved that zone change; they were *applying* it. In
doing so, the county board of commissioners was acting in much the
same way as a court—in a 'quasi-judicial' manner. Quasi-judicial
decisions are not entitled to a presumption of validity in court, and
they are subject to substantive and procedural requirements.

The substantive requirements are these. A zone change (and by
extension, many other land-use decisions) must conform to the comprehensive plan; and

In proving that the change is in comformance with the comprehensive plan in this case, the proof, at a minimum, should show *(1)* there is a public need for a change of the kind in question, and *(2)* that need will be best served by changing the classification of the particular piece of property in question as compared with other available property. (*Fasano v. Washington Co. Comm.*, 264 Or 584, 507 P2d 28)

The procedural issues have come to be known as "the Fasano requirements":

Parties at the hearing before the county governing body are entitled to an opportunity to be heard, to an opportunity to present and rebut evidence, to a tribunal which is impartial in the matter—i.e., having had no pre-hearing or ex parte contacts concerning the question at issue—and to a record made and adequate findings executed. (*Fasano v. Washington Co. Comm.*, 264 Or 588, 507 P2d 30)

The implications of *Fasano* are extraordinarily significant. The case changed the entire permit process, lightening the burden on the appellant and greatly increasing the burden for the applicant—and for the city or county that approved the applicant's permit. The case also provided many more grounds from which to launch an appeal.

Most people see planning in Oregon almost wholly in terms of Senate Bill 100, the 1973 legislation that created a statewide planning program. It needs to be remembered, however, that the state Supreme Court's decision in *Fasano* in that same year also had profound effects. Even if Senate Bill 100 had never been adopted, the entire planning process after 1973 would have been greatly changed—simply because of *Fasano*. See **finding, land-use decision,** and **quasi-judicial.**

Fee simple estate. A freehold estate that gives to its holder the largest number of rights to a piece of real property; the highest form of ownership of real property. Also known as a 'fee' or 'fee simple absolute' estate. See **property.**

Field representative. A member of the Department of Land Conservation and Development's staff who acts as a liaison between local governments and the DLCD. There are six 'field reps' for the state. They work from field offices in Portland, Newport, Bend, Medford, and La Grande and from the main DLCD office in Salem.

DLCD's field representatives are sometimes confused with coordinators. The coordinator is a local officer employed by a county or a council of governments. The field representative is a state employee whose job is to convey information for the LCDC to local jurisdictions, to monitor their planning, and to report on local planning to the LCDC.

Fill. "The placement by man of sand, sediment, or other material, usually in submerged lands or wetlands, to create new uplands or raise the elevation of land" (LCDC Goals).

This particular definition was written with an eye to the coastal goals. In general usage, the term simply means the deposit of any materials, organic or inorganic, on a site using a truck, bulldozer, or other mechanical device. The word is often heard as a part of the phrase 'cut and fill,' which means to remove material from one place (a borrow pit or some high place to be leveled) and put it in another (usually a low area that is to be raised).

Cutting and filling has been a common practice in the construction of roads and the development of subdivisions, but many jurisdictions have adopted regulations to restrict this practice. The act of cutting causes erosion and creates a great deal of sediment that pollutes surface water. Cutting also may lead to hazards from mass wasting and may alter drainage patterns in undesirable or unforeseen ways. Many development ordinances regulate the angle of 'cut slopes' and 'fill slopes' in order to control such problems. Chapter 70 of the state's structural code, an optional set of standards for excavation and grading, has been adopted by many local governments.

A specialized definition of fill from the statutes on state lands and waterways is this: "the total of deposits by artificial means equal to or exceeding 50 cubic yards or more of material at one location in any waters of this state" (ORS 541.605(5)). Such fill (and removal of the same amount) requires a permit from the Director of the Division of State Lands. Placing fill materials in "waters of the United States" requires a permit from the US Army's Corps of Engineers. See *404 permit* and *wetlands.*

Final approval. The last stage in the review of complex land-use decisions such as planned unit developments or subdivisions. The more substantive action in such reviews occurs with tentative or preliminary approval. Final approval usually is not much more than rubber-stamping of what has already been agreed on by the planning commission and the developer during earlier phases of the review process. See **subdivision.**

Finding. A statement of the standards, facts, and conclusions used in making a decision. Oregon's laws generally require that land-use decisions be supported by findings. Moreover, the laws (ORS 215.416(7) for counties; 227.173(2) for cities) specify three elements that must go into those findings: *(1)* a statement of the criteria and standards applied in making the decision; *(2)* a description of the facts relied on; and *(3)* an explanation of the "justification for the decision based on the criteria, standards and facts set forth."

Findings are the foundation for a decision. There is more to them than mere documentation. Fifty pages of facts and figures would be inadequate as findings if they lacked any of the three elements listed above. A single page, on the other hand, might suffice if all the right elements were included.

'The findings' and 'the record' for a case are not the same thing. The record for a permit to partition farmland, for example, might contain information to show that the land involved is good for farming. That same record might also contain information to suggest that the land is poorly suited for agriculture. The findings for such a case should make it clear which of those pieces of information the decision makers decided to rely on.

Having proper findings is the single most important factor in most land-use decisions. The importance of findings stems from three facts. First, state law requires that findings be made. Second, the preparation of findings leads to better decisions; it is an exercise in logic. Finally, most land-use appeals rely on a review of the record. If the farmland partition mentioned above got appealed to LUBA, for example, LUBA would not conduct a *de novo* hearing (a legal term for starting a trial from scratch). Rather, LUBA would look at the county's findings to see whether they support the decision. Those findings must describe the standards the county applied to the case, the facts that the decision makers chose to rely on, and the rationale for their decision. If any of those key ingredients is missing, LUBA cannot fill in the gaps by substituting its own conclusions. LUBA must send the case back.

A finding that simply asserts a position without describing the facts that support it is referred to as a conclusional finding. Example: "The application satisfies all of the requirements for a variance." Without a description of what those requirements are and how the application addressed them, the statement is a conclusional finding and is inadequate to support a decision. One also encounters the terms 'conclusory' or 'conclusionary findings,' but those usages are not grammatical.

Fire-protection rating. An objective measure of the type of fire protection available to a certain area. A common system is that used by the Insurance Service Office (ISO), a national nonprofit insurance rating organization. The ISO evaluates various features (respone time, type of equipment, etc.) of a fire-protection system and then rates that system on a scale from one to ten. 'One' represents the highest level of service, and 'ten' indicates the lowest level or a complete absence of fire protection. Areas with the best ratings generally pay less for fire insurance; those with low ratings pay more.

Fiscal zoning. The use of zoning to enhance the property tax revenues of a community or to screen out 'undesirable' land uses that do not generate much revenue. There are two main methods of fiscal zoning: *(1)* zoning inordinately large amounts of commercial and industrial land (also called overzoning); and *(2)* using large minimum-area requirements in residential zones so that only expensive homes can be built there.

Flag lot. A lot that is mostly separated from a street by other lots but that has a long, narrow extension that reaches to the street. Also called a panhandle lot.

Sometimes the flag configuration is a way of providing access. The 'pole' provides a narrow strip of land on which a driveway to the otherwise landlocked lot can be built. Often, however, the flag design is merely a way of satisfying requirements in the subdivision ordinance that call for some minimum amount of frontage, typically 50 or 60 feet. Such requirements are meant to ensure adequate access, but they often fail to do so. It is quite common for landowners to divide their holdings into flag lots and then build driveways to them not along the poles of the flags but on easements over adjoining lands. In such cases, the poles are useless appendages. See **easement.**

Even when the pole or panhandle serves the purpose for which it was intended, the flag lot still is considered to be an inefficient design. It wastes land, delays or precludes the development of public roads,

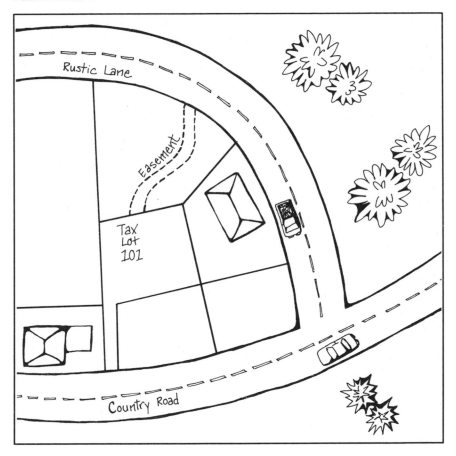

Figure 8. Tax lot 101 is a 'flag' or 'panhandle' lot. It seems to have access to Country Road via the long flagpole or panhandle. The lines on the map imply the existence of a road there, but in fact none may exist. And if there is a hill or gully in that narrow strip of land, it may be impossible to build a road or driveway there. The owner of tax lot 101 then would have to negotiate for an easement across a neighbor's land.

and often causes conflict among neighbors when access roads are not built precisely on the flag's staff. People who want to divide their land may want to use flag lots rather than dedicate land for and share in the cost of a new segment of public road. But many jurisdictions have strong policies against flag lots precisely to ensure that public roads or other forms of access will be built where they are needed.

Floating zone. A special zone that exists in the text of a local government's ordinances but that is not applied generally to large tracts of land, as are the conventional residential, commercial, and industrial zones. Rather, the floating zone is applied on a case-by-case basis in response to requests by individual landowners. This process is often used for mobile-home parks and planned unit developments. The floating zone may be an overlay zone, but the two terms are not synonymous.

Flood. The inundation of land adjoining a stream, river, estuary, or ocean. Floods can be defined in several different ways. They are most commonly described according to their frequency of occurrence expressed in years. A 100-year flood, for example, is a flood that has a probability of occurring once every hundred years. Oregon's 1964 flooding was considered to be a 100-year flood in many areas. This terminology is, of course, only a way to describe a certain probability; a 100-year flood could happen two years in a row.

Frequency of flooding is also described in percentages. A '1 percent flood' is that which can be expected to happen in one out of every hundred flood seasons. The 1-percent flood and 100-year flood, then, are simply different terms to express the same thing. The 100-year (or 1-percent) flood is sometimes referred to as 'base flood' or the 'regional flood.'

The LCDC Goals describe a regional flood as:

A standard statistical calculation used by engineers to determine the probability of severe flooding. It represents the largest flood which has a 1-percent chance of occurring in any one year in an area as a result of higher than normal rainfall or streamflows, extremely high tide, high winds, rapid snowmelt, natural stream blockages, tsunamis, or combinations thereof.

Floodfringe. "The area of the floodplain lying outside of the floodway, but subject to periodic inundation from flooding" (LCDC Goals). Development may be permitted in such areas if it satisfies certain conditions and requirements regarding the height of the structure's main floor above floodwaters, 'floodproofing' construction, displacement of floodwaters, and similar matters. Development typically is *not* permitted in the more hazardous floodway. See *floodplain* and *floodway.*

Flood insurance. Although this phrase could mean any insurance for structures subject to the hazards of flooding, it usually refers specifically to federally subsidized insurance obtained in accordance with the National Flood Insurance Act of 1968. That act provides that flood-prone communities may receive federally subsidized flood insurance only if they adopt a floodplain management program consistent with federal standards.

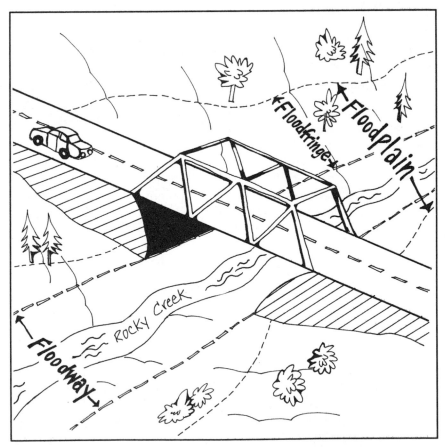

Figure 9. The floodplain for Rocky Creek consists of the floodway (including the channel) and the floodfringe. In a steep gorge, most or all of the floodplain would be floodway. In more level areas (as in the Willamette Valley), the floodfringe might reach far beyond the floodway.

The standards are of two kinds. Relatively minimal standards apply to those communities where detailed hydrologic data are not available. This phase is known as the emergency program. Higher standards come into effect when detailed data become available. A community then enters what is known as the regular program.

Floodplain. "The area adjoining a stream, tidal estuary or coast that is subject to regional flooding" (LCDC Goals). A floodplain comprises two areas, the floodway and the floodfringe. Floodplains are described according to the frequency of the floods that inundate them. A 100-year floodplain, for example, is the land that would be submerged when a 100-year flood occurs. The area that has been covered by the highest known floods is sometimes described as the flood basin.

Floodway. "The normal stream channel and the adjoining area of the natural floodplain needed to convey the waters of a regional flood while causing less than one foot increase in upstream flood elevations" (LCDC Goals).

In less formal usage, the floodway is where floodwaters are moving, as opposed to the floodfringe, where floodwaters are standing or moving very slowly. Many zoning ordinances prohibit development in the floodway but permit some development in the floodfringe. A significant problem with such provisions is that many jurisdictions have no way to tell the two areas apart prior to an actual flood.

Floor area. The total area of all the floors in a building. Gross floor area is measured from the outside of the building, and thus includes the thickness of walls and the area in stairwells, elevator shafts, etc. Net floor area is measured from the interior walls, and excludes the so-called 'dead areas' under walls, stairs, etc.

Floor-area ratio (FAR). A formula used in many urban zoning ordinances to regulate the dimensions of multistory buildings. Suppose, for example, that the ordinance establishes a maximum building area of 20,000 square feet and a floor-area ratio of 3 for a particular lot. Such a combination would permit a one-story building of no more than 20,000 square feet, a three-story building with 20,000 square feet on each floor, a ten-story building with 6,000 square feet per floor, and so on. The building may have any combination that does not exceed a total of 60,000 (3 x 20,000) square feet nor extend beyond the 20,000 square-foot building area limit.

Forecast. See *projection.*

Foredune, active. "An unstable barrier ridge of sand paralleling the beach and subject to wind erosion, water erosion, and growth from new sand deposits. Active foredunes may include areas with beach grass, and occur in sand spits and at river mouths as well as elsewhere" (LCDC Goals).

Foredune, conditionally stable. "An active foredune that has ceased growing in height and that has become conditionally stable with regard to wind erosion" (LCDC Goals).

Foredune, older. "A conditionally stable foredune that has become wind stabilized by diverse vegetation and soil development" (LCDC Goals).

Forest dwelling. An informal term from planning jargon to refer to a dwelling that is associated with an activity permitted in a forest zone. For example, the home of the resident owner and operator of a 100-acre tree farm would be a forest dwelling. A cabin located in a forest and used for recreation by an owner who lives 100 miles away would be a nonforest dwelling.

This pair of terms derives from a similar distinction made between farm and nonfarm dwellings. The farming terms, however, are more precise because they are defined by statute (ORS 215.283). The terms 'forest dwelling' and 'nonforest dwelling' are not so defined. Since 1982, LCDC's standard for distinguishing the two is that the former is "necessary for and accessory to commercial timber production."

Forest lands.
(1) lands composed of existing and potential forest lands which are suitable for commercial forest uses; (2) other forested lands needed for watershed protection, wildlife and fisheries habitat and recreation; (3) lands where extreme conditions of climate, soil and topography require the maintenance of vegetative cover irrespective of use; (4) other forested lands in urban and agricultural areas which provide urban buffers, wind breaks, wildlife, and fisheries habitat, livestock habitat, scenic corridors and recreational use. (LCDC Goal 4)

The state's Forest Practice Rules (OAR 629-24-101) define the term differently: "'Forest land' means land for which a primary use is the growing and harvesting of forest tree species." See *commercial forest land.*

Forest Practices Act (FPA). The state laws (ORS 527.610 to 527.730 and subsection (1) of 527.990) that govern commercial activity involving the growing, harvesting, or processing of forest tree species. These statutes are implemented with a set of administrative rules (OAR 629-24-101 to 629-24-648) known as the Forest Practices Rules.

The FPA has great significance to land-use planning in counties because of what is usually called the '3008 conflict.' The number refers to House Bill 3008 in the 1979 legislature. That bill amended the FPA, adding several paragraphs regarding the regulation of forest operations. One section (ORS 527.722) can be read to declare that, in effect, counties are barred from all regulation of forest operations; regulation must be left to the state and the FPA. But Goals 5, 15 and 17 require counties to protect certain resources that occur on forest lands—wildlife habitats and riparian vegetation, for example. Therein lies the conflict: one state law seems to say that counties cannot regulate forest operations, while another says that under certain circumstances they must.

The Forest Practices Act and related rules contain some provisions for protecting natural resources. Therefore, LCDC and the state's Attorney General ruled (in a series of reviews and opinions from the early 1980s) that counties could rely on the FPA in order to satisfy the goals that involve resources on forest land. Several environmental groups challenged that conclusion. They argued that the FPA is not a suitable measure to implement Goal 5, and that HB 3008 does not preclude counties from regulating some commercial forest operations if such regulation is necessary to protect habitats, waterways, and other Goal 5 resources.

The state's Court of Appeals agreed with the environmentalists. In what is usually referred to as the Tillamook case, the court said that ORS 527.722 "does not eliminate county land use planning authority over forested lands"; counties *must* regulate forest operations when "it is necessary that they do so to fulfill their land use planning duties" (*1000 Friends of Oregon v. LCDC,* A32117, 30 October 1985, p. 6).

Forest uses.
(1) the production of trees and the processing of forest products; *(2)* open space, buffers from noise, and visual separation of conflicting uses; *(3)* watershed protection and wildlife and fisheries habitat; *(4)* soil protection from wind and water; *(5)* maintenance of clean air and water; *(6)* outdoor recreational activities and related support services and wilderness values compatible with these uses; and *(7)* grazing land for livestock. (LCDC Goal 4)

404 permit. A permit from the US Army's Corps of Engineers to discharge dredge spoils or place fill material in waters of the United States. The number refers to the applicable section of the federal Clean Water Act. See **wetlands.**

FPA. *Forest Practices Act.*

Framework plan. A document that establishes the overall policies for a jurisdiction; sometimes referred to as 'the policy element.' It is usually supplemented with several, more detailed plans that deal with specific functions (e.g., transportation) or geographic areas. The detailed plans that deal with specific functions are known as functional plans, development plans, or elements. The more detailed policy documents that deal with specific geographic areas are described as community, neighborhood, district, unit, area, or subarea plans. All of these documents together—that is, the framework plan plus any functional and community plans—make up the **comprehensive plan.**

Frontage. 1. A building's exterior that faces a street.
2. The part of a lot that borders a street or waterfront, often expressed as a distance: "The lot has 300 feet of lake frontage."
3. The direction property faces: "The cabin has a lake frontage."
4. The land between a building and the street it faces: "If they put in a sidewalk, it will decrease my frontage."

Frontage road. A local street that runs parallel with and adjacent to an arterial. If all of the properties that adjoin an arterial are allowed direct access to it, its efficiency and safety are greatly decreased. On the other hand, the adjoining properties are likely to require some access to the arterial. The solution is the frontage road, which is also known as a 'marginal access street.' It provides access to all of the properties adjacent to the arterial, collects their traffic, and brings it on and off the arterial at a few controlled intersections.

Front-end costs. The costs incurred at the beginning of a project. Subdivisions, for example, are said to have high front-end costs because the subdivider must buy the land and spend thousands of dollars to install streets, sewers, water lines, fire hydrants, street lights, and other facilities before selling a single lot and beginning to receive some return on this investment.

Front foot. A unit of measure to describe a property's frontage along a public way or a body of water. The value of commercial land and some recreational property depends more on frontage than on gross area. A quarter-acre lot with 200 feet of street frontage thus will be worth more than a half-acre lot that has only 50 feet of frontage. For that reason, commercial land is often described and priced in terms of front feet: e.g., "Land in that district costs $200 a front foot." Special assessments for sewers, water lines, or streets in local improvement districts are usually made at a rate of so many dollars per front foot.

Front yard. An area between the front lot line and the front building line, within which the placement or construction of buildings is prohibited. See **yard.**

Functional plan. A set of detailed information, policies, and standards regarding some function of local government—transportation, for example. Functional plans usually deal with capital improvements or public services, e.g., municipal water supply, sewers, fire protection, transportation. They are also known as development plans, or may be referred to as elements (as in 'the transportation element of the comprehensive plan'). A comprehensive plan often contains several functional plans, community plans, and a framework plan.

G

Garage. 1. A building or place to shelter motor vehicles.
2. A building or place to repair motor vehicles.

Most zoning ordinances permit small, private garages outright, as accessory uses. They may limit the floor area of such structures (1,000 square feet is the standard used in the state's structural code) and restrict the activities that can occur in the building. Such restrictions ensure that a commercial or industrial use won't be started in a residential neighborhood under the guise of a private garage. Public parking structures or commercial repair shops are usually restricted to commercial and industrial zones.

Garden apartment. A low-rise, multifamily dwelling with extensive landscaping or open space. Such apartments usually are walkups of two or three stories and have medium densities of ten to twenty units per acre.

General plan. See **comprehensive plan.**

Goals. " . . . mandatory statewide planning standards adopted by the commission pursuant to ORS 197.005 to 197.855" (ORS 197.015(8)). The commission referred to in this quotation is of course the Land Conservation and Development Commission (LCDC). Since receiving its mandate from Senate Bill 100 in 1973, LCDC has adopted nineteen statewide goals. They are found, verbatim, in the Appendix of this book.

Among planners in Oregon the terms 'Goals' (capitalized), 'the goals,' or 'the planning goals' usually refer specifically to the nineteen statewide standards. Many local plans, however, contain their own 'goals,' and they use the term in various ways. Generally, a goal is the broadest statement of a community's aims. See **comprehensive plan** and **policy.**

Government-assisted housing.
 Housing that is financed in whole or part by either a federal or
 state housing agency or a local housing authority as defined in
 ORS 456.005 to 456.720, or housing that is occupied by a
 tenant or tenants who benefit from rent supplements or housing vouchers provided by either a federal or state housing
 agency or a local housing authority. (ORS 197.295(2))

Grade. *1.* The ground level at a building site. Most land-use ordinances contain complicated definitions of this term. There is of course
no problem defining the grade of a structure that is to be built on a level
site: it is simply the point where the ground meets the structure, and it
will be the same on all sides of the building. But what is 'the grade' of
a building site on a steep slope? Is it set on the uphill side, the downhill
side, or as some average between those two levels? Most ordinances
specify some type of average; that is why the definitions are often
complicated. A precise definition in the ordinance is important because it is used in applying various regulations, such as those that limit
the heights of buildings.
2. Slope or gradient; the inclination of a road, building site, etc., with
the horizontal, usually measured in degrees or percent. See **slope** for
more details.
3. To make level or reduce the angle of inclination of a surface.

Gradient. *1.* An inclined surface.
2. The degree of inclination, or rate of ascent or descent, of such a
surface. See **slope.**

Grandfathered. Permitted to continue, despite the imposition of new
laws that would otherwise prohibit the activity. Land-use regulations
are rarely retroactive. The activities that do not conform with new
regulations but are permitted to continue are said to be 'grandfathered
in.' A land use that operates under such a 'grandfather clause' is
described as a 'pre-existing non-conforming use,' or, more commonly, a
nonconforming use. See also **vested right.**

Grant. *1.* The act of transferring (conveying) real property.
2. The real property that is transferred.
3. A sum of money given by one party to another. In the field of
planning, the most significant money grants are those from federal

agencies to state and local governments or from state agencies to local governments. Several different types are discussed in the paragraphs immediately following this.

Grant, maintenance. Money from DLCD to a local government for the purpose of maintaining a comprehensive plan after it has been acknowledged.

Grant, planning assistance (PAG). Money provided to local governments by DLCD for purposes of developing comprehensive plans and implementing ordinances that satisfy statewide standards. PAGs made up the bulk of DLCD's grant expenditures in the first decade of the program.

Grant, 701. A federal grant to local governments for the development of comprehensive plans in accordance with Section 701 of the Housing Act of 1954. Formerly a major source of grant money to planning agencies, the program now is defunct; it has been largely absorbed by the Community Development Block Grant process.

Grant, technical assistance. Money paid by DLCD to other governmental agencies (e.g., Bureau of Governmental Research and Service, Department of Fish and Wildlife) or to private consultants and contractors for special research and technical studies; also called 'data and inventory grant.'

Grant, 305. A matching grant from the federal government to a state to establish a program to manage resources in a state's coastal zone. Such grants are authorized under the provisions of the Coastal Zone Management Act of 1972.

Grant, 306. A federal grant to a state for the purpose of administering and maintaining a management program established under the provisions of the Coastal Zone Management Act of 1972.

Greenbelt. An area of parks or open space that surrounds or adjoins a community. In addition to providing recreational and scenic amenities, the greenbelt is a device to prevent urban sprawl; its development is restricted by the government that owns or regulates it. Its effects are similar to those of the urban growth boundary. The greenbelt has not been widely used in this country, presumably because of the great cost to local government in acquiring title to or scenic easements on the land. Boulder, Colorado, is a city often cited as a successful user of this planning technique.

Greenway. In general usage, greenway is a synonym for greenbelt (see above). In Oregon, the word most often refers to the Willamette River Greenway, a natural, scenic, historical, and recreational area adjoining the Willamette and protected by the state in accordance with ORS Chapter 390 and statewide planning goal 15. The Greenway extends from south of Eugene all the way to Portland and into Columbia County. Its average width is 150 feet from the low water line on either side of the river, but in some places it is much wider.

Gross density. See *density.*

Growth. An important, but often ambiguous, word in the literature of planning. It most often means one of three things: economic growth, as measured by some standard such as per capita income; the expansion of a city onto surrounding rural land; an increase in the population of a particular jurisdiction.

Growth management; growth control. In its broadest sense, 'growth management' is little more than a synonym for planning. Frequently, however, 'growth management' (and certainly 'growth control') means a special type of planning through which a community seeks to directly limit the amount of development or growth of population. The techniques for accomplishing that are varied: restrictive zoning; differential taxation; tight 'urban growth boundaries'; greenbelts; moratoria on development; limits on the number of building permits issued per year, etc.

Some people assume that growth controls have been widely used in Oregon. In fact, however, few communities have adopted policies or measures designed to restrict their growth. Most cities and counties have estimated future population growth by extrapolating past trends, and they have then developed plans to accommodate the expected growth. See *Petaluma.*

Guest house. A small cottage on the same lot as a larger single-family dwelling and intended to provide sleeping quarters for guests. Guest houses, cottages, bunkhouses, and similar quarters for guests are permitted outright as accessory buildings in many residential zones, but subject to important limitations. Single-family residential zones are specifically intended to limit the number of dwellings per lot to one. In order to prevent guest houses from turning into second dwellings, as they might otherwise tend to do, land-use regulations typically prohibit kitchen or bathroom facilities, or both, in such units.

Guidelines.

. . . suggested approaches designed to aid cities and counties in preparation, adoption and implementation of comprehensive plans in compliance with goals and to aid state agencies and special districts in the preparation, adoption and implementation of plans, programs and regulations in compliance with goals. Guidelines shall be advisory and shall not limit state agencies, cities, counties and special districts to a single approach. (ORS 197.015(9))

Each of Oregon's statewide planning goals (except number 15) is accompanied by several paragraphs of such guidelines. Since the goals are mandatory and the guidelines are not, the former have received great attention and the latter almost none at all. Although local governments are not compelled to heed the guidelines, these "suggested approaches" to planning are helpful in their explanation and elaboration of the goals.

H

Habitable room. " . . . a space in a structure for living, sleeping, eating or cooking. Bathrooms, toilet compartments, closets, halls, storage or utility space, and similar areas are not considered habitable space" (State Structural Code, Section 409).

Halfway house. A boarding house for persons recently released from prisons, mental hospitals, or similar institutions. Such houses are meant to provide a homelike environment in which their residents can make the transition from institutional life to normal society. For that reason, it is desirable to locate halfway houses in conventional dwellings in residential areas. Proposals to locate halfway houses in such areas, however, often draw the ire of neighborhood residents, who fear an increase in crime and a decrease in property values. Some zoning ordinances do not mention the topic. Others clearly define halfway houses as institutional land uses, and ban them from residential zones. Others provide for them as conditional uses, often in the higher-density residential zones.

That variety of approaches is likely to be short-lived. With Senate Bill 478, the 1983 legislature required that halfway houses with five or fewer persons be allowed outright in residential and commercial zones. See *residential home,* the term seized on by the legislature in their search for a euphemistic alternative to 'halfway house.'

Hammerhead street. See *cul-de-sac.*

Hard copy. The final subdivision plat that is filed with a local government. The hard copy usually is required to conform to very precise standards regarding what must be shown and how the plat is to be drafted. See *subdivision.*

Hardship. Some condition that is difficult to bear or endure. Financial, medical, or other forms of personal hardship often are cited by applicants for some land-use action as reasons why their requests should be granted. Such reasons may be very real and compelling, but they are often wasted on a planning commission. This is not because planning commissioners (and other planning officials) are cruel or unfeeling. It is because they must apply the ordinances as they are written, and most ordinances do not list personal hardship as justification for approving a land-use action.

There are two partial exceptions to the general rule that a showing of hardship is irrelevant. First, almost all ordinances do require such a showing for a **variance.** Second, some contain special provisions that allow a mobile home to be placed temporarily on a lot to provide a residence for an ill or infirm relative of homeowners who already have a home on that lot: in such cases, it must be shown that a medical hardship necessitates the placing of the mobile home there.

Health-hazard annexation. The annexing of an area so that polluted wells and failing septic-tank systems can be replaced with urban water and sewer services. Such annexations can be initiated by a city council, boundary commission, local board of health, or the residents of an area where a hazard to health is believed to exist. The state Department of Human Resource's Health Division is responsible to determine whether a "danger to public health" does exist in the area proposed for annexation (ORS 222.850-222.915).

Hearing. A public meeting at which a tribunal hears comments from various parties, reviews information submitted to it, and (usually) makes some type of land-use decision. The characteristics of a hearing depend on what body is conducting it and on whether the subject is quasi-judicial or legislative. The following statements, however, will generally hold true:

• Some type of advance notice—mail, newspaper ad, radio announcement—is provided at least 10 days before the hearing.
• The hearing, deliberation, and decision are open to the public.
• The hearing is informal: there are no dress codes, formal terms of address, or swearing in.
• Everyone has a chance to speak.
• There is no cross-examination.
• Few persons are represented by attorneys.
• An official record of the meeting is maintained.

All in all, a newcomer to the planning process can expect a relatively informal and unintimidating forum in which he or she will have an opportunity to express an opinion. The trend, however, is toward more formality and a stricter observance of due process. Certain types of state agency hearings may be classified as contested case hearings, and will have more courtroom formalities.

Hearings officer. An official appointed by a local governing body to hear and decide on applications for various quasi-judicial permits or actions (e.g., conditional uses, variances, zone changes, partitions). The hearings officer often is a private attorney on contract to rather than an employee of the city or county. Decisions of the hearings officer usually can be appealed to the local planning commission or governing body.

Height of buildings. You may not think that this phrase deserves a definition, but most zoning ordinances take at least one long paragraph to do it. They usually use the definition found in the state's structural code (Section 409). Such a definition is meant to answer this question: from what point on the ground to what part of the building does one measure height? A one-story home with a half-basement on a steep slope might be 10 or 30 feet high, depending on which side of the house you choose to stretch your tape measure. The ordinances solve the problem by carefully defining grade (the elevation of the building site) and by specifying what part of the roof should be regarded as the top of the building. Residential zones quite often restrict the height of dwellings to 35 feet or two-and-a-half stories, whichever is lower. They frequently exempt antennas, chimneys, or other projections from the height limitations.

One reason for the height limitations is to keep buildings within the reach of standard fire-fighting equipment. Height limitations also help to ensure adequate sunlight and circulation, preserve the residential appearance of a neighborhood, maintain some privacy for backyard sunbathers, etc. In those jurisdictions that do not exempt rooftop projections, however, the height restriction may cause a contemporary problem by prohibiting the construction of solar-heating devices on roofs.

Highest and best use. The use or development of land to its greatest potential for income or economic advantage. The phrase describes a concept basic to land economics and appraisal, that is, that the value of land derives from the maximum net income that could be made if the land were used or developed as intensely as possible. The concept is loathsome to most environmentalists, who point out that short-run economic gains to a few individuals are often not good for the larger human community or the natural environment.

High-rise. A tall, multistory office building or apartment. How many stories does it take to make a high-rise? There is no consensus among planners: some would say as few as seven, but ten stories seems more typical. However many stories it has, a high-rise is always served by an elevator. Conversely, a 'low-rise' is a building with no more than two or three stories and (usually) no elevator.

Historical resources. "Those districts, sites, buildings, structures, and artifacts which have a relationship to events or conditions of the human past" (LCDC Goals). Historical resources are those from an era begun when the first white settlers moved into an area. Those that relate to an earlier time are archeological resources.

The words 'historic' and 'historical' are not interchangeable. 'Historic' means 'well known or important in history.' 'Historical' is a broader term that means 'pertaining to history or past events.' Almost every community has some buildings and sites that are historical resources. Few communities, however, have any places that can truly be said to have *historic* significance.

Holding capacity. A less commonly used synonym for **carrying capacity.**

Holding zone. A zone used to restrict the development of land temporarily until some anticipated event or condition occurs. Land in an urban growth area, for example, may be placed in a holding zone that establishes a minimum-area requirement of 10 acres. That zone is left in place until the nearby city grows and extends its boundaries and facilities closer. In the meantime the holding zone keeps the land that will one day be annexed to the city from being divided haphazardly and inefficiently.

Home occupation. A commercial activity that is conducted within a dwelling unit in a residential zone. Home occupations usually are explicitly defined and limited in zoning ordinances. They sometimes

are allowed outright in residential zones, or more often are listed as
conditional uses, but some ordinances do not provide for them at all.

Most local ordinances restrict the persons that a home occupation
can employ to those living in the residence plus, perhaps, one or two
outsiders. But the 1983 legislature broadened the enabling legislation
for home occupations "in any zone" *in counties* considerably; ORS
215.448 allows home occupations to employ up to five full-time
persons.

The home occupation is a difficult activity to administer. The
community that does not allow for them at all discourages fledgling
businesses and cottage industries that cannot afford expensive commercial or industrial property. The local government that does provide
for them, however, often encounters complaints from disgruntled
neighbors and finds it impossible to keep the home occupations from
growing beyond the limits established by the ordinance.

Homeowners' association. An organization made up of those who
own units in a condominium and through which the condominium is
managed. The owner of a unit in a residential condominium, for
example, shares in the ownership of the condo's common areas: the
halls, yards, parking lot, swimming pool, etc. That owner has a voice
in the management of those common areas through his or her
homeowners' association (or "association of unit owners," as Oregon's
statutes phrase it, at ORS 94.146). The association hires maintenance personnel, pays them with dues collected from the unit owners,
decides whether to re-surface the parking lot, and so on. Also known as
a property owners' association or maintenance association.

Homesite. The ground on which a home is or will be located, and the
land immediately around and associated with the structure; *curtilage.*
This concept is particularly important to the tax assessor, who usually
separates rural parcels into two or more pieces for purposes of appraisal.
A 40-acre parcel of forest land with a dwelling on it, for example,
might be appraised according to two systems, 39 acres as timberland,
and 1 acre—the homesite—as residential property. The same sort of
division is also useful to a planner who surveys or maps existing land
uses. In analyzing a large lot that could be divided in the future and
that has only a single dwelling on it now, the planner will count only a
part of the lot as 'residential land use' and classify the remainder as
vacant.

In an urban setting, the area of the homesite ranges from 3,000 to 6,000 square feet. The components to be counted are the area actually occupied by the dwelling (2,000 to 4,000 square feet), the area taken by a garage or other accessory buildings (250 square feet for a typical single-car garage or carport), and the driveway and parking area (300 square feet or more). Required yards and setbacks may also be counted; they would add 2,000 square feet or more.

The more or less standard figure for rural homesites is 1 acre. The much larger figure is due to four factors. First, the rural home usually

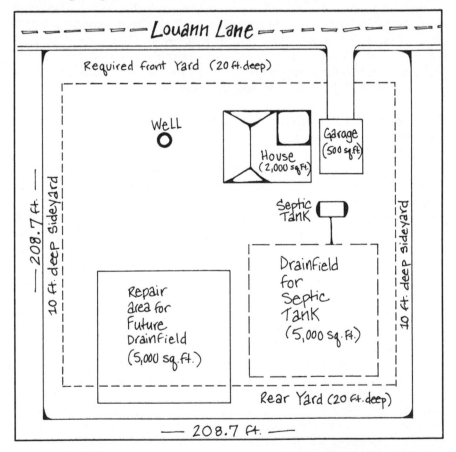

Figure 10. A 1-acre rural homesite, showing some of the typical dimensions and areas required for setbacks, yards, drainfields, and structures.

requires a septic tank and drainfield. No structures can be built over these facilities, and they typically occupy at least 5,000 square feet. Second, state law requires that an area be reserved for a 'repair,' i.e., a new drainfield to replace a failing older system. For that, another 5,000 square feet would be needed. Third, the rural home is assumed to require a well, which will occupy some small area. Finally, the well and the subsurface sewage treatment system must be separated from property lines and from each other a specified distance, typically 100 feet.

Homestead partition. A modification of the minimum-area requirements of a rural zone to allow longtime residents in that zone to remain in their homes while selling off most of their acreage. Suppose, for instance, that an elderly farmer and his wife own 100 acres which they have lived on and farmed for many years. They want to retire because they are no longer able to work the farm, but they also want to keep their home. Farm zoning, however, establishes a minimum-area requirement of, say, 40 acres. Under such circumstances, the farm couple could only sell 60 acres of their farm, and keep their home with a 40-acre yard. Such a division would serve neither the community, which hopes to keep farm lands from being divided into small parcels, nor the couple, who cannot maintain or farm 40 acres. One answer is a homestead partition, which permits the creation of a 1- or 2-acre homestead for the couple, while the remaining acreage is left undivided. Those ordinances that provide for homestead partitions usually set standards regarding the maximum size of homestead (typically less than 5 acres) and the length of time the owners have lived there. They also frequently prohibit any redivision of the acreage separated from the homestead. Homesteads in EFU zones must be reviewed against the nonfarm-dwelling standards of ORS 215.283(3). A more effective alternative to the homestead partition in many cases is a transaction that gives the homestead owners a life estate in their 1 or 2 acres.

Hotel. " . . . any building containing six or more guest rooms intended or designed to be used, or which are used, rented or hired out to be occupied, or which are occupied for sleeping purposes by guests" (State Structural Code, Section 409).

The smaller version of a hotel—a building containing five or fewer rooms for paying guests—is a lodging house. See also **boarding house.**

Household.

A household includes all persons who occupy a group of rooms or a single room which constitutes a housing unit.

A group of rooms or a single room is regarded as a housing unit when it is occupied as separate living quarters, that is, when the occupants live and eat separately from other persons in the building and have direct access from the outside of the building or through a common hall.

The measure 'persons per household' is obtained by dividing the number of persons in households by the number of households.

These are the definitions used by the federal Bureau of the Census. What the Bureau refers to as 'persons per household' is called 'average household size' or just 'household size' in many plans. Note that the word 'household' is not a synonym for the word 'family'; the members of a household may or may not be related.

Household size. The average number of persons per household in a community. The figure is important in the calculation of a community's future need for housing. The smaller the average household size, the larger will be the number of units of housing needed.

A typical household size for Oregon cities is 2.6 persons per unit. The figure falls to 2.0 or lower in urban areas that have a large number of multifamily dwellings. It rises to 3.5 or higher in suburban or rural areas where most of the population is families living in single-family dwellings.

The way in which household size is calculated makes some difference in the figures. If one simply divides the total population of a community by its total number of dwellings, the resulting figure is artificially low because it includes vacant dwellings. Some authorities feel that the proper label for such a calculation should be 'average number of persons per dwelling' and that 'household size' should be used only to mean the average number of persons per *occupied* dwelling. Such a distinction is useful, but it is not widely recognized or maintained.

Housetrailer. See **mobile home.**

Housing assistance plan (HAP). A four-part plan that includes an evaluation of a city's housing conditions, an analysis of need for housing, a statement of the city's goals for housing assistance, and a statement of where such assistance will be directed. The HAP is a prerequisite for federal aid through the Community Development Block Grant program.

Housing authority. A public corporation that manages housing assistance programs in a city or county. A housing authority may be run directly by a local governing body or by a special board appointed by the governing body. The state law regarding housing authorities is found in ORS 456.005-456.235. It enables local governments to establish housing authorities, but does not require that they do so.

Housing code. A set of local regulations that control the use and maintenance of dwellings. A building code and a housing code are not the same. The former specifies how a building is to be constructed. The latter specifies how a dwelling is to be used and maintained after it is constructed. All jurisdictions in Oregon have a building code, because it is required by state law; few have a housing code.

Housing mix. The combination of housing types found in a community. It is usually expressed in percentages. For example, a small city may have a housing mix of 70 percent single-family dwellings, 15 percent multifamily dwellings, and 15 percent mobile homes.

HUD. Department of Housing and Urban Development (federal).

I

Impact fee. See *systems development charge.*

Implementation measures.
> . . . the means used to carry out the plan. These are of two general types: *(1)* management implementation measures such as ordinances, regulations or project plans, and *(2)* site or area specific implementation measures such as permits and grants for construction, construction of public facilities or provision of services. (Goal 2, "Land Use Planning")

The most common devices for implementing a comprehensive plan are zoning and subdivision ordinances, but such regulations are not the only measures available. Capital-improvement programs, grants, special property tax programs (e.g., farm tax deferral), and the construction or withholding of public facilities all can be used to effect the plan. All are encompassed by the term 'implementation measure.'

Improved land. Land that has the services and facilities necessary for its development either on the property or extending to it. An urban lot with sewers, water lines, a street, etc., running by it, for example, would be improved land. Because the tax assessor speaks of buildings as 'improvements,' some persons use the phrase 'improved land' to mean property that has been developed with structures. 'Developed land' would be a better usage, one consistent with a useful three-part hierarchy:

- *raw* — land that has not been developed (that is, with structures) and that lacks most of the services and utilities needed for development
- *improved* — land that has not been developed but that does have the services and utilities necessary for development
- *developed* — land that has buildings or other permanent structures built on it.

126

Figure 11. (a) Raw land.   (b) Improved land.   (c) Developed land.

Improvements. 1. The facilities needed to develop raw land. Typical improvements required in a new urban subdivision include streets, sanitary sewers, storm sewers, water lines, fire hydrants, curbs, sidewalks, street signs, and street lights.
2. As the term is used by the tax assessor, the buildings and other structures affixed to a piece of land. Real property in Oregon is assessed according to the value of the land and the improvements on it. Each property tax statement thus includes a column labeled 'improvements' that shows the assessed value of those structures.

Inclusionary zoning. Land-use regulations intended to increase the diversity of the community, to bring in ethnic or socioeconomic groups formerly excluded, to encourage types of housing other than single-family dwellings alone; the opposite of exclusionary zoning.

Incorporation. The act of creating a city as a legal entity; the organization of a community into a municipal corporation in accordance with ORS Chapter 221. Incorporation is a land-use decision as defined in the statutes and thus is subject to the statewide goals (ORS 197.175). LCDC's administrative rule governing the matter is OAR 660, Division 14. The incorporation of the city of Rajneeshpuram in 1981 spawned considerable litigation and case law on the process of incorporation and its relation to the state's land-use laws.

Incrementalism. The management of one's resources and affairs through a series of uncoordinated, short-term reactions to problems as they occur. The term describes a process that is the opposite or absence of planning. Incrementalism is also known as 'adaptive planning,' 'contingency planning,' 'ad hocism,' and 'fighting brushfires.' Incrementalism and planning can be contrasted on three main points. The former is short-term, largely reactive, and narrow in scope. The latter is long-term, goal-oriented, and comprehensive or holistic.

Industrial lands inventory. A list of sites available for industrial development and a description of their features (acreage, zoning, services, slope, access to rail and air transportation, etc.) Most communities have such inventories in their plans. The state's Economic Development Department maintains a computerized inventory of some 1,500 industrial sites throughout the state. Prospective industrial developers can call (503) 373-1560 and quickly get detailed information on likely sites in any part of the state.

Industrial park. A tract of land that has been planned, divided, and improved for industrial uses. Improvements may include water and sewer lines, fences, railroad spurs, and roads and parking areas designed for large trucks. In some cases an industrial park may be little more than a lot with standard urban utilities and industrial zoning. In others, park may indeed be the appropriate term to describe a well-designed, heavily landscaped property subject to many covenants and managed by a property owners' association. A synonym for this term is 'industrial estate.'

Industry. In popular usage the word means business activity in general, as in 'the tourist industry.' In planning, however, the term almost always denotes only those businesses that process raw materials or that manufacture, repair, or store products. A mill, furniture factory, and a warehouse would all be industrial uses. The word 'commercial' is applied to all nonmanufacturing business activities, such as retail stores, offices, and tourism. A furniture store thus would be counted as a commercial, not an industrial, land use.

Infill. Development (usually residential) that occurs on isolated vacant lots in a city. Such development usually is considered to be a boon to the community because it conserves land, reduces sprawl, and uses lots that otherwise become weed-filled eyesores, dumps, or attractive nuisances for neighborhood children. Infill is, however, usually more expensive for builders because it deprives them of the economies of scale they might gain from building a much larger project on a bigger tract. The units built on isolated urban lots are sometimes called 'vest-pocket housing.'

Infrastructure. The public facilities and services that support the functions and activities of a community. The entire collection of public facilities for a city is sometimes called 'urban plant.' See **public facilities and services.**

Intensity. The extent to which a land use affects a given property or area. Low-intensity uses are those that preserve some of the natural features of their sites, involve little construction, and require few public services and facilities—parks and farms, for example. High-intensity uses require major alterations of their sites, a lot of building, and a maximum of supporting services and facilities—shopping centers and high-rise apartments, for instance.

Interchange. A junction consisting of a system of several road levels arranged so that vehicles can move from one road to another without directly crossing the stream of traffic. This term is to be contrasted with 'intersection,' any place where two or more roads meet.

Interpretation of boundaries. Almost all zoning ordinances have a section with this or some similar title. The purpose of the section is to explain in detail how the boundaries of zones are to be determined in those cases where the zoning map does not provide enough clarity. Zone boundaries usually follow the centerlines of streets, railroads, and streams, and conform to property lines. Large or irregularly shaped lots, however, may be crossed by one or more boundaries. A deep, narrow lot fronting on a highway, for example, may be zoned commercial to a depth of 200 feet while the remainder is zoned residential.

Interstate Land Sales Full Disclosure Act (ILSFDA). Federal legislation passed in 1969 to regulate the interstate selling of lots in large subdivisions. This was primarily a consumer protection measure rather than a federal attempt to control land use. The act is administered by the Office of Interstate Land Sales Registration (OILSR), an arm of HUD (the US Department of Housing and Urban Development). See **subdivision.**

Intervenor. A third party to a court case who volunteers to enter into the case in order to protect his or her own interests as they relate to that case. See for comparison **amicus curiae.**

Inventory. The findings, data, and technical analysis on which a plan's policies are based. Statewide Planning Goal 2 requires inventories for all applicable goal topics. Each city and county plan thus contains a wealth of information on topics such as housing, commercial and industrial lands, natural resources, and hazardous areas. Much of the technical information is presented on maps, although only Goal 4, "Forest Lands," specifically requires a map. In smaller jurisdictions the inventory material often is included in the same document as the plan's policies and is adopted with them. The entire document then is described as 'the Plan.' In larger jurisdictions the inventory usually comprises several separate volumes. The governing body often formally adopts only the policies, but then must refer to the inventory in the plan or in its adopting ordinance.

The separate volumes of inventory material are variously described as background reports, technical reports, or support documents. Common synonyms for 'inventory' include 'factual base,' 'data base,' and 'background material.'

Inverse condemnation. See **taking.**

Island lot. See **landlocked.**

J

Joint Legislative Committee on Land Use (JLCLU). A committee to advise the legislative assembly about various aspects of the state's land-use planning program. It comprises seven members: four from the House of Representatives (appointed by the Speaker of the House) and three from the Senate (appointed by the President of the Senate). The committee's responsibilities are set forth in ORS 197.125-197.135.

K

Key facilities. "Basic facilities that are primarily planned for by local government but which also may be provided by private enterprise and are essential to the support of more intensive development, including public schools, transportation, water supply, sewage and solid waste disposal" (LCDC Goals).

L

Land. That part of the earth's surface not covered by water. Land can be classified in many different ways: by soil type, geologic origin, density of development, dominant plant community, climate, elevation, resources, type of ownership, and the way in which people use it ('land use').

The total land area of the United States is approximately 2.3 billion acres. The federal government owns a third of that. State and local governments own roughly 6 percent. The remainder, 61 percent, is owned by private corporations and individuals.

Oregon's land area is 61.6 million acres. That land is distributed as follows:

Owner	Percentage
federal government	52
state government	2
local governments	1
private parties	45
inland water areas	(less than 1)
	100

(*Source:* Loy et al. 1976: p. 20)

Economists often use this word to mean land and all the natural resources associated with it (timber, minerals, water, etc.). Land (in this very broad sense), capital, and labor make up the three basic factors of production.

Land banking. The buying and holding of land by a public agency for resale to private parties at some time in the future for some specified form of development. The main disadvantage of land banking is that it is an expensive means of controlling land use. Its principal advantage is that it gives a community the greatest amount of power to determine how the acquired land will be used. Land banking is most commonly

133

used in cities, where the municipal government buys a strategic lot (or assembles several of them) and later sells the land to a private developer. In exchange for a lower price on the land, the developer allows the city to control the design of the project.

Land conservation and development action. This phrase was used at the outset of Oregon's statewide planning program to mean local government actions, usually quasi-judicial, that involve the regulation of land use and that are subject to the statewide planning goals. The term is likely to see little use since a slightly less cumbersome synonym, *land-use decision,* was added to the statutes in 1981.

Land Conservation and Development Commission (LCDC). A seven-member commission established by Senate Bill 100 in 1973 to develop and administer Oregon's statewide planning goals. Its members are lay persons appointed by the governor and confirmed by the Senate. The governor is required to choose one member from each of Oregon's congressional districts. (As a result of the increased population shown in the 1980 Census, Oregon gained a new congressional district, bringing its total to five.) The remaining two members can be selected from the state at large. At least one member of the commission, but no more than two, must be from Multnomah County. The laws governing the commission's membership, duties, and powers are found in ORS 197.030-197.060.

LCDC had three main roles in the first decade of Oregon's statewide planning program: to adopt the statewide planning goals and related policies and standards; to review and acknowledge city and county comprehensive plans; and to review and certify state agency programs. In the post-acknowledgment era, LCDC's role is more limited. Appeals of plan amendments go to LUBA, not to LCDC. Periodic reviews come to LCDC only if appealed or called up. LCDC's role thus has shifted more toward policy making and general supervision of the state planning program.

Landlocked. Not having frontage on or access to a public way. 'Island lots' suffering from this condition are often found in older urban neighborhoods and in rural areas where land was divided before the advent of subdivision ordinances. Access to landlocked lots may be provided through an *easement* or *way of necessity.*

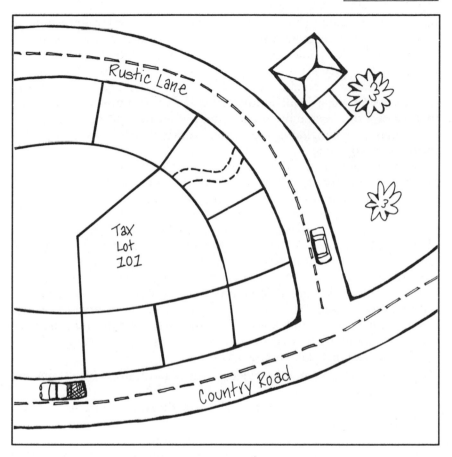

Figure 12. Tax lot 101 is an island lot. Ribbon development and land division along Country Road and Rustic Lane have left it landlocked, with no direct access to either road. The owner must negotiate with neighbors to obtain an easement.

Landlord-tenant laws. The laws that set forth the rights and responsibilities of landlords and those persons who rent or lease property from them. Some cities have ordinances governing this matter. The state's landlord-tenant laws are contained in ORS Chapter 91.

Land use. The main activity that occurs on a piece of land, or the structure in which the activity occurs. Planners generally classify land use by its intensity—its effect on the site, the environment, and the community. The least intensive, of course, is no use at all, so at the bottom of this list comes open space and vacant land. The intensity hierarchy then moves up: farming and forestry, rural residential, single-family residential, multifamily residential, neighborhood commercial, general commercial, light industrial, and heavy industrial. It is from this concept of a hierarchy of uses that the terms 'upzone' and 'down-zone' derive. Changing a zone from residential to commercial, for example, is upzoning.

Terms such as 'residential' or 'commercial' are, of course, very general. There are thousands of different types of land uses. For a more precise means of describing them, see *standard land-use code.*

The proportions of land devoted to different types of land uses vary widely from city to city. An older city with small blocks, numerous alleys, and several rail lines may have an extraordinary amount of land—35 or 40 percent—devoted just to transportation. A small city with a state college in it (Monmouth, for example) may have unusually large amounts of land in institutional uses but almost none in industry. Despite this variety, the following patterns can be observed in many Oregon cities. Note that these proportions are simply reflections of past development patterns; they are not necessarily indicators of how a city should allocate land in the future.

• *Residential uses*—the biggest user of land; takes 30-40 percent of the total area.

• *Street rights-of-way*—typically the second biggest user; takes 20-30 percent of total.

• *Public and institutional uses*—15-20 percent.

• *Commercial uses*—not a big user of land; less than 5 percent of the total urban area.

• *Industrial uses*—varies greatly, but generally not as big a user of land as might be expected; 5-15 percent.

• *Vacant*—varies greatly; 10-30 percent.

Land Use Board of Appeals (LUBA). A board established by the state legislature in 1979 to hear and decide on contested land-use cases (Sections 1-6a, Chapter 772, Oregon Laws 1979). The purpose for creating LUBA was to provide a means of resolving a growing number of land-use cases without taking them through the courts or to the LCDC. LUBA comprises three members: a "chief hearings referee" and two referees. They are appointed by the governor and confirmed by the state senate. All must be "members in good standing of the Oregon State Bar" (ORS 197.810).

LUBA originally was an arm of LCDC, and submitted recommendations to that commission for final action. The 1983 legislature changed that with House Bill 2295, making LUBA an independent land-use court. The statutes that govern it are found at ORS 197.805-855.

Land-use decision.

(A) A final decision or determination made by a local government or special district that concerns the adoption, amendment or application of:

 (i)   The goals;
 (ii) A comprehensive plan provision;
 (iii) A land use regulation; or
 (iv) A new land use regulation; or

(B) A final decision or determination of a state agency other than the commission with respect to which the agency is required to apply the goals. (ORS 197.015(10))

The term does not include " . . . a ministerial decision of a local government made under clear and objective standards contained in an acknowledged comprehensive plan or land use regulation and for which no right to a hearing is provided by the local government under ORS 215.402 to 215.438 or 227.160 to 227.185" (ORS 197.015(10)).

To reduce all that to general terms, a land-use decision is a legislative or quasi-judicial action of the type that usually involves a public hearing (e.g., a variance or a subdivision request). The phrase does not encompass most over-the-counter ministerial actions (building permits, for example). For descriptions of the three general kinds of decisions involving land and development, see entries under *legislative, ministerial,* and *quasi-judicial actions.*

Land Use Policy and Planning Assistance Act.
Abortive federal legislation to establish a national policy on land use and to provide planning grants to state governments. It was based on the American Law Institute's model land-development code. The legislation was introduced in 1971 and defeated in committee in 1974.

Land-use regulation.

 . . . any local government zoning ordinance, land division ordinance adopted under ORS 92.044 or 92.046 or similar general

ordinance establishing standards for implementing a comprehensive plan. 'Land use regulation' does not include small tract
zoning map amendments, conditional use permits, individual
subdivision, partitioning or planned unit development approvals or denials, annexations, variances, building permits and
similar administrative-type decisions. (ORS 197.015(11))

This definition was added to ORS Chapter 197 in 1981 by House
Bill 2225. The term is roughly synonymous with 'implementing
ordinance.' See **implementation measures.**

Large-lot zoning. Zoning that establishes large minimum-area requirements. Large is, of course, a relative term. In a city a 1-acre
minimum-area requirement would be considered large-lot zoning. In
rural areas, anything from a 20- to a 160-acre minimum constitutes
large-lot zoning. The purposes of such zoning are many. In urban
settings the purpose may be to enhance aesthetics, to maintain low
density consistent with the capacities of municipal services, or to keep
out 'undesirables' by not providing small, lower-priced homesites.
Urban large-lot zoning in residential areas that is largely for aesthetic
purposes is called 'estate zoning.' When similar zoning is used as a
means to keep other persons out of the community, the appropriate
label is 'snob zoning' or 'exclusionary zoning.' In rural situations the
purpose of large-lot zoning usually is threefold: to ensure that resource
land remains in parcels large enough to be used for commercial
farming or forestry; to limit the density of residential development so
that it will not overload small rural public facilities and services; and to
prevent environmental problems such as excessive drawdown in wells.

LCDC. Land Conservation and Development Commission.

League of Oregon Cities (LOC). An organization "aimed at helping
Oregon cities to be strong, efficient units of government, effectively
answering the needs of their citizens, and representing the interests of
city residents before both the state and federal governments" (LOC
pamphlet *'League of Oregon Cities,'* p. 1). The League was formed
in 1925. It now has a membership that includes 235 of the state's 241
cities. It is directed by an executive committee of twelve members,
who are all elected or appointed city officials. The League maintains
an office and staff in Salem.

Leapfrog development. Development that occurs some distance from the main concentration of similar land uses and the facilities that serve them. The classic form of leapfrog development is the subdivision which develops a mile or two from similar tracts in a nearby city. Developers like the leapfrog subdivision because they find a greater variety of land and lower land prices the farther they go from the city. The new residents like the leapfrog subdivision because the lots are cheaper and they are 'in the country.' City officials and taxpayers, however, will not like the new subdivision when they have to pay for the costs of extending sewer and water lines and other services over the extra mile or two.

Legal description. A description of the precise location and boundaries of a particular parcel of land. The description usually is written in one of three general forms. See *metes-and-bounds, plat,* and *township-and-range survey system.* Planners and others who deal with land often refer to a legal description as 'the legal.'

Legislative action. The making of law, as opposed to the application of existing law to a particular case. When a city council adopts an ordinance making mobile homes a conditional use in certain residential zones, it is taking a legislative action. When it applies the provisions of that ordinance to a specific request for a conditional use, it is taking a quasi-judicial action.

Governing bodies generally have a great deal of discretionary power in taking legislative actions. Unlike quasi-judicial actions, legislative actions have a presumption of validity in court, and they are not subject to many of the formalities of procedural due process. See *Fasano* and *quasi-judicial.*

LOAC. Local Officials Advisory Committee.

LOC. League of Oregon Cities.

Local access road. "A public road that is not a county road, state highway or federal road" (ORS 368.001(3)). The difference between a county road and a local access road is that the county government is responsible for maintaining the former. The county does not have the responsibility to maintain the latter: owners of adjoining property must pay to fill the potholes, renew the gravel, or oil the roadway.

Local government. " . . . Any city, county or metropolitan service district formed under ORS Chapter 268 or an association of local governments performing land use planning functions under ORS 197.190" (ORS 197.015(12)).

Local improvement district (LID). A small district formed for the purpose of carrying out local improvements (paving of streets, construction of storm sewers, development of a park). Property owners within the LID are assessed for the cost of the improvements in accordance with ORS 223.387-223.485.

Local Officials Advisory Committee (LOAC). A committee of elected officials from cities and counties in Oregon. Its members are chosen by the LCDC. The purpose of the committee, as set forth in ORS 197.165, is to "advise and assist the commission [LCDC] on its policies and programs affecting local government." The group is moribund; it has not met in years.

Local street. A public roadway designed to provide access to the properties that adjoin it and to move local traffic onto collectors. Also called a minor street. See **road.**

Lodging house. " . . . any building or portion thereof containing not more than five guest rooms where rent is paid in money, goods, labor or otherwise" (State Structural Code, Section 413). Structures with more than five guest rooms are considered to be hotels. Almost all zoning ordinances count hotels as commercial uses and restrict them to the appropriate zones. Many such ordinances, however, do list lodging houses as conditional uses in some residential zones. The local definitions of lodging house may differ from that above.

Boarding house is often used as a synonym for lodging house. Indeed, many zoning ordinances mention only the former. That usage is unfortunate. A boarding house is, after all, one that provides board— that is, daily meals. A lodging house provides lodging; it may or may not provide meals. The distinction between the two remains useful.

Lot. "A unit of land that is created by a subdivision of land" (ORS 92.010(1)). Since Oregon's statutes define subdivision to be a division of land that creates four or more new units of land, the word 'lot' is not properly applied to the units that result from simple divisions that create only two or three new units. These simpler divisions are called partitions, and the resulting pieces of land are called parcels. Although Oregon's lawmakers carefully distinguish lots from parcels, they have not provided us with any broader term that encompasses both. Thus, one will continue to hear the word 'lot' used both in its narrower statutory sense and in the broader sense of 'any piece of land divided from some larger tract.'

The planner's lexicon includes many terms for special kinds of lots. Those defined in this glossary include **double-frontage, flag, island, panhandle, reversed-frontage, ribbon, shoestring,** and **through lots.** See also **subdivision.**

Lot coverage. The percentage of a lot's total area that is covered by buildings and accessory structures. Many zoning ordinances limit such coverage on residential lots: a maximum coverage of 35 percent is typical. The intended purpose of this and other bulk regulations is to ensure adequate light, privacy, open space, and circulation to individual dwellings. An unintended and increasingly important effect is to hinder more efficient use of and higher densities on urban land. See **building area.**

Lot depth-to-width ratio. Long, narrow shoestring or ribbon lots are difficult to develop and are considered to be an inefficient use of land. To prevent their creation, many land-use ordinances require that new lots and parcels not exceed a certain ratio of depth to width: 2½ to 1 is a common standard.

Lot line. The boundary of a lot or parcel. Most subdivision and zoning ordinances define the various types of lot lines (front, rear, and side) quite carefully; such lines provide the basis for determining setbacks, yards, vision clearance, etc.

Lot-line adjustment. The relocation of a common boundary line between two lots or parcels. When no new parcel is created and when no existing parcel is reduced below the minimum area required by zoning, such an adjustment is not considered to be a partition (ORS 92.010(8)).

Lot number. The number used to distinguish a lot in a certain block of a subdivision. Lot and block numbers together provide a legal description of the property in a subdivision. Example: Lexington Heights, Second Addition, Block 7, Lot 12.

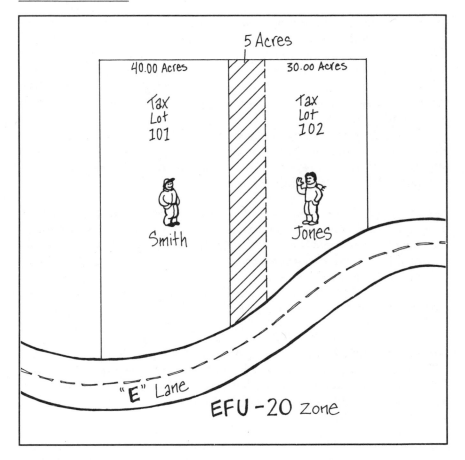

Figure 13. If Jones wants to sell Smith the 5-acre strip along the western boundary, he can do so without going through a partition. This would be a simple lot-line adjustment. No new lot would be created, and tax lots 101 and 102 would both remain larger than the 20-acre minimum lot size required in the EFU-20 zone. But Jones cannot sell Smith any more than 10 acres, because that would leave tax lot 102 smaller than the required minimum.

Note that this type of lot number, from a subdivision plat, is not the same thing as a tax-lot number. Tax-lot numbers are assigned to lots and parcels by the tax assessor for accounting and record keeping. The lot described above—number 12 from the Lexington Heights Subdivision—also may have a separate and distinct tax-lot number.

Lot of record. A broad, nonlegalistic definition is a lot or parcel that, because of its existence prior to the passage of a certain regulation, retains development rights that would otherwise be prohibited by that regulation. Oregon's legislature defined the term more narrowly: " . . . a lot or parcel in the unincorporated area of a county outside of the Willamette Greenway and outside of areas designated in a county comprehensive plan as being in a flood plain or geological hazard area or designated for urban, industrial or commercial development and which was lawfully created by or transferred to the present owner by a deed or sales contract executed after January 1, 1948, and before January 1, 1975" (Section 9(1)(c), Chapter 884, Oregon Laws 1981). The law from which that quotation comes also provided that one dwelling could be built on any lot encompassed by that definition. The law contained a 'sunset clause,' however, which terminated thatprovision on 1 July 1985.

The concept underlying lots of record is simple. Zoning and subdivision ordinances are not retroactive. The owner of a store is not made to tear it down if the property is zoned residential after the store has already been built. And the owner of a legally created, 1-acre parcel generally retains the right to build a home on the land even after the property is zoned residential with a 5-acre minimum-area requirement.

The question of what lots and parcels should be 'grandfathered in' becomes more difficult with other examples. Should an undeveloped subdivision of 1-acre lots recorded in 1890 in the midst of prime farmland be allowed to develop with a house on each lot even though the land now is zoned exclusive farm use with a 40-acre minimum-area requirement? Should land divisions that occurred before the counties had standards for and kept records of partitions be counted for lots of record? Should two parcels created by a contract that was never recorded with the county be considered lots of record? These are some of the questions that planners and legislators wrestled with in arriving at the temporary statutory provisions described above.

Lot yield. The number of lots per acre obtained in a subdivision. The yield will depend on many variables: topography; type of public services and facilities available; minimum-area requirements in local land-use regulations; amount of land needed for parks or school sites, etc. A subdivider usually attempts to maximize the lot yield of the subdivision. See ***commercial acre.***

M

Maintenance association. See *homeowners' association.*

Major partition. "A partition which includes the creation of a road or street"(ORS 92.010(2)). See *partition.*

Major revision. Any change of a comprehensive plan and its implementing ordinances that will have widespread and significant effects beyond the immediate area that is subject to the change. Amending the plan map for a small city to redesignate a four-block residential district for industrial uses would constitute such a revision. Major revisions are to be contrasted with minor changes, such as redesignating a single small parcel from residential to industrial.

Major revisions are discussed in Section 5A of the guidelines for Goal 2. That section suggests that major revisions of a comprehensive plan not be made more frequently than once every two years. Compare with *minor change* and *quasi-judicial action.*

Manufactured home. Housing that is built partly or entirely in a factory rather than at the site where it is to be placed. The term embraces *mobile homes, modular homes,* and *panelized homes.*

ORS 197.295 (3) defines manufactured homes as follows:
. . . structures with a Department of Housing and Urban Development (HUD) label certifying that the structure is constructed in accordance with the National Manufactured Housing Construction and Safety Standards Act of 1974 (42 U.S.C. Article 5401 et seq.), as amended on August 22, 1981.

Marginal. 1. Situated near the edge or border.
2. Almost insufficient.
3. In economics, the selling of goods at a price per unit which just equals the additional cost of producing the last unit supplied.

144

This adjective is often used as a synonym for 'bad,' 'inefficient,' or 'unsuitable.' Many persons use the phrase 'marginal farmland,' for example, to mean land not suitable for farming. Such usage is incorrect. 'Marginal' serves the useful purpose of describing that which only comes near to being unsuitable or uneconomical. There are plenty of other words to describe that which crosses the line—submarginal, for example, if one wants to use the jargon of economists.

Marginal-access street. See *frontage road.*

Marginal lands. Certain farm or forest lands exempted from the requirements of Goals 3 and 4 because of their low productivity. The standards for determining marginal lands are found in ORS 197.247. Those standards and the less stringent planning and zoning requirements for marginal lands apply only in counties that have chosen to use this optional set of statutory provisions. The marginal lands bill (Senate Bill 237) was adopted in 1983. It is a classic example of legislative compromise, giving tougher farmland planning standards to conservation interests and less stringent standards on marginal lands to pro-development factions.

Few counties have chosen to use the marginal land provisions. The main reason for that probably is that the provisions are complicated and difficult to administer. The 1985 legislature directed LCDC to take another look at the problem and to "provide a practical means of identifying secondary resource lands and allow[ing] specified uses of those lands" (Section 11, Chapter 811, Oregon Laws 1985).

Market factor. The inclusion of extra land within a city's urban growth boundary (UGB) in order to allow for unexpected growth. Goal 14 requires that a UGB be designed to provide enough buildable land to meet a city's projected needs to some target date, usually the year 2000. Some cities have projected their growth to that year, and then adopted a UGB that is large enough to accommodate that growth plus 10 or 20 percent more—the market factor. The argument put forth for such a reserve of buildable land is that future growth cannot be predicted accurately. If it occurs more rapidly than expected, land costs will soar because of a restricted supply, and new businesses will go to other cities where land is more readily available. The argument against the market factor is that the UGB is not cast in concrete. If growth occurs more rapidly than expected, the UGB can be expanded, long before the year 2000 if need be. And if growth occurs as predicted or less rapidly, the city is not committed to providing expensive urban services to areas where they are not needed, sprawl is reduced, and farm and forest lands near the city are not sacrificed for unrealized growth.

LCDC has consistently rejected the overt use of market factors. In practice, however, many plans have achieved the same result through other means. In some cases, excess land is included in the UGB inadvertently, as when projections of population growth are done incorrectly. See *population growth*. In other cases, the projected need for urbanizable land is inflated by a combination of unrealistic assumptions about population growth, densities, household size, and availability of urban services.

Market value. The price that a buyer would pay and that a seller would accept for a particular piece of property, assuming that the following conditions exist: *(1)* the seller is willing to sell; *(2)* the buyer is willing to buy; *(3)* neither is under abnormal pressure to make the transaction; and *(4)* the transaction is 'arms length,' i.e., the two parties do not have some special relationship that might affect the price. The price that a father might ask in selling a home to his son, for example, would not necessarily indicate the true market value.

'True cash value' is a synonym for market value used by the tax assessor. ORS 308.205 defines it this way:

"True cash value of all property, real and personal, means market value as of the assessment date. True cash value in all cases shall be determined by methods and procedures in accordance with rules and regulations promulgated by the Department of Revenue. With respect to property which has no immediate market value, its true cash value shall be the amount of money that would justly compensate the owner for loss of the property. With respect to property that is subject to governmental restriction as to use on the assessment date under applicable law or regulation, true cash value shall not be based upon sales that reflect for the property a market value that the property would have if the use of the property were not subject to the restriction unless adjustments in value are made reflecting the effect of the restrictions."

The last line of the definition means that real property should be assessed according to its value as zoned, not according to its potentially higher value if unrestricted by zoning. See *highest and best use, user value,* and *value.*

Master plan. A comprehensive plan. Although a few planners discern some differences in the meanings of 'master,' 'comprehensive,' and 'general' plans, most do not: the three terms are largely interchangeable. In Oregon, 'comprehensive plan' is clearly the predominant usage, with 'general plan' coming in a poor second. 'Master plan' is the least popular of the three, but it is beginning to be used in another way, as a synonym for 'functional plan': for instance, a 'parks and recreation master plan.' See *comprehensive plan.*

Material recovery. See *resource recovery.*

Meridian. **1.** An imaginary line on the earth's surface extending directly from the north pole to the south pole on a great circle route; a reference for describing one's position (longitude) east or west of the Greenwich meridian. Salem's longitude, for example, is roughly 123 degrees west (of the Greenwich meridian).
2. A north-south reference used in the township-and-range survey system.

For both types of meridian, the complementary east-west lines used to establish the other half of the reference grid are called parallels.

Metes and bounds. A 'mete' is a limit or boundary, as is a 'bound.' Together, the two words refer to a system for describing property in terms of a set of directions and distances. Metes-and-bounds descriptions invariably start with the words "Beginning at a point . . . ," go on to describe that point, and then proceed through directions and distances until the description closes: e.g., "thence southerly 100 feet and thence westerly 235 feet to the point or place of beginning." In older legal descriptions the point or place of beginning may be a tree, body of water, or some other natural feature that has changed or no longer exists.

Metes-and-bounds descriptions are often difficult for the uninitiated to read because of all the 'thences,' 'southerlies,' 'westerlies,' and so on. Further complication occurs when the description uses a unit of distance other than feet. Two units often encountered in older descriptions are 'rods' and 'chains.' A rod equals 16½ feet. A chain equals 4 rods or 66 feet. A mile (5,280 feet) contains 320 rods or 80 chains. See *legal description.*

Metro. See *Metropolitan Service District.*

Metropolitan. In general usage, anything having to do with a large city. The US Bureau of Census uses the word specifically to describe populations that reside in Standard Metropolitan Statistical Areas.

Metropolitan Service District ('Metro'). A district formed under the provisions of the Metropolitan Service District Act of 1969 (ORS Chapter 268) to consolidate governmental functions in the Portland area. The purpose of the act was "to provide for the consolidation of those regional governments [in the Portland metropolitan area] and to establish an elected governing body and thereby to increase the accountability and responsiveness of regional government officials to the citizenry through the election process" (ORS 268.015). Metro encompasses all of Portland and Multnomah County, several other cities, and parts of Clackamas and Washington counties.

Mineral rights. The rights to extract minerals (soil, aggregate, ores, etc.) from a piece of land. The definition of minerals varies: it may or may not include oil, for example. Statutes relevant to this topic are found in ORS Title 43, "Mineral Resources."

Minimum-area requirement. See **minimum lot size.**

Minimum lot size. 1. The smallest area permitted by ordinance for any new lot or parcel in a particular zone. In this sense, the phrase implies a land-division standard, which applies only to new partitions or subdivisions. (See **lot-line adjustment.)**
2. The smallest lot or parcel on which a new building can be constructed in a particular zone. Used this way, the term is a development standard applicable to all existing lots and parcels.

In most zoning ordinances, both of the above meanings are intended. Many of those same ordinances contain provisions that exempt some legally created lots of record from area requirements. In a zone where the minimum is 2 acres, for example, the owner of a 3-acre lot could not divide this land. The owner of a 1-acre lot of record, however, could build a dwelling on it, assuming that all other applicable bulk requirements were met. The lot-of-record provisions in most city ordinances are so broad that the minimum lot size is essentially only a land-division standard. County lot-of-record provisions are greatly restricted by state law: in counties, then, the minimum lot size is as much a development standard as a land-division standard.

It is common to refer to minimum lot size as a density standard. Lot-size requirements do affect density, but the relation is less direct than it might seem at first glance. A thousand-acre district under 10-acre zoning, for example, is highly unlikely to be carved into one hundred lots. There are several reasons why. First, there will be some lots larger than 10 acres that cannot be divided: a 10-acre minimum prohibits the division of lots as large as 19 acres. Second, streets, schools, and other public uses will take some of the thousand acres. Third, constraints such as steep slopes, poor drainage, or a lack of roads will hinder division and development of some areas.

Lot-size requirements vary greatly from zone to zone. Urban zoning ordinances usually express such requirements in square feet. A typical figure for a single-family residential zone is 6,000 square feet. County ordinances deal in acres. Suburban or rural residential zones typically require 1 to 10 acres per lot. There is no typical figure for farm and forest zones: the range extends from 10 to several hundred acres.

Although the phrase 'minimum lot size' is standard planning jargon, it suffers from a flaw: the word 'lot' is often inappropriate. A lot is a unit of land created by a subdivision; a parcel is a unit created by a partition. Subdivisions and partitions both are subject to the requirements of zoning ordinances, but the phrase 'minimum lot size' implies that only subdivisions are. The remedy suggested here is to replace that phrase with 'minimum-area requirement.'

Ministerial action. A routine governmental action that involves little or no discretion. The issuance of a building permit is such an action; if construction plans conform to the building code and other related requirements such as zoning, for example, a building permit will be issued.

Unlike quasi-judicial actions, a ministerial action usually does not involve notice to affected parties, public hearings, and similar procedures. And unlike legislative actions, it is not dependent on the judgment, opinion, or discretion of the issuing authority. Very few of the land-use decisions made by a planning department, planning commission, or hearings officer are ministerial. However, most of the permit decisions made by local environmental health and building departments are ministerial. See **land-use decision, legislative action,** and **quasi-judicial action.**

Minor change. Any change of a comprehensive plan and its implementing ordinances that will have no significant effects beyond the immediate area subject to the change. The term encompasses, but is not identical to, small-tract zone change and quasi-judicial action. It is discussed in Section 5B of the guidelines for Goal 2. That section suggests that minor changes "should not be made more frequently than once a year, if at all possible." Some jurisdictions honor that suggestion. They accumulate proposed plan amendments, ordinance revisions, rezonings, and other minor changes for a specified period, often one year, and then act on them all at the same time. Many jurisdictions, however, continue to make minor changes piecemeal.

Minor partition. "A partition that does not include the creation of a road or street" (ORS 92.010(4)). See **partition.**

Mitigation. The act of alleviating, abating, or lessening some problem or affliction. The word is significant in planning because of its use in Goal 16, "Estuarine Resources," which states: "When dredge or fill activities are permitted in intertidal or tidal marsh areas, their effects shall be mitigated by creation, restoration or enhancement of another area to ensure that the integrity of the estuarine ecosystem is maintained." The precise statutory definition of mitigation and the rules for carrying it out are set forth in ORS Chapter 541. The statute's requirements are administered by the Division of State Lands.

Mobile home. A structure intended for residential use, manufactured in a factory, and built on a chassis so that it can be towed from factory to homesite or from one site to another. A mobile home is one type of **manufactured home.**

    The definitions of and standards for mobile homes vary from one jurisdiction to another. Some ordinances use a definition similar to that in ORS 446.003(19): "A vehicle or structure constructed for movement on the public highways, that has sleeping, cooking and plumbing facilities, is intended for human occupancy and is being used for residential purposes."

    Many local ordinances use more restrictive definitions. Some specify that the structure must have a certain minimum floor area to be considered a mobile home: minimums of 200 to 800 square feet are typical. Other ordinances specify a minimum width: 12 feet is a common standard. Some require that a mobile home be a 'double-wide.' And many require that a mobile home have an 'insignia of compliance,' as set forth in ORS Chapter 446. Finally, some ordinances use several or all of these standards.

By building standards into a definition, a local government narrows the range of structures that are permitted as residences. Units that do not qualify as mobile homes are considered to be travel trailers or recreational vehicles. Such types of structures are not permitted to be used for extended occupancy.

Despite the restrictions found in some ordinances and disapproval from some residents of conventional frame dwellings, mobile homes have come to occupy a significant share of the typical community's **housing mix.** In many jurisdictions more than half of the total permits issued for dwellings in recent years have been for mobile homes. At one time, mobile homes were known as house trailers, trailer homes, or trailers. Those names are shunned by today's owners and makers of mobile homes. Those persons believe (properly so) that the older terms conjure up images of tinny little boxes occupied by transients. They declare (correctly) that the modern mobile home is rarely tinny, little, or occupied by persons any more transient than the owners of 'stick-built' houses. And they note that the mobile home is rarely trailered behind anything except the truck that brings it to its first (and often only) homesite. Despite all that, many local ordinances still contain the outmoded terms for this important type of housing.

Mobile home park.
Any place where four or more mobile homes are located within 500 feet of one another on a lot, tract or parcel of land under the same ownership, the primary purpose of which is to rent space or keep space for rent to any person for a charge or fee paid or to be paid for the rental or use of facilities or to offer space free in connection with securing the trade or patronage of such person. 'Mobile home park' does not include a lot or lots located within a subdivision being rented or leased for occupancy by no more than one mobile home per lot if the subdivision was approved by the local government unit having jurisdiction under an ordinance adopted pursuant to ORS 92.010 to 92.190. (ORS 446.003(22))

Modal split. The proportions of different types (modes) of transport that comprise a transportation system. For example, the modal split on a typical weekday in a small town might be 90 percent of the trips by privately owned vehicles (called POVs by the transportation planners), 6 percent by bus, and the remaining 4 percent by walking and bicycling.

Model cities. A federal program to provide aid to low-income districts in central cities. It grew out of the Demonstration Cities and Metropolitan Development Act of 1966. It was replaced by the broader programs of the Housing and Community Development Act of 1974.

Modular home. A residential structure made up of units that are built in a factory and then brought to and assembled at the homesite. The term is often limited to structures made from modules that are entire rooms or groups of rooms. Structures assembled from sets of standardized floor, wall, and ceiling components are then referred to as panelized homes.

Monument. A fixed object used as a reference point in a survey of land. Galvanized pipe, steel rods, stone, or concrete are used for monuments at the beginning points of surveys, at lot corners, and at other points where a survey boundary changes. ORS 92.060 sets forth the requirements for monuments in the surveying of subdivisions.

Moratorium. ORS 197.505 defines 'moratorium on construction or land development' to mean
> engaging in a pattern or practice of delaying or stopping issuance of permits, authorizations or approvals necessary for the subdivision and partitioning of, or residential construction on, urban or urbanizable land. It does not include actions engaged in, or practices in accordance with a comprehensive plan or implementing ordinances acknowledged by the Land Conservation and Development Commission under ORS 197.251, nor does it include denial of permits or authorizations because they are inconsistent with applicable zoning or other laws or ordinances.

The statute goes on to state that moratoria "may be both necessary and desirable," but may also have harmful effects. It establishes methods by which local governments may adopt moratoria, and procedures for their review by LUBA.

MSD. Metropolitan Service District (usually known as 'Metro').

Multifamily dwelling. A residential structure designed to accommodate more than one family in separate dwelling units. The term includes apartment houses, townhouses, row houses, and garden apartments. It may or may not include duplexes; comprehensive plans and land-use regulations are often vague or contradictory on this point. The preferred and more common usage is for the term not to encompass duplexes. 'Multiple-family dwelling' and 'multiple-unit housing' are synonyms. In casual usage, a multifamily dwelling is sometimes called a 'multiple.'

Municipal. Of or pertaining to a local governmental unit. The term is commonly used in regard only to city governments, but some persons use it in reference to county and special district governments as well. The Oregon Bar states, "Both the Oregon Supreme Court and Court of Appeals have referred to cities as being the only true municipalities or municipal corporations" (Oregon State Bar 1979; p. 7).

N

Natural areas.

Includes land and water that has substantially retained its natural character, which is an important habitat for plant, animal, or marine life. Such areas are not necessarily completely natural or undisturbed, but can be significant for the study of natural, historical, scientific, or paleontological features, or for the appreciation of natural features.

This definition appears in Goal 5 and in the list of definitions that accompanies the goals. A survey of natural areas in Oregon has been published by The Nature Conservancy, a private nonprofit organization dedicated to the identification and preservation of ecologically significant natural lands.

Natural estuaries.

Estuaries lacking maintained jetties or channels, and which are usually little developed for residential, commercial, or industrial uses. They may have altered shorelines, provided that these altered shorelines are not adjacent to an urban area. Shorelands around natural estuaries are generally used for agricultural, forest, recreation, and other rural uses. (OAR 660-17-010(1))

OAR 660-17-015(1) lists five estuaries that have been classified as natural: Sand Lake, Salmon River, Elk River (Curry County), Sixes River, and Pistol River. Oregon's other major estuaries are classified as conservation, deep-draft development, or shallow-draft development. See Goal 16 in the Appendix.

Need. In planning, the topic of need (defined in terms of the public interest) occurs mainly in two areas. First, several of the statewide planning goals require that a local comprehensive plan contain evaluations of and policies on several different types of community need: needs for recreational facilities, commercial land, industrial land, and buildable residential land all must be addressed. Second, some types of quasi-judicial requests (zone changes, for example) can be approved only if the applicant shows that there is some public need for the action requested. Personal need is not germane in most quasi-judicial cases. See *Fasano* and **hardship.**

Needed housing. ORS 197.303 defines this term as follows:

As used in ORS 197.307, until the beginning of the first periodic review of a local government's acknowledged comprehensive plan, 'needed housing' means housing types determined to meet the need shown for housing within an urban growth boundary at particular price ranges and rent levels. On and after the beginning of the first periodic review of a local government's acknowledged comprehensive plan, "needed housing" also means *(a)* housing that includes, but is not limited to, attached and detached single-family housing and multiple family housing for both owner and renter occupancy and manufactured homes, and *(b)* government assisted housing.

The statute goes on to require that cities of 2,500 or more persons and counties of at least 15,000 persons must permit needed housing "in a zone or zones with sufficient buildable land to satisfy that need" (ORS 197.307(3)). See *St. Helens Policy.*

Net density. See **density.**

New land use regulation. " . . . a land use regulation other than an amendment to an acknowledged land use regulation adopted by a local government that already has a comprehensive plan and land regulations acknowledged under ORS 197.251" (ORS 197.015(13)). See **land use regulation.**

Noise inventory. Planner's jargon for the description of major sources of noise in the community. LCDC has consistently applied Goal 6 to require that such an inventory be in each community's comprehensive plan.

Nonconforming use. In its most general sense this phrase means any land use that does not comply with the zoning or other land-use regulations that apply to it. It thus would encompass both a structure built before the enactment of the regulation that made it nonconforming and a prohibited structure built after the regulation's enactment. The former would usually be considered legal, because land-use regulations are not retroactive. The latter would be illegal, having been constructed in spite of the regulations that prohibit it. It is common to find in the planning literature, however, that the term is used to mean only the former: i.e., a use that conflicts with the land-use regulations that govern it but that may continue to operate legally because it is 'grandfathered in.' Those who wish to distinguish between legal and illegal types often use the phrase 'pre-existing,' 'true,' or 'valid' nonconforming use to describe the former.

A pre-existing nonconforming use generally may continue to operate, but cannot expand or intensify its activities. If a nonconforming use is stopped for a certain period (typically six months or one year), it usually is not allowed to resume operation. Most zoning ordinances contain provisions that prohibit the reconstruction of nonconforming uses if they are destroyed or heavily damaged (by fire, etc.). Some ordinances contain amortization provisions that allow a nonconforming use to operate only for a limited period after it becomes nonconforming. See *grandfathered* and *vested right.*

Nonfarm dwelling. See *farm dwelling.*

Nonpoint source. See *point-source pollution.*

Nonresource land. In casual usage among planners this term means rural land not subject to the farm- or forest-land goals. OAR 660-04-005(3) defines it to be land not subject to those two goals or to the coastal goals. The term is somewhat misleading: so-called nonresource land often has many resources—waterways, wildlife habitats, minerals, etc. Such lands and resources are subject to statewide planning Goal 5, "Open Spaces, Scenic and Historic Areas, and Natural Resources," which is every bit as much a 'resource goal' as Goals 3 and 4.

Notice. Information about a land-use decision or about a hearing to be held regarding such a decision. Statutory and ordinance requirements about how notice must be provided vary. Some type of notice is required for most meetings of local planning commissions, hearings officers, city councils, boards of county commissioners, LUBA, and LCDC. Notice for local hearings is provided through several or all of the following: *(1)* posting placards on the property that is the subject of the hearing; *(2)* advertising the hearing one to two weeks in advance in the legal ads of a local newspaper; *(3)* mailing information about the hearing to the owners of properties near the subject property; and *(4)* posting announcements in the city hall, courthouse, and other public buildings.

Attorneys differentiate 'actual notice' from 'constructive notice.' The former means information that can be shown to have been directly received by a person—a letter sent by return-receipt mail, for example. The latter means knowledge or information that is made available in such a way that any interested party should be able to find it—a legal ad, for example.

Note: It is entirely possible for property to be rezoned without its owner receiving individual notice of the action. This might occur, for example, where a county rezones hundreds of parcels and tens of thousands of acres. For this type of legislative action, a local government simply cannot afford to send individual letters to all the affected parties. ORS 215.503 requires that such notice be given if funds are available from the state's Department of Land Conservation and Development (DLCD), but the legislature has not provided such money to the DLCD.

Nuisance. That which substantially interferes with the enjoyment and use of one's land, e.g., noise, smoke, odor, water pollution. The word 'substantially' is used here advisedly; not every annoyance is considered a nuisance in the eyes of the law.

In its early days zoning was essentially a means of regulating nuisances—a way of keeping a smoky, noisy factory from locating next door to a tidy, vine-covered cottage. Modern land-use regulations are considerably broader in scope, but still are based partly on the need to regulate nuisances. Whether a particular nuisance case is actionable depends on several factors. First, the amount of harm done must be substantial. Second, the harm must actually be caused by the party sued (a difficult proposition to prove in cases involving pollutants). Third, the relative value of the complainant's use and enjoyment of his or her land versus the value to society of the defendant's activities must be weighed. Fourth, the ease with which the nuisance could be alleviated must be considered.

O

O-and-C lands. Lands given by the federal government to the Oregon and California Railroad Company in 1866 to subsidize the building of a railroad through western Oregon into California. The company later violated some provisions of the agreement, and had to give much of the land back to the federal government. This action took 2½ million acres in western Oregon off the property tax rolls. In order to compensate the eighteen Oregon counties that had been receiving property tax revenues from O-and-C lands, the Congress passed legislation in 1938 to pay the counties a percentage of the money earned from timber sales on those lands. Since then, the eighteen counties have received approximately 50-75 percent of that timber revenue each year.

OAR. Oregon Administrative Rule. See *rule.*

Objections. " . . . statements or positions by persons (including the local coordinating body, affected agencies or districts) opposing the granting of an Acknowledgment of Compliance" (OAR 660-03-005(4)). Objections to a plan submitted by a local government to LCDC may be filed with the Department of Land Conservation and Development prior to LCDC's action on the plan. If the objection is received prior to the deadline announced by the department, it will be addressed by the department's staff when they prepare their report on the plan. This system has proved to be an effective means of bringing to LCDC detailed information and general concerns from a wide range of citizens and organizations.

OCCDC. Oregon Coastal Conservation and Development Commission.

Occupancy permit. See *certificate of occupancy.*

Occupancy rate. *1.* The proportion of a community's housing that is occupied. In this sense, the term is a complement to vacancy rate: if the vacancy rate is 2 percent, then the occupancy rate is 98 percent. *2.* The number of residents per room in a dwelling; persons per room. Because of this term's ambiguity it is preferable to use 'persons per room' if the second meaning is intended. See also *household.*

Ocean flooding.
The flooding of lowland areas by salt water owing to tidal action, storm surge, or tsunamis (seismic sea waves). Land forms subject to Ocean Flooding include beaches, marshes, coastal lowlands, and lowlying interdune areas. Areas of ocean flooding are mapped by the Federal Emergency Management Agency (FEMA). Ocean flooding includes areas of velocity flooding and associated shallow marine flooding. (LCDC Goals)

OCZM. Office of Coastal Zone Management.

OCZMA. Oregon Coastal Zone Management Association.

OEDP. Overall economic development program.

Office of Coastal Zone Management (OCZM). An agency in the Department of Commerce's National Oceanic and Atmospheric Administration (NOAA) that administers the programs mandated by the Coastal Zone Management Act of 1972.

Official map. The zoning map or plan map actually adopted by ordinance; the original map, recorded, kept on file, and continuously updated, as opposed to unofficial maps that may be produced and distributed in large numbers. Unofficial copies of the plan or zoning map suffer from two major deficiencies: they are soon out of date, since they do not reflect the zone changes and plan amendments that occur after they are printed, and they are often of such small scale that one cannot readily identify individual lots and boundaries. If you want to know the precise zoning or plan designation on a particular piece of property, it is wise to check the official map or a reliable copy of it.

Off-street parking. A designated area on private property for the parking of motor vehicles. To prevent traffic congestion and problems with on-street parking, most local land-use regulations require that parking spaces of a certain type and number be provided in conjunction with all new development. For example, new multifamily dwellings may be required to provide one to two offstreet parking spaces per dwelling unit. Commercial land uses have to provide a certain number of spaces per hundred square feet of floor area. Most jurisdictions get such figures by taking them from some standard text on urban design. The standard numbers do bear some examination, however. If they are very low, the city and its drivers will suffer from an excessive demand for on-street parking. If they are high, the developer loses land available for building and must spend more money on asphalt.

OILSR. Office of Interstate Land Sales Registration (federal).

One-hour wall. See **wall.**

1000 Friends of Oregon. An organization of persons interested in land-use planning and resource management in Oregon. It was founded in 1975 to help citizens participate in and to monitor Oregon's new statewide planning program. The organization is directed by an advisory board and a board of directors. It maintains an office and a staff of planners and attorneys in Portland. 1000 Friends has played a significant role in local and statewide planning programs, particularly in matters pertaining to citizen involvement, agricultural lands, forest lands, the state's economy, and housing.

Open-meeting law. An Oregon statute that requires the decisions of public bodies (including county boards of commissioners, city councils, and LCDC) to be made in meetings open to the public. Advance notice of such meetings must be provided. The statute (ORS 192.610-192.990) does not specify exactly what type of notice must be given, but it does state that special sessions must be announced at least 24 hours in advance. It also provides for executive sessions that may be closed to the public when they deal with certain topics (labor negotiations, personnel matters, etc.).

Open space. Land that is undeveloped and that can be expected to remain so indefinitely. The term encompasses parks, forests, and farm land, but in many plans it refers only to open spaces that are available to the public and that have been officially designated and zoned as such. Examples include playgrounds, watershed preserves, and parks, which are usually zoned 'open space' or 'public.' The terms 'vacant land' and 'open space' are not synonymous: see *vacant land.*

Open-space deferral. A reduction in property taxes on certain lands maintained in an undeveloped or natural state. Provisions for such deferral are found in ORS 308.740 to 308.790.

Ordinance. A law enacted by a local legislative body, such as a city council or board of commissioners.

Oregon Coastal Conservation and Development Commission (OCCDC). A body created in 1971 by ORS Chapter 191 to administer a program for protecting Oregon's coastal resources. In 1975 OCCDC was disbanded. Its functions were given over to LCDC, which continues to carry them out. See *coastal zone management.*

Oregon Coastal Zone Management Association (OCZMA). An organization of coastal counties, cities, port districts, and soil and water conservation districts formed in 1975. Its purpose is to advise state and federal agencies about local concerns pertaining to coastal zone management and to keep local officials informed of the various management programs. The association is not a governmental agency.

Oregon recreation trails system. A statewide system of public trails established pursuant to ORS 390.950 to 390.990. Each trail is designated a 'footpath,' 'horseback riding trail,' or 'bicycle path.' The system is far from complete: the majority of trails have only been proposed, not yet developed. Many miles of trails have been built, however. The system is managed by the Parks and Recreation Division of Oregon's Department of Transportation.

Oregon water quality index (OWQI). A convenient summary measure of water quality developed by the state's Department of Environmental Quality. The index combines six key indicators of pollution: dissolved oxygen (DO), biological oxygen demand (BOD), fecal coliform bacteria, dissolved solids, acid-alkali balance (pH), and inorganic nitrogen and ammonia. The index ranges from zero to 100 and has five general categories: excellent (90-100); very good (85-89); good (80-84); fair (60-79); and poor (under 60) (Department of Environmental Quality 1981: p. 16).

ORS. Oregon Revised Statutes.

Outright use. Planning jargon, shorthand for "a land use permitted outright in a particular zone." See *permitted outright, permitted use, conditional use.*

Overall economic development program (OEDP). A regional plan for economic development prepared in accordance with guidelines set by the federal Economic Development Administration (EDA). Such plans are prepared by counties or associations of local governments. An OEDP contains data on various aspects of the regional economy, a description of "development strategies," and an analysis of "potentials for economic development" (Cortright 1977: Section III, pp. 5-10). Not all of Oregon's counties have such plans, but a majority do. Preparation of an OEDP is a prerequisite for obtaining money from the EDA.

Overcrowding. The presence of too many residents in a dwelling; a housing problem usually described in terms of persons per room. The criterion by which to define overcrowding varies: 1.00, 1.25, and 1.50 persons per room are commonly accepted thresholds. See Ragatz 1979, p. 60.

Overlay zone. A special zone that is applied 'over' or in addition to a base zone. The most common example is the floodplain overlay zone, which is applied to properties that already are subject to the provisions of conventional residential, commercial, and industrial zones. Such properties then become subject to the requirements of both the base zone and the overlay zone. Many zoning ordinances specify that if there is a conflict between a base and an overlay zone the more stringent requirement shall prevail. The overlay zone is also known as a 'combining zone.'

Overzoning. 1. The zoning of more land than is necessary for commercial uses. Overzoning was common in many cities two or three decades ago, and it is still seen in a few communities today. The incentives to overzone are mainly these. First, the individual property owners think that commercial zoning will enhance the value of their land. Second, the city's governing body sees such zoning as a device to increase property tax revenues. (Overzoning for this purpose is also described as fiscal zoning.) Finally, business persons may see overzoning as a way to ensure a large supply of commercial land at low prices.

The three incentives described above, however, are often illusory. Less than 5 percent of a typical community's land is needed for commercial uses. Zoning far in excess of that often provides little gain to the individual property owner, and brings unnecessary costs to the city and its business persons. The vacant commercial land may be divided prematurely or lost to residential development when no commercial development materializes. It may turn into blighted areas because its owners are anticipating commercial development, and do not want to maintain or invest further money in structures already on the land. And the city may be unable to plan its public facilities and services adequately. Commercial uses generate large volumes of traffic, for example, thus requiring a city to plan its streets for such areas to be sized for heavy traffic. If the city has many times as much land zoned commercial as will ever develop in commercial uses, it may wind up building arterials where none are needed or having to respond to a sudden demand for an arterial where none was planned.

2. Zoning more land than is needed for any type of use. If a city's projected need for residential lands for the next quarter century is 500 acres, and it has zoned 1,000 acres for such uses, it has overzoned.

Owner. One who holds title to real property. Contract purchasers or mortgagors, however, are often counted as 'owners,' even though they do not hold title to the property that they are buying. ORS 215.503, for example, defines owner to be "the owner of the title to real property or the contract purchaser of real property of record as shown on the last available complete tax assessment roll." This has been cause for confusion in some localities, where notice of impending land-use decisions may be sent to contract purchasers but not to the true owners of affected property. Such owners are entitled to notice and may have grounds to challenge a decision made without notice to them.

Owner-built dwelling and outbuildings. "A single-family residence and adjacent auxiliary structures the structural components of which are constructed entirely by the owner who intends to occupy the structures or by that owner and friends and relatives of the owner assisting on an unpaid basis" (ORS 456.920(1)(b)). Such a building "shall be exempt from any requirements of the structural code for

164 · *Owner-built dwelling*

ceiling heights, room sizes, and the maintenance of specific temperature levels in those structures" (ORS 456.920(2)). If the owner/builder
chooses to use the exemption, that information must be recorded on
the deed for the property (ORS 456.920(2) and (3)).

Ownership. For a discussion of different forms of ownership see
estate and **property.**

P

Panelized home. See *modular home.*

Panhandle lot. See *flag lot.*

Parallel. **1.** An imaginary line on the earth's surface formed by the intersection of a plane through the earth parallel to the equator; a reference for describing one's position north or south of the equator in terms of latitude. Salem, for example, is roughly halfway between the equator and the north pole, a position described as latitude 45 degrees north. The line passing through that position and parallel to the equator is the forty-fifth parallel.
2. A baseline; a reference line in the township-and-range survey system.

For both types of parallel, the complementary north-south lines used to establish the other half of the reference grid are called meridians.

Parcel. "A unit of land that is created by a partitioning of land" (ORS 92.010(6)). The complementary term for units of land created by subdivision is 'lot.' The Oregon planner's lexicon lacks a general term to describe a unit of land created by a partition or subdivision. See *partition.*

Parcelization. Planning jargon for the division of rural land into many small, undeveloped parcels.

Parent parcel. The original unit of land from which the lots or parcels of a subsequent subdivision or partition were created.

Parent zone. See *base zone.*

Parking space. The area required for the parking of a single passenger car. The typical dimensions of such a space are 10 by 20 feet.

165

Additional area is needed, however, for maneuvering, so the average area required for one parking space in a larger parking lot usually is at least 300 square feet. The area varies according to the design of the parking lot. Right-angle head-in parking generally requires more maneuvering room than parking spaces arranged at acute angles. Most local governments require off-street parking in accordance with standards set forth in the zoning or subdivision ordinance.

Partition. 1. To divide a unit of land into two or three parcels.
2. The act of partitioning land.
3. An area or tract of land that has been partitioned.

The word denotes simple divisions of land into only a few parcels, as opposed to 'subdivision,' which denotes a complex process that creates many lots. Oregon's statutes (ORS 92.010(8)) define the verb phrase 'partition land' as follows:

> To divide land into two or three parcels of land within a calendar year, but does not include: *(a)* A division of land resulting from a lien foreclosure, foreclosure of a recorded contract for the sale of real property or the creation of cemetery lots; or *(b)* An adjustment of a property line by the relocation of a common boundary where an additional unit of land is not created and where the existing unit of land reduced in size by the adjustment complies with any applicable zoning ordinance.

Partitions are classified as major or minor. A major partition involves the creation of a road or street; a minor partition does not. ORS 92.044 requires local governments to regulate major and minor partitions in exclusive farm use zones. ORS 92.046 gives them the option to regulate minor partitions in other zones as well.

If a large tract of land is partitioned repeatedly by its owner over several years, the process is called a series partition. The 1983 legislature defined that term as follows:

> 'Series partitioned lands' and 'series partition' mean a series of partitions of land located within this state resulting in the creation of four or more parcels over a period of more than one calendar year and whether composed of a series of minor partitions, a series of major partitions or a series combining both major partitions and minor partitions. (ORS 92.305(10))

See **subdivision.**

The word 'partition' also has another meaning in real estate law: to separate or divide land held by tenants in common or by joint tenants, so that the resulting parcels are owned individually.

Payment in lieu of dedication. Many jurisdictions require a subdivider to dedicate to the public a certain percentage of the land area of a new subdivision as a future site for a park or school. As a series of subdivisions is approved, however, the jurisdiction may begin to have a group of small, widely separated lots that are not suitable for parks or schools and that are expensive to maintain. Moreover, the dedicated sites are in public ownership, and thus provide no property tax revenues to the jurisdiction. For these reasons, many subdivision ordinances contain provisions that allow the local government to require money from the subdivider instead of raw land. The amount of money often is fixed in the ordinance as a percentage of the assessed value of the tract that is to be sudivided. See *exactions.*

Peak-value intersection. The street intersection at a city's commercial center where land is most valuable.

Performance bond. A bond required of a subdivider or developer to ensure that specified improvements will be carried out after approval for the development is given by the local government. Performance bonds are widely used for a broad range of improvements—not only sidewalks but also streets, curbs, storm sewers, street lighting, etc. They are one type in a broader category known as surety bonds. Performance bonds are sometimes called completion bonds.

Performance standard. A standard regarding the effects of a land use on some aspect of the environment or community—on noise, air quality, traffic, etc. Performance standards are commonly found in the ordinance provisions for industrial zones. They often are cited as a type of implementing measure that is superior to conventional use zoning, and thus are sometimes used in commercial and residential zones as well. See *performance zoning.*

Performance zoning. The regulation of land use through performance standards rather than zoning restrictions. Conventional Euclidean and exclusive zoning are based on the premise that the many different types of land uses can be lumped into several categories and then segregated into corresponding zones. Such segregation ensures that incompatible uses will not conflict with each other, and allows the community to regulate the amount of different types of land uses that will occur. A city can limit industrial development, for instance, simply by zoning very little land for industrial uses. Performance zoning, on the other hand, aims to control the harmful effects from the uses rather than the uses themselves. Under this system a community would establish districts on the basis of standards for noise, bulk of structures, air and water pollution, etc. A 'residential district' would have the most stringent standards, but it would not specify that only residential uses could occur there. An industrial plant would be able to locate in such a district if it met all of the standards. Performance zoning is theoretically superior to conventional zoning, and many zoning ordinances have come to use some performance standards. But such standards are very hard to write and administer. Conventional zoning is indeed a crude device with which to implement complex plans and policies. It will endure, however, precisely because of its simplicity.

Periodic review. 1. The regular review by the Department of Land Conservation and Development of acknowledged local comprehensive plans and land-use ordinances. ORS 197.640 and OAR 660, Division 19, establish the procedures for such reviews. The statute provides that a city or county must revise its plan, again bringing it into compliance with the goals, if certain types of changes have occurred since the plan was acknowledged. See Chapter 1, section titled "After Acknowledgment."
2. "The review of an acknowledged comprehensive plan and land-use regulations by a local government in accordance with the schedule for plan review and revision adopted as part of the acknowledged comprehensive plan" (ORS 197.295(4)). Goal 2 requires such periodic reviews. Its guidelines suggest that the reviews take place "at least every two years," but they also recommend that major revisions "should not be made more frequently than every two years, if at all possible."

Permit. An order (usually written) from a governmental agency officially authorizing an individual to do something. Many activities that involve land or buildings require permits, most of which must be obtained at city or county agencies. Common local permits include those for building, septic tanks, mobile homes, plan amendments, zone changes, variances, conditional uses, partitions, and subdivisions. The term 'local permit' may be misleading for some of these in that it is state law that requires them. Permits for septic tanks, for example, are required by the state's Department of Environmental Quality (DEQ). Such permits are local only in the sense that they can be obtained at city or county offices rather than at state offices in Portland or Salem. Local governments administer such permit programs as a convenience to their citizens. See Chapter 3, "How To Get a Permit."

A second type of permit is that which must be obtained directly from a state agency. For a discussion of the various types of state permits, see **Class A Permits** and **Class B Permits** and Chapter 2.

A third type of permit is that obtained from a federal agency. Few activities on private lands are subject to federal permits.Some activities that involve bodies of water require review by and permits from the Army's Corps of Engineers. Large subdivisions involving interstate selling of lots must be registered with HUD's Office of Interstate Land Sales Registration.

Permitted outright. Allowed to be built or used without special permits or conditions. Most zoning ordinances specify three types of land uses in each zone: those that are permitted outright (outright uses); those that may be permitted, subject to certain conditions (conditional uses); and those that are prohibited. Note: That a particular use is permitted outright by a zoning ordinance does not imply that no permits are necessary. A single-family dwelling is permitted outright in many zones, but the builder of such a dwelling still must obtain building permits, sanitation permits, etc. An outright use also must conform to all applicable requirements for setbacks, off-street parking, building height, etc.

Permitted use. A land use that is permitted outright in a particular zone. See **conditional use, outright use.**

Person. " . . . Any individual, partnership, corporation, association, governmental subdivision or agency or private organization of any kind" (ORS 197.015(14)). Most local land-use regulations define this word just as broadly as the state does, so as to include not only individuals but also organizations and agencies.

Persons per room. The number of residents per habitable room in a dwelling. A habitable room is one other than a bathroom, closet, garage, or (usually) kitchen. This statistic is an indicator of crowding. See **overcrowding.**

Petaluma. An important court case regarding growth control. The City of Petaluma, California, adopted a plan that limited the number of building permits that could be issued each year. The county's construction industry challenged the plan on the grounds that it was arbitrary and exclusionary. The industry won in District Court but that decision was reversed by the federal Court of Appeals in 1975. The full citation for the Petaluma case is *Construction Industry Association of Sonoma County* v. *City of Petaluma*, 522 F2d 897 (9 Cir 1975).

Phasing. The development of a subdivision in several distinct stages. Typically this process works as follows. A subdivider receives final approval from a local government for, say, a two-hundred-lot subdivision. Streets, sidewalks, streetlights, fire hydrants, storm drains, etc., to serve the first fifty lots are installed. The subdivider then sells as many of those lots as possible, and puts the cash received into the development of the next fifty lots—phase two of the subdivision.

Phasing is a compromise between the developer and the local government. If that government allows the subdivider to sell most of the two hundred lots before the utilities are installed, it loses its power to ensure that the needed facilities will be constructed and paid for by the subdivider. More than a few cities have had to foot the bills for such development after a subdivider took the profits and a powder. On the other hand, the development of streets, sidewalks, and all the other essential amenities in a subdivision requires a great deal of money. Few developers can afford to pay several hundred thousand dollars for such improvements before they receive even a dollar of cash flow from the sale of lots. The solution is phasing—allowing the subdivider to install the needed improvements to some of the lots and then sell only those lots to recoup some gains from the initial investment.

'Phasing' also refers to the process in which a city plans and provides its services to an urbanizing area in clearly defined stages.

Physical life. The length of time that a structure remains intact. See for comparison *economic life.*

Plan. 1. A concept, design, or statement of how one intends to carry out some action. For a discussion of the many different types of governmental plans, and how they relate to each other, see *comprehensive plan.* Also, see separate entries for *community, framework, functional, master, public facility* and *site plans.*
2. An architectural drawing or blueprint.

Plan amendment. An official change made by a local governing body to the adopted comprehensive plan of a city or county. Since a plan comprises two main parts, a map and a text, the term encompasses changes to both. In practice, however, it usually means a change to the plan map, often as the result of a quasi-judicial action affecting a single piece of property. A zone change (rezoning) often necessitates a plan amendment as well. A landowner wanting to change his or her property's residential zoning to commercial would have to seek a rezoning and a plan amendment. As was determined in the *Baker v. Milwaukee* case, the plan is the controlling document: the zoning map must not allow uses more intensive than those permitted by the plan map.

Local governments must submit proposals to amend acknowledged plans to the state's Department of Land Conservation and Development (ORS 197.610). DLCD reviews the proposals and may comment on them. If DLCD suggests that a particular proposal is not consistent with the statewide goals, the local government can still go ahead and adopt it. DLCD does not have the authority to overturn such a decision, but it can appeal the decision to the Land Use Board of Appeals. See Chapter 1, section titled "After Acknowledgment."

Plan-checking fee. A fee charged by the building official to review a plan for a proposed building for compliance with construction standards and regulations. See ***building permit.***

Plan designation. A general description of what uses are planned to occur in a district described on the comprehensive plan map. In most cases, plan designations are indicated on the plan map with various colors, symbols, or hatching, labeled in the map's legend, and then described in greater detail in the plan's text. For example, an older residential district near the center of a city may be shown on the city's plan map to be designated 'multifamily residential, medium density.' The plan's text explains that areas so designated may be developed with residences up to a density of 20 units per acre, subject to certain policies on access, siting, etc.

It is very important to note that a plan designation is not a zone, and vice versa. The two are complementary. The former establishes some broad policies for a particular area; the latter implements those policies with specific regulations. For example, an area is designated "industrial" on the plan map. The plan's text indicates that manufacturing and wholesaling may occur in areas so designated, but that residential uses are not appropriate. The area is zoned industrial park, and the zoning ordinance sets forth several dozen standards for how development in that district shall occur. The plan designation only describes generally what uses may develop; the zoning specifies how they may develop. See **Baker conflict.**

Although the terms 'zone' and 'zoning' are almost universally understood and agreed on by planners, the same is not true of the words 'designate' and 'designation.' Some planners simply use the verb 'plan' to describe the process of defining areas on the plan map; e.g., "That area is planned (i.e. designated) industrial." Others occasionally use the word 'designation' as a synonym for district or zone.

Planned unit development (PUD). The bulk regulations of zoning and subdivision ordinances are based on the assumption that most development will occur on a lot-by-lot, house-by-house basis. Such regulations aim at ensuring that each lot will have adequate access, building area, open space, etc. That aim may be laudable, but when one's focus shifts from the individual lot to an entire neighborhood, some serious problems become apparent. Monotony is one, with every house set back from the street precisely 20 feet, from its neighbor by 15 feet, and so on. Wasted land is another: the mandatory yards often serve little purpose, are nuisances to their owners, and increase the cost of housing. Inflexibility is another problem. The bulk requirements limit development to detached single-family dwellings. Innovative or cheaper forms of construction, such as row houses, are not possible.

One solution to the problems described above is to provide for larger-scale development—to diminish monotony, waste, and inflexibility by planning large developments as units. Most land-use ordinances now contain provisions for such PUDs. Typically the ordinances specify that a PUD may be built only on a lot or group of contiguous lots with an area greater than 5 (or occasionally 3) acres. A design team, comprising an architect, engineer, landscape architect, or other professionals, is required. Conventional bulk requirements are waived, in return for which the PUD must provide for adequate access, open space, offstreet parking, etc. In an effort to provide incentives rather than restrictions, many PUD ordinances provide density bonuses: if the plan is well designed and provides amenities such as landscaped open space, a certain percentage of dwelling units beyond the number normally permitted in the zone will be granted to the developer.

The review and approval of PUDs is a process similar to that for subdivisions, with a preliminary and final plan and one or more quasi-judicial hearings. It is a process that takes several months.

PUDs almost always use some form of cluster housing. This enables the developer to concentrate the dwellings in one corner of the parcel, which reduces costs by requiring fewer and shorter streets and utility lines. Cheaper forms of common-wall housing can be built. And the remaining expanse of land can be used for gardens, playgrounds, and golf courses, options that are not possible in the conventional subdivision with its 6,000-square-foot lots. A well-designed PUD provides graphic proof that there are desirable alternatives to the expensive and inefficient single-family dwelling. Giving up the 2,000-square-foot home on a tract lot need not mean moving into a 600-square-foot apartment in a twenty-story high-rise.

PUDs are provided for in local ordinances in three different ways. Perhaps the most common is the PUD overlay zone. It usually is placed over a residential base zone, and is bound by the base zone's density (plus whatever bonus may be offered). A second approach is to list PUDs in residential zones as a conditional use. This approach gives a city more discretion in approving or denying individual requests. It sacrifices some predictability, since no specific residential areas are mapped to show where PUDs may occur. A third approach establishes a PUD base zone, in which planned development is the main permitted use. This zone usually is not applied in advance of specific requests. Rather, it is applied to individual properties as developers initiate requests. Each PUD, then, involves a zone change.

Planner. Although this word commonly is used to denote only professional planners, its meaning should be broadened. Comprehensive plans really are made by four types of planners. First are the policy makers. These are the county commissioners and city council members who adopt the plans and their implementing ordinances. Second are the planning commissioners, who advise the policy makers and decide upon many quasi-judicial cases. Third are the many citizens involved in the planning process. They serve on citizen advisory groups and technical advisory committees, and attend public hearings. Fourth, of course, are the professional planners.

The larger cities and counties have planning departments with one or several professional planners. These departments are usually headed by a planning director. Larger departments often are divided

into a 'code section' and a long-range planning section, each of which
is managed by a 'section chief' or 'division head.' From there the
hierarchy descends through senior planner, planner 3, planner 2,
planner 1, and code administrator. The planner 3 or planner 2 may
also be called an associate planner, while the planner 1 may also be
referred to as an assistant planner. The labels vary from one department to another.

The entry-level position for a professional planner with a bachelor's
degree and little or no experience is at planner 1 or assistant planner.
The newcomer's work often starts at the counter as a code administrator.
The entry-level position for a planner with a master's degree and
limited experience typically is a planner 2.

Probably because it is a relatively new field, planning is not well
defined or organized as a profession. It lacks a counterpart to the
attorney's bar or the medical association. Planners are not required to
have licenses in the state of Oregon, and they serve no formal
apprenticeship, as do architects. All of this apparent lack of formality
and organization has had its costs: anyone can call him- or herself a
planner. The benefit from all of this, however, is that the field has not
been restricted to a hidebound, elitist few. It has profited from its
diversity, for planning is not a narrow, technical profession. Rather, it
is a place for the eclectic and generalist.

The planners do have a national professional organization known
as the APA—the American Planning Association. Oregon has a local
chapter of APA, which publishes a newsletter, runs workshops, and
holds an annual statewide conference. Associated with APA is the
national American Institute of Certified Planners. As the name suggests,
this body evaluates and accredits planners. A planner who has been so
accredited may use the initials 'AICP' after his or her name. There are
no requirements that a planner be accredited, so the proportion of
professional planners who are 'AICP' remains small.

Planning commission. A group of lay persons appointed by the
governing body of a city or county to advise it in matters pertaining to
comprehensive planning. The primary duties of such commissions
are, first, to recommend to the governing body how the local comprehensive plan and implementing measures should be developed and
maintained and, second, to assist the governing body in carrying out
the plan. In the second capacity, planning commissions may hear and
act on land-use decisions, such as variances, conditional uses, and

zone changes. Some commissions emphasize their long-range advisory function, and do little review of quasi-judicial actions, leaving those matters to a hearings officer. Other planning commissions act largely as zoning administrators, and are little involved in long-range planning.

The enabling legislation for county planning commissions is ORS 215.010-215.035. It provides that such commissions may have five, seven, or nine members, and that commissioners must be "appointed by the governing body for four-year terms." Despite the statute's use of the word "appointed," at least one jurisdiction, Polk County, has an elected planning commission. Counties may have more than one planning commission. Lane County, for example, has one for its coastal area and another for the larger inland region.

The enabling legislation for city planning commissions is found in ORS 227.020-227.090. It does not specify how many members must be on a commission or their term of office, and does not provide for existence of more than one planning commission in a city. It does set forth a long list of the activities such a commission may do.

Both the county and the city enabling statutes state that "no more than two members of a planning commission shall be engaged in the same kind of occupation, business, trade or profession." Both statutes provide that no planning commissioner shall participate in any commission action in which he or she would have a conflict of interest.

Planning commissions typically meet once or twice a month, most often on a weekday evening. Their meetings are informal and usually provide an open forum. The length of the meetings often provides graphic evidence that citizen participation is alive and well in Oregon.

A special note: planning commissioners do not get paid. Their compensation is typically limited to 15 or 20 cents per mile for travel to the meetings, and an occasional mediocre dinner. A commissioner must endure long meetings, boring staff reports, and stressful decisions. Anyone who does so can truly be said to have a strong sense of civic responsibility.

Planning period. The period of time during which a plan is expected to operate. Although not specified by the statewide goals, a period of fifteen to twenty years has become the convention for local plans in Oregon.

Plat. A map of a subdivision. The plat usually shows the location of all public rights-of-way and easements, the dimensions of lots, and various other items as required by the local subdivision ordinance. The plat also establishes block and lot numbers by which the different lots can be described for legal purposes. The original copy of the plat that is filed with the local government is referred to as the 'hard copy.' The plat is sometimes called a plat map, a redundancy since the term plat itself means a map.

Plats must be prepared as specified in ORS 92.080. They must be filed with the county clerk, who maintains them in a book called "Record of Town Plats" (ORS 92.120). A copy of each plat also must be filed with the county surveyor "if requested by him" (ORS 92.120).

Plat book. The official "Record of Town Plats" maintained by each county clerk in accordance with ORS 92.120.

Plot. 1. A small piece of land or area of ground, e.g., a garden plot, a burial plot.
2. A unit of land made up of several contiguous pieces. It is from this meaning that the term 'plottage' derives.
3. A plan, map, or diagram of land and buildings, e.g., "a plot of the proposed mobile home park." The phrase 'plot plan' is seen and heard often, but the expression is redundant. Plot alone would do the job.
4. As a verb, the word means to divide land into plots. This usage is not common.

Plottage. An increase in value that occurs when two or more lots or parcels are combined under one ownership. The 'plottage increment' is the amount by which the value of the combined plots exceeds the sum of their values as individual plots. Four 1-acre lots, for example, may be worth $5,000 a piece. If they are assembled into one 4-acre lot, however, the new value of the combination may be $25,000, $5,000 more than the sum of the individual lot values. The plottage increment, then, is $5,000.

Plottage is significant in cities, where commercial and industrial developers may spend years and millions of dollars to assemble a plot large enough for a particular project. In rural areas, however, the opposite process may occur. Developers or property owners may work to create smaller parcels, since the value of a small holding in an area subject to large-lot zoning is disproportionately large. In an area subject to farm or forestry zoning with large minimum-area requirements (typically 20 to 40 acres), the value of 1 acre of land that is part of a 40-acre holding might be $2,000. The value of that same land, separated from the larger tract and available as a rural homesite, might be five or ten times as much. See **assemblage.**

Point-source pollution. Pollution of the air or water from a single, concentrated source. The dumping by a factory of a large volume of effluent into a river is an example of point-source pollution. The pollution of the same river by dozens of septic tank drainfields over a course of several miles would be described, somewhat clumsily, as 'nonpoint-source' or 'nonpoint' pollution. The terminology grows out of the federal Clean Water Act of 1977. Generally, that act subjects point sources to federal regulations but leaves the nonpoint sources of pollution to state and local control (Oregon State Bar 1982, p. 26-32).

Police power. The power of a government to regulate the conduct of its citizens for the common good, within the limits of its constitution. The regulation of real property through zoning ordinances and other land-use regulations is generally held to be a legitimate exercise of the police power. See **eminent domain.**

  Under the federal system of government, the broadest police—or 'plenary'—powers belong to the states. State legislatures may pass any law on any matter, and in so doing are restricted only by the limits of the federal constitution. The federal government, on the other hand, does not have plenary powers. The constitution confers specific powers on the federal government: the Congress may legislate and regulate only in accordance with those specified powers. Likewise, local governments do not have plenary powers. Their authority to make law derives from the state, through enabling legislation or the home-rule provisions of the Oregon constitution.

Policy. A statement in a comprehensive plan that expresses clearly what an agency or individual is required to do. Such statements usually contain the verb "shall" or similar positive wording, as in, "The city shall require all buildings to be set back 50 or more feet from any property line adjoining a major arterial."

  Although the term 'comprehensive plan' is carefully defined in ORS 197.015(5), the word 'policy' is not. It also is not defined in the statewide planning goals. This omission is unfortunate, because many local plans do not make clear which of their statements are truly policies and which are simply gloss.

The policies of a comprehensive plan have the force of law. In order to determine which of the plan's statements are indeed policies, the reader of the plan must do two things. The first is to find which of the various statements in the plan are defined to be policies. Many plans contain a vast array of goals, objectives, recommendations, 'directions for the future,' standards, criteria, functions, findings, or other types of statements, but will define only one or a few of those types to be mandatory. The labels themselves may be misleading. Some plans, for example, will label their mandatory policies as 'recommendations.'

Once the reader has determined which statements in a plan are defined to be policies, he or she must then examine the wording of each. Statements that contain the verbs 'shall,' 'will,' or 'must' usually are mandatory. Imprecise statements mired in a verbal swamp of 'encourages,' 'suggests,' 'mays,' and 'recommends' usually indicate one of two things: *(1)* the jurisdiction does not want to take action on the topic addressed, but feels it must have some sort of statement on it; or *(2)* the jurisdiction would like to take action, but lacks the money or political clout to do so.

Oregon's statewide goals and case law have clearly established that the plan is the controlling document. The meat of a plan—the real controlling language—is the mandatory policies. Vague and discretionary statements of what a local government may do or want have little control or effect.

Population estimates. ORS 190.510 requires the state Board of Higher Education each year to estimate the population of every city and county in Oregon as of 1 July and submit that estimate to the Secretary of State by 15 December of the same year. Those estimates are quite important to each jurisdiction because they are the "official and exclusive basis for determining per capita allocation and payments of funds" from various state revenue sources, such as liquor and cigarette taxes (ORS 190.540). The Board of Higher Education has delegated the job of preparing the official estimates to the Center for Population Research and Census, an agency associated with Portland State University. See **census, population growth,** and **projection.**

Population growth. The populations of countries, states, and counties grow as a result of two processes, natural increase and net inmigration. The former is simply the excess of births over deaths, while the latter is the moving of more persons into an area than move out of it. The same two processes also cause the populations of cities to grow, but a third factor influences the figures: annexation. The population of a city may increase dramatically as the municipal boundaries expand to take in suburban subdivisions. Such 'growth' may involve little increase in the actual numbers of persons living in an area.

The analysis and projection of population growth presented in comprehensive plans often reflect political forces and methodological errors. A common political force that may affect the projection of future population is the desire of a community to grow. Opponents of growth will seek to adopt low projections; proponents of growth will call for higher figures. Some grant requirements and formulas for sharing state revenues encourage a local government to exaggerate its present or projected population. The wish to attract new business firms may also act as an incentive for unrealistic projections of growth.

Two common technical problems also cause distortions in population projections. One is to make a "straightline projection" of growth from some brief period when the community was growing unusually fast. Many cities have experienced a year or two when the rate of growth was 5 to 10 percent or even higher. Projecting growth to continue at such rates for the next twenty years, however, is almost always unrealistic. Sustained growth at annual rates in excess of 3 percent is quite unusual.

The other common technical error is to miscalculate past rates of growth. A typical example is this: *City A has 100 people in 1970. Its population grows to 200 in 1980, an increase of 100 percent. The annual rate of growth, then, over the decade is 100 percent divided by 10, or 10 percent per annum. City A's average annual rate of growth, therefore, can be projected to the year 2000 at the same rate — 10 percent.*

The process may appear to be correct at first glance, but it is not. The *annual* rate of growth cannot be found by dividing the *decade's* rate by 10. If the growth rate *were* 10 percent per year, at the end of year 1 the population would be 110. A growth rate of 10 percent in year 2 would add not 10 but 11 new inhabitants. By the end of the decade, City A would have a population of not 200 but 259.

The correct formula to find the annual rate is $r = (P_2/P_1)^{1/n} - 1$, where 'r' is the rate of growth, 'P_2' is the later population (the 1980 population in the example), 'P_1' is the earlier population (the 1970 population in the example), and 'n' is the number of years (ten in the case of City A). Applying that formula to the example, one finds that City A's average annual rate of growth between 1970 and 1980 is $(200$ divided by $100)^{1/10} - 1$, or 7.2 percent. The difference between 7.2 percent and 10 percent is highly significant when one projects rates over a twenty-year period. For populations that have been growing, this incorrect method described above *always* inflates the past annual rates. If those inflated rates are projected into the future, the resultant projection will always be larger—perhaps much larger— than if the proper rates had been used.

Post-acknowledgment. Of or pertaining to planning activities that occur after a local comprehensive plan has been acknowledged by LCDC to be in compliance with all of the statewide goals. House Bill 2225, adopted by Oregon's 1981 legislature, established standards and procedures for land-use planning by cities and counties with acknowledged plans. It thus was known as the post-acknowledgment bill. But before the post-acknowledgment era was really entered, the 1983 legislature again modified the statutes, this time with House Bill 2295 (the 'post-post-acknowledgment bill,' perhaps?). The applicable statutes are found in ORS 197.610 to 197.650.

The post-acknowledgment statutes are designed to ensure that acknowledged comprehensive plans remain up-to-date and consistent with the statewide goals. The statutes establish two processes, one for the review of individual plan amendments, the other for broader periodic reviews. See **periodic review, plan amendment,** and Chapter 1, section "After Acknowledgment."

Pre-existing use. A use that existed prior to the enactment of a land-use regulation that now applies to it. Such a use can be one that conforms to the regulation, but most often this phrase means a **nonconforming use.**

Prescription. In real estate law, the process of acquiring rights to real property as the result of an assertion of those rights over a long period. The assertion (occupying or using property persistently over a long period, for example) is known as **adverse possession.** The rights obtained from it are described as a **prescriptive easement.**

Prescriptive easement. A right or rights to real property obtained as the result of adverse possession. See **adverse possession** and **prescription.**

Private zoning. See **covenant.**

Projection. An extrapolation or estimate of future conditions that will occur if one or more explicitly stated assumptions hold true. A projection is not a prediction or forecast. It is simply a statement, often in mathematical form, of what must result if certain conditions occur. For example, a city's present population is 2,000; if it increases by 2 percent a year for five years, its population will be 2,208. A prediction or forecast, on the other hand, is based on a consideration of all the forces that may affect the population, to the extent that they can be foreseen. Often the assumptions about those forces are left unstated. The distinction between a projection and a prediction or forecast is subtle but useful. Perhaps the best way to remember it is this: a plan may have many projections about population growth—a low, medium, and high range, for example—but it probably will have only one forecast. The projection is analytical: "If conditions A and B take place, then C will occur." The forecast involves elements of judgment: "Having observed A and B, I believe that C is likely to occur."

Property. Although this word is commonly used to mean objects, structures, or lands that are owned or possessed, it also has a more complex meaning: the legal right to possess, use, enjoy, and dispose of objects, structures, or land. Real property thus is sometimes described as a 'bundle of rights' associated with the land. There are, for example, air rights, water rights, mineral rights, development rights, and so on. Fee simple ownership gives one the biggest bundle, but that bundle is not complete or unlimited. For any piece of land, the government reserves three rights: to tax the land and buildings on it; to take it (with just compensation) under the power of eminent domain; and to regulate it in accordance with the government's police power. See **estate.**

Property owners' association. See **homeowners' association.**

Property tax. An *ad valorem* tax on property (real property, for the most part). The theory works like this. A taxing jurisdiction, a county for example, projects its need for revenue in the coming year. It then appraises the actual value (market or true cash value) of each property in its jurisdiction. Using that appraisal as a guide, the county then assigns a value to each property for purposes of taxing. That assigning is called 'assessment,' and the number that results from it is the assessed value of the property. It is theoretically possible for taxing officials to assess property at some value other than its appraised value. In Oregon, however, real property is assessed at 100 percent of its true cash value (ORS 308.232).

Once the county has assessed all the properties, it determines the tax rate by dividing the projected budget by the total of all those assessed values. Finally, the county taxes each property owner for an amount equal to the assessed value of his or her property times the tax rate.

If a certain county projects its need for revenues to be $100,000 and it finds a total assessed value of $10,000,000 in the county, the tax rate then will be $100,000 divided by $10,000,000 or 0.1. That rate is commonly expressed as so many dollars and cents per thousand dollars of appraised value—$10 per thousand in the preceding example. The rate may also be expressed in mills. A mill equals one tenth of a cent. The figures in the example yield a rate of 10 mills (per dollar of assessed valuation).

The actual practice of administering the property tax is far more difficult than the theory suggests. There are many different properties in a typical jurisdiction, and they are constantly changing in value. The tax assessor—a county official—and his or her staff of appraisers are not able to appraise each property each year. The law, in fact, requires only that each piece of real property be appraised at least once every six years. In the intervening years, the property is assessed through an averaging system known as indexing or trending. If property owners feel that their property has been assessed incorrectly, they may appeal the assessment to the local Board of Equalization.

The property tax paid by the typical homeowner is actually a combination of several taxes from different governments and special districts, one for city government, one for the county, one for a school district, etc. The composite or total rates paid by homeowners vary widely over the state. $15 to $35 per thousand is a typical range. The owner of a $50,000 home in a taxing district with a rate of $20 per thousand (or 20 mills) would then pay $1,000 per year in property taxes.

Property taxes provide the single largest source of revenues to local governments in Oregon. The state government does not tax real property. State laws governing assessment and other aspects of property taxation are found in ORS Chapters 306 to 313.

Public facilities and services. "Projects, activities and facilities which the planning agency determines to be necessary for the public health, safety and welfare" (LCDC Goals).

For a city, this term typically would include schools, police, fire protection, sewage collection and treatment, storm drainage systems, water distribution and treatment, public health services, zoning and subdivision control, public recreational programs and facilities, electrical power generation and distribution, natural gas distribution, telephone systems, solid waste disposal, streets and sidewalks, street lights, transportation services, library services, and community government. The whole combination is often called the urban infrastructure. The collection of structures needed to distribute the various services is the urban plant.

Public facility plan. A rather specialized term from Oregon planning law meaning a plan for the sewer, water, and transportation facilities needed to serve a city with a population greater than 2,500 people. Such a plan is less specific than a *capital improvements program (CIP),* but more detailed than the general facilities planning required under Goal 11. State law requires that any city with an urban growth boundary encompassing a population greater than 2,500 have a public facility plan (ORS 197.712(2)(e)). OAR 660, Division 11, sets forth the details of how such a plan is to be developed.

Public housing. Dwellings leased or owned by a public agency and rented at a reduced rate to low-income persons who cannot afford to pay normal market rents. Public housing is sometimes called low-income housing, but the two terms are not synonyms. Public housing always involves ownership or subsidies by a public agency. Low-income housing is simply cheap: it may be privately or publicly owned. See *government-assisted housing.*

Public road. See road.

PUD. Planned unit development.

Q

Quasi-judicial action. A legal action that involves the application of general policies or laws to specific persons or properties. One example would be a request by an individual for a conditional use permit to place a mobile home on a lot. In making its decision, the local planning commission would apply the plan's general policies on mobile homes and the zoning ordinance's provisions regarding conditional uses to that specific request. This type of action is to be contrasted with **legislative actions,** which involve the creating of policies and law, and with **ministerial actions,** which involve routine administration of clear and objective requirements.

For many years conditional use permits, rezonings, variances, and similar land-use decisions were regarded as legislative actions. This allowed local governing bodies considerable latitude in the use of their plans and ordinances. All of that changed, however, in the 1970s, when Oregon's courts established that many of those land-use decisions are quasi-judicial. The watershed case was *Fasano v. Washington County Board of Commissioners* (264 Or 574, 507 P2d 23, 1973). See **Fasano.**

The effect of *Fasano* and subsequent cases was to limit the discretionary powers of local governments and to increase the burdens on applicants for various land-use decisions. Planning commissions and governing bodies had to begin making findings to support their conclusions and had to keep records of their findings and decisions. Applicants had to show that there was a public need for their proposals and that the proposals were consistent with the comprehensive plan. It should be noted, however, that the prefix 'quasi-' does have some significance. Quasi-judicial hearings are not full-blown trials, and planning commission meetings have not become adversary proceedings with a brace of lawyers needed to argue every point.

It is not always clear whether a particular action is quasi-judicial or legislative. A request for a variance, a conditional use permit, or a rezoning of one small parcel surely would be regarded as quasi-judicial. And a change of the text in a plan or zoning ordinance, or a map change involving dozens of properties, would be legislative. A change of the plan map or zoning map for several contiguous lots or for one large tract, however, could be either. How it is treated depends on the circumstances of the case and the judgment of the reviewing body. See *finding* and *land-use decision.*

Quasi-public. Of or pertaining to a land use that is owned or operated by a church, service club, fraternal organization, philanthropy, or charitable institution. Such land uses are not owned by governmental bodies and do not necessarily operate in the interests of a very large part of the community. Their effects on neighboring land uses may be great, so most zoning ordinances give the governing body some control over their development, typically through the conditional use process. On the other hand, quasi-public uses are not run solely for the gain of any one person or firm, and they may provide useful services, so they are often provided for in almost all of a city's or county's zones.

R

Ramapo. A town in New York state noted for its innovative approach to controlling urban growth. It adopted a system to synchronize development with the construction of public facilities. The system was attacked in the courts, but New York's Court of Appeals upheld its validity (*Golden* v. *Town Planning Board of Ramapo*, 285 NE 2d 291 (NY 1972)).

Range. A column of land 6 miles wide and described in terms of its location east or west of reference lines called 'meridians.' See **township-and-range survey system.**

Rangeland. Land—also called simply 'range'—on which the predominant types of vegetation are grasses, forbs, and shrubs, and which is suitable for grazing or browsing by big game or livestock. In Oregon, particularly in the eastern part of the state, much rangeland is classified as agricultural land and is subject to the provisions of Goal 3, "Agricultural Lands." Although rangeland is typically arid, open land with few trees, it may include forested areas that have undergrowth of grasses and shrubs suitable for grazing or browsing.

Real Estate Division. A division of Oregon's Department of Commerce. Among other things it regulates real estate transactions and administers the state's Subdivision Control Law. Its office is located in Salem. The policy-making body that directs the Division is the Real Estate Board, whose six members are appointed by the director of the Department of Commerce (subject to approval by the governor).

Real property. Land and the appurtenances to it, such as buildings, crops, mineral rights, etc. Property in general is classified as either personal or real. Personal property is also known as personalty or chattels. Real property is also called realty or real estate. The standard legal phrase to describe real property is "land, tenements, and hereditaments." A tenement is a freehold interest in some object affixed to the land. A heriditament is an inheritable estate or interest in real property. See also *property.*

Record. To place a document on file with some public official so as to make it a matter of public record. That an instrument has been recorded does not mean that it has received official approval. Most deeds, for example, are recorded in a county clerk's office, but that does not imply that the parcels created by such deeds have been legally partitioned.

Recreational vehicle (RV).
   A vacation trailer or other unit with or without motive power which is designed for human occupancy and to be used temporarily for recreational or emergency purposes and has a floor space of less than 220 square feet, excluding built-in equipment such as wardrobes, closets, cabinets, kitchen units or fixtures and bath or toilet rooms. The unit shall be identified as a recreational vehicle by the manufacturer. (ORS 446.003(26)).
See *camping vehicle* and *mobile home.*

Recycling. See *resource recovery.*

Redevelopable land. As used in the Metropolitan Housing Rule (OAR 660-07-005(8)) this phrase means "land zoned for residential use on which development has already occurred but on which, due to present or expected market forces, there exists the strong likelihood that existing development will be converted to more intensive residential uses during the planning period." Such land is most often found in old urban neighborhoods with good central locations but declining stocks of decrepit single-family dwellings. Such neighborhoods usually are planned and zoned for multifamily dwellings.

Redivision plan. A plan to describe how a proposed subdivision with large lots can be subdivided again in the future. A redivision plan usually is required for any subdivision proposed in an urban growth area. Such a project initially will not have a full range of urban services, particularly sewers, because it lies outside the present city limits. It therefore will have large suburban lots, typically 1 acre or more in size. But the area will be annexed to the city someday. When that occurs, the large existing lots will be divided into smaller units. If that redivision has been planned for, the city's sewer lines and streets can be readily extended through the area. If, however, there are houses in the path of the proposed extensions, if the suburban subdivision's streets do not jibe with the city's, if the 1-acre lots have the houses centered on them—then efficient redivision cannot occur.

Many cities and counties have an urban reserve zone for land in the urban growth area. Such a zone often requires that a redivision plan be submitted with any proposal for a subdivision in that district. The zone also usually has standards for the location of houses, structures, utilities, and streets to provide for efficient urbanization in the future.

Redline. **1.** The practice by lending institutions of delimiting certain urban neighborhoods and charging excessively high interest rates for mortgage loans in such areas or not making loans at all for development there. The neighborhoods that are redlined typically are transitional districts of older homes. The decline of such neighborhoods into slums is virtually assured if money for improvement is withheld.
2. To delete some item from a budget: "The budget committee redlined the Planner 2 position."

Red tag. A slang term for an action taken by the building official to stop the construction of a building that has not met the standards of the building code. The term refers to the red placard that is placed upon the structure to warn the builders not to proceed.

Regional (100-year) flood. See *flood.*

Regional government. See **Metropolitan Service District** and *voluntary association of governments.*

Regional planning. The planning of land use for some area larger than a city in a coordinated effort involving two or more governments. Such planning is theoretically desirable in that it can reduce some of the duplication and inefficiencies that result from having several small cities and special districts each regulating land use and providing services in the same region. In practice, regional planning is difficult to carry out because there is no single unit of government that has regional powers. Counties do not have the authority to zone land within cities, and cities cannot zone land beyond their corporate limits.

There are, however, several means by which some regional coordination is achieved. First, each city usually has a management agreement with its county that provides for joint planning of the city's urban growth area. Second, some parts of Oregon have voluntary associations of local governments that coordinate the planning functions of a region's cities, counties, and special districts. (See *voluntary association of governments*.) These associations are sometimes called regional governments, but they do not have the full range of land-use controls available to cities and counties. The exception to that is Metro, Portland's Metropolitan Service District, which exercises considerable control over land use and services in an urban region comprising several counties and cities. Third, state law (ORS 197.190) requires coordination of the planning done by a region's local governments. That coordination must be carried out by the appropriate county, or be assigned to a voluntary association of local governments. Fourth, boundary commissions in the Portland and Eugene metropolitan areas (and formerly in Salem) exercise control over annexations and extensions of public services near those cities. Finally, federal laws require regional coordination and planning for certain programs involving water quality, highways, coastal resources, air pollution control, and economic development.

Remand. To send back a case to some lower tribunal for reconsideration. Example: A county's decision to permit a partition of farmland gets appealed to LUBA. LUBA sends the case back to the county because the findings to support the county's decision were inadequate. Such a remand does not necessarily address the merits of the decision itself. It only declares that the findings to support the decision are inadequate.

A remand by LUBA is a 'final order' that can be appealed to the state's Court of Appeals (ORS 197.835 and .850). More often, however, a LUBA remand is reconsidered by local government, which may stand by its original decision but reinforce it with additional findings. Such a 'reinforced decision' can be appealed to LUBA again. It thus is possible for a local government to issue the same permit several times, with each new decision being appealed to LUBA and then remanded.

Remedy. The legal means to correct some wrong action or enforce some right; legal redress. If, for example, the local planning director denies your request for a partition, and you feel that the case was not handled properly, your remedy is an appeal to the local hearings officer, planning commission, or governing body. The remedy for a permit applicant typically is such an appeal, but there are many other forms of remedy: injunction, mandamus, compensation, etc. The remedies appropriate to a particular situation depend on the circumstances and on what is being challenged.

Remonstrate. To protest or object. The word can mean an informal, verbal objection, but in planning it usually refers to a vote against the formation of a local improvement district. Such votes are conducted according to provisions contained in the charters of many cities.

Removal. As it relates to the extraction of rock, gravel, sand, and other fill material, this word means "the taking of more than 50 cubic yards or the equivalent weight in tons of material in any waters of this state in any calendar year; or the movement by artificial means of an equivalent amount of material on or within the bed of such waters, including channel relocation" (ORS 541.605(10)). Such removal requires a permit from the Division of State Lands.

Renewable resource. A resource that people can use indefinitely without depleting it. The term is commonly used to include two types of resources: those that are affected by human activities (e.g., forests) and those that are largely inexhaustible and unaffected by human use of them (solar energy, wind, rain, etc.). The former are mostly organic, and are renewable only to the extent that they are managed effectively. The latter are mostly inorganic and are renewed by natural processes independent of human actions. Nonrenewable resources are those that have a finite supply and that cannot be renewed within any reasonable period. Nonrenewable resources are usually abiotic materials: petroleum and uranium are examples.

Repair area. See **subsurface sewage disposal system.**

Replacement cost. The cost of replacing a destroyed structure with one of similar, but not identical, utility. For example, the cost of duplicating an old wood-frame barn with hand-hewn posts and beams would be very high. The replacement cost of that barn, however, refers only to the smaller costs needed to build a modern counterpart—perhaps a pole barn with metal siding. The cost of rebuilding the old barn exactly as it was before would be called the 'reproduction cost.'

Reservation. *1.* A clause in a contract or other conveyance with which a grantor or seller retains some right or interest in the property granted. *2.* A tract of land set aside or reserved for some public purpose, as for a school or a park site. Some subdivision ordinances enable the local government to require such reservations in a new subdivision. Note that reservation is different than dedication. With the former, no change of ownership occurs: the subdivider who reserves the land for a school site still owns it, and will be paid for it if a school is built there. If the government does not exercise its option to use the reserved land within specified time limits, the land may be sold or developed by the subdivider. Dedication, on the other hand, means that the subdivider gives land to the local government. See *exactions.*

Reserve strip. A narrow strip of land located at the end of a street or right-of-way and owned or controlled by a local government. The purpose of such a strip is to enable the city or county to control access to the street or right-of-way until it can be extended or widened. A common synonym is 'streetplug.'

Residence. *1.* The place where one dwells at any given time. See *census* for an explanation of the difference between *de facto* and *de jure* residence. *2.* An informal planning term to describe a home, usually a single-family dwelling. Some land-use regulations use the word without making clear whether it encompasses mobile homes and multifamily housing as well as detached single-family dwellings.

Residential home. "A residence for five or fewer unrelated physically or mentally handicapped persons and for staff persons who need not be related to each other or to any other home resident" (ORS 443.580(3)).

The 1983 legislature came up with this strained euphemism for halfway house (are there nonresidential homes?) in Senate Bill 478. The bill provides that residential homes as defined above "shall be a permitted use in all areas zoned for residential or commercial purposes."

Resource. Anything that is valuable or useful. 'Valuable' and 'useful' are, of course, highly subjective words; what one person considers worthless, another may find to be a resource. Resources are often thought of as being only materials that occur in nature, but some are created as a result of human activities—proximity to a highway may be a resource for a business firm, for example. Some writers describe the natural resources as 'intrinsic,' and those that gain their value from human activities as 'extrinsic.'

Resource land. A term used informally by planners to describe areas that are outside of urban growth boundaries and are agricultural or forest lands as defined in Goal 3 or 4. Those goals' definitions are quite broad, so the great majority of rural land in Oregon is resource land.

OAR 660-04-005(2) formally defines resource lands to include not only farm and forest lands but also estuarine resource lands, coastal shorelands, and beaches and dunes as defined in the coastal goals. The same OAR then defines nonresource lands to be all lands not subject to Goals 3, 4, 16, 17, and 18.

Resource recovery.
The process of obtaining useful material or energy resources from solid waste and includes:
- *(a)* "Energy recovery," which means recovery in which all or a part of the solid waste materials are processed to utilize the heat content, or other forms of energy, of or from the material.
- *(b)* "Material recovery," which means any process of obtaining from solid waste, by presegregation or otherwise, materials which still have useful physical or chemical properties after serving a specific purpose and can, therefore, be reused or recycled for the same or other purpose.
- *(c)* "Recycling," which means any process by which solid waste materials are transformed into new products in such a manner that the original products may lose their identity.
- *(d)* "Reuse," which means the return of a commodity into the economic stream for use in the same kind of application as before without change in its identity. (ORS 459.005(16))

Restrictive covenant. See *covenant.*

Reuse. See *resource recovery.*

Revenue withholding. A sanction used by LCDC against local governments that fail to bring their plans into compliance with statewide planning standards. The state of Oregon distributes money received from certain taxes (on liquor, gasoline, cigarettes) to cities and counties. Under Section 12, Ch. 827, Oregon Laws 1983, LCDC can withhold such shared revenues until a tardy jurisdiction gets its plan acknowledged. The maximum amount that LCDC could withhold equals the total given by LCDC to the jurisdiction in planning grants since the program started.

Reverse condemnation. Inverse condemnation. See *taking.*

Reversed-frontage lot. A lot that has its frontage at right angles to the general pattern that prevails in a block or neighborhood. Such lots are considered undesirable, and some land-use ordinances prohibit them. Also called a 'reverse frontage lot,' or a 'reversed corner lot.'

Ribbon development. 1. Strip development; a long line of commercial buildings and signs along a highway or urban arterial.
2. The development of a single row of houses along each side of a road from a city into the country; chiefly a British usage.

Ribbon lot. A very long, narrow lot poorly suited for most forms of development because of its limited frontage and inefficient shape. Also called a shoestring lot, spaghetti lot, etc.

Right-of-way (ROW). 1. The right to pass across another person's land.
2. The ground over which such a right exists. The strip of publicly owned land on which a city street is built, for example, is a right-of-way. Such a strip usually is wider than the actual street surface in order to leave an area on which to construct sidewalks and curbs, to place utility structures such as sewer lines and power poles, and to provide for expansion of the roadway. A typical local street, for example, has a paved surface 34 to 36 feet wide, but a right-of-way width of 60 feet. The extra area within the right-of-way also gives the street builder more flexibility: if one part of the ROW has some obstacle in it, the street can be moved one way or the other within the 60-foot strip. Because of this, one should not assume that the centerline of a street is congruent with the centerline of its right-of-way.
    The term 'right-of-way' usually refers to land that is owned in fee simple by the public. Easement is the word to describe the legal

arrangement that allows one to use another's land for access or other purposes. Despite this useful distinction, right-of-way is often used as a synonym for easement.

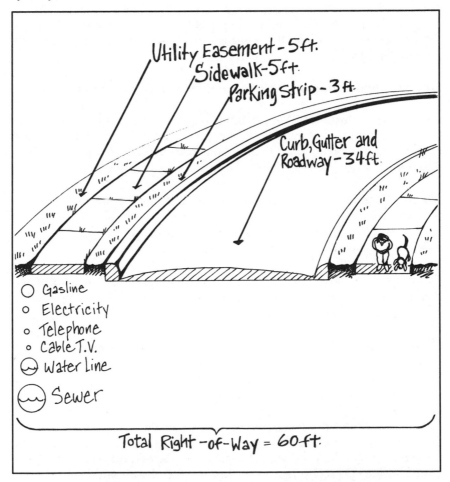

Figure 14. *A cross section of the right-of-way for a local street, showing typical dimensions and elements. The parking strip provides a buffer from traffic for pedestrians, a planting strip for shrubs and trees, and a place to deposit snow after plowing. The right-of-way can be made smaller if the parking strip is eliminated, sidewalks are reduced to 4 feet and installed on only one side of the street, utilities are put in under the roadway, and so on—but each of those measures has some drawbacks.*

Riparian. "Of, pertaining to, or situated on the edge of the bank of a river or other body of water" (LCDC Goals). The word is commonly seen with the word 'vegetation.' Riparian vegetation is a significant habitat for birds and certain animals. It also has an important effect on the temperature of the surface water that it adjoins. It keeps that water temperature cooler and more stable, thus helping to maintain a habitat for fish. Many local governments have stream setbacks or other regulations to preserve riparian vegetation.

Riparian rights. The rights of a landowner to the water on, under, or abutting his or her property. See *water right.*

Road. A long, narrow way with a graded or paved surface constructed for travel by motor vehicles; a street, highway, lane, etc. The word often is given a rural connotation, and is thus distinguished from its urban counterpart, street. The word also is used with a broader meaning, to encompass all types of public thoroughfares for vehicles, from highways to culs-de-sac. In that sense, the word would include street.

Roads (in the broader sense of the word) serve two main functions, to provide access and to enable movement of vehicles from one place to another. These two functions often conflict. A local street lined with houses and driveways every 50 feet provides access to many dwellings but is not efficient at moving many vehicles at high speeds. Conversely, a freeway may enable vehicles to move freely at 55 miles per hour, but it provides no access to the properties that border it.

There are dozens of different kinds of roads, but all can be classified in a three-part hierarchy according to the extent that they provide access, movement, or both. Roads that are designed primarily to provide access are described as 'local' or 'free access.' This category includes local streets and culs-de-sac. Such roads usually have only two travel lanes, two lanes for parking, very low speed limits (15 to 25 miles per hour), and frequent stop signs.

A second type of road, the collector, does double duty. It provides some access, but also is intended to move traffic. The collector usually is wider than the local street, may not provide for on-street parking, has a moderate speed limit (25 to 40 miles per hour), and has fewer stop signs.

The third type of road, the arterial, is designed to move traffic as efficiently as possible. Direct access from adjoining properties is restricted and may be prohibited entirely. Arterials often have more than two traffic lanes, no on-street parking, and higher speed limits, and are controlled with street lights rather than stop signs. A feeder that brings traffic to a highway is called a minor arterial. The highway itself (i.e., the principal mover of traffic in a region) is a major arterial.

The word arterial covers many different types of roads. Expressway, turnpike, freeway, parkway, beltway, and highway are the most common. The first four usually have more than two travel lanes, no on-street parking, completely controlled access, and an absence of signals or stop signs.

Oregon's laws on county roads give an extended definition of 'road' at ORS 368.001. The same statute makes a distinction between two types of public road: a 'county road' and a 'local access road.' Both are open to the public and both are under the jurisdiction of the county. But maintenance for the former is the responsibility of the county. Maintenance for the latter is the responsibility of the property owners served by the road (ORS 368.001).

Roadway. The part of a road or street that actually carries traffic. The term is used to distinguish the paved surface of a road or street from the broader **right-of-way.**

Rollback. A penalty imposed for allowing farm land that was under a farm tax deferral to convert to nonfarm use. The penalty is an amount equal to the extra taxes that would have been required in the past had the land been assessed at market value rather than at its lower farm-use value. The period of time for which the deferral may be rolled back is a maximum of ten years. Farm tax deferrals (and the rollback) are established in accordance with ORS 308.370-308.406.

Room. A space within a building, separated from other spaces by walls or partitions. The rooms in a dwelling usually are classified as habitable or nonhabitable. The former includes living rooms, kitchens, and bedrooms. The latter includes bathrooms, closets, and halls. These neat classifications are confounded by dining areas, breakfast nooks, balconies, foyers, and other spaces that are not quite rooms in their own right but that are distinct spaces. As a result, what one person calls a six-room house may be a ten-room dwelling to another. See **habitable room** for the Building Code's interpretation.

ROW. Right-of-way.

Rule. An Oregon Administrative Rule (OAR). ORS 183.310(8) defines 'rule' to be "any agency directive, standard, regulation or statement of general applicability that implements, interprets or prescribes law or policy, or describes the procedure or practice requirements of any agency." The definition goes on to specify several types of statements not considered to be rules.

Rural facilities and services. Goal 11 defines this phrase to mean public "facilities and services which the governing body determines to be suitable and appropriate solely for the needs of rural use." That a power transmission line extends across rural land, then, does not in itself mean that it is a rural facility. Only if it is intended to serve the area it passes across would it be considered 'rural.'

Rural land.
Rural lands are those which are outside the urban growth boundary and are: *(a)* Non-urban agricultural, forest or open space lands or, *(b)* Other lands suitable for sparse settlement, small farms or acreage homesites with no or hardly any public services, and which are not suitable, necessary or intended for urban use. (LCDC Goals)

S

St. Helen's Policy. An important policy of the Land Conservation and Development Commission regarding Goal 10, "Housing":

> Where a need has been shown for housing within an urban growth boundary at particular price ranges and rent levels, housing types determined to meet that need shall be permitted in a zone or zones with sufficient buildable land to satisfy that need. This policy shall not be construed as an infringement on a community's prerogative to *(1)* set approval standards under which a particular housing type is permitted outright, *(2)* impose special conditions upon approval of a specific development proposal, or *(3)* establish approval procedures. However, approval standards, special conditions, and the procedures applicable to both *(1)* must be clear and objective and *(2)* must not have the effect, either of themselves or cumulatively, of discouraging, such as through unreasonable cost or delay, the needed housing type.

That statement was adopted by LCDC in 1979 as a part of an official paper titled "Land Conservation and Development Commission Housing Policy," later became an administrative rule, and finally was made a statute (ORS 197.307). The statement is widely known as the St. Helen's Policy because it was developed as a response to issues that arose in LCDC's review of the City of St. Helen's comprehensive plan in 1978. The gist of the policy is that a city may not use its discretionary review process (as for conditional uses) to discriminate against types of housing (e.g., mobile homes, multifamily dwellings) that are needed in the community. See ***conditional use.***

Sanitary landfill. A place where solid waste is deposited, compacted, and covered with soil. A sanitary landfill is not a dump. At a dump, solid waste is disposed of without being compacted or covered with soil. The former presents fewer health and aesthetic problems, and can eventually be reclaimed for other uses, such as golf courses.

198

Sanitary sewage. **1.** The liquid wastes generated by normal house-hold operations; human waste and graywater. The term is also described as 'domestic sewage.' Sanitary sewage in this sense is to be contrasted with the other main component of sewage, industrial effluent.
2. Domestic sewage, and industrial effluent; the main components of waste in a sanitary sewer, as contrasted with the storm runoff that flows through a storm sewer.

Sanitary sewer. A sewer designed to carry only sanitary sewage—human waste, graywater, and industrial effluent—and not intended to convey storm drainage. When a sewer system must carry both sanitary sewage and storm runoff, the sewage treatment plant often is unable to handle the greatly increased volume of liquids that occurs during periods of heavy rainfall. As a result, the treatment plant may have to be bypassed, thus allowing millions of gallons of untreated effluent ('raw sewage') to be dumped into the receiving body of water. For this reason a combined sewer is considered less effective than a dual system with separate sewers for sanitary sewage and storm drainage.

Scale. **1.** The relationship between a true distance on the ground and its corresponding distance measured on a map. Scale may be expressed in several ways. A 'representative fraction' on a map indicates that one unit on the map represents the number of units in the denominator on the ground. For example, the scale 1:63,360 (or 1/63,360) means that 1 inch on the map represents 63,360 inches (or 1 mile) on the ground. This is the most difficult scale for untrained persons to use at first because it has no familiar units of measure, such as inches or miles. But the absence of such units is precisely why it is so popular in the scientific community. The simple fraction remains the same no matter what units are used. The same 1:63,360 scale, for example, is just as easy to use for metric measurements: e.g., 1 centimeter on the map equals 63,360 centimeters on the ground.
　　A more commonly used system is the verbal scale. It simply makes a brief statement: e.g., 1 inch (on the map) = 1 mile (on the ground).
　　A third type of scale is the graphic scale. It uses a small diagram in the map's legend to show distances as they appear on the map.
　　Maps are often said to be 'large scale' or 'small scale.' That terminology is sometimes confusing, because it is hard to recall whether a large-scale map is one which shows a large area in little detail or a

small area in great detail. (It's the latter.) The confusion is compounded by the fact that small-scale maps have large numbers in their scales (e.g., 1 inch = 100,000 feet) and often show large areas. One way to remember the correct relation is this: on a large-scale map (from the tax assessor's office, for example), your property will appear large; on a small-scale map (from a world atlas, for example), your property will appear very small or not show up at all.

Maps used in planning and zoning are usually large scale. Such maps are sometimes called plans by cartographers, but that usage will be avoided here, where the word is already overused. Large-scale maps of urban property, such as a tax assessor's cadastral maps, often have a scale of 1 inch = 50 or 100 feet. The tax assessor's maps of rural property typically use a scale of 1 inch = 400 or 800 feet. The drawings required for partitions or site plans often call for a very large scale—1 inch = 10 feet, for example.

2. Scale also has another meaning, from architecture. Here the word refers to the relative or proportionate size of two or more structures. A ten-story apartment building in the midst of a subdivision of one-story houses is said to be "out of scale" with its surroundings. Buildings that are designed to accommodate rather than intimidate human beings are said to be in 'human scale.'

Scenic easement. An easement to preserve a scenic view by restricting the use of land where the view might be blocked—along a scenic highway or river, for example. A scenic easement is one type of conservation easement. One occasionally sees the former term used, however, as a synonym for the latter, broader expression.

Scenic river. See **Wild and Scenic Rivers Act of 1968.**

Scenic waterway. "Waldo Lake, river or segment of river (*sic*) that has been designated as such in accordance with ORS 390.805 to 390.925 or any subsequent Act, and . . . related adjacent land" (ORS 390.805(2)).

Waldo Lake and all of the Minam River have been designated scenic waterways. Parts of the following have also been so designated: the Rogue, Illinois, Deschutes, Owyhee (South Fork), Owyhee (Main Fork), John Day, and Clackamas Rivers. Effective 1 July 1987, Opal Lake, Opal Creek, and a segment of the Little North Fork of the Santiam River will also become scenic waterways (ORS 390.825).

The aim of this program is to keep these waterways in a "free-flowing condition" and to preserve their natural features. State law declares that the "highest and best uses" of the scenic waterways are "recreation, fish and wildlife uses" (ORS 390.835). Dams, placer mining, and fill and removal in the waterways are limited. Development on lands adjacent to the waterways is controlled by the state's Department of Transportation. Note that this term applies to a state program. For explanation of a similar federal program, see *Wild and Scenic Rivers Act of 1968.*

SCORP. Statewide Comprehensive Outdoor Recreation Plan (administered by the Parks and Recreation Division of Oregon's Department of Transportation).

Secondary activities. Jobs involving manufacturing or the processing of raw materials. Primary activities are those that involve growing, harvesting, or extracting of raw materials. Tertiary activities comprise the services, or white-collar jobs. A community or regional economy usually has all three sectors.

Secondary lands. See *marginal lands.*

Secondary uses. See *accessory uses.*

Section. 1. The basic unit of land area in the township-and-range survey system. A section is (theoretically) a square 1 mile on a side. The township-and-range system, however, is a two-dimensional grid that has been applied to the earth's curved and irregular surface. The grid must be corrected every few miles in order to compensate for the curvature and irregularities. As a result many townships contain one or more sections that are neither perfectly square nor 1 square mile in area.
2. A representation of a building, object, or part of the earth's surface (e.g., a river channel) as it would appear if cut by a plane to show its internal structure; a cross-section. The term is often used in the phrase 'to show something in section.'

Senate Bill 100 (SB 100). The popular name for the Oregon Land Use Act, the 1973 legislation that established Oregon's statewide land-use planning program and a Land Conservation and Development Commission to administer it; codified as ORS Chapter 197.

Senate Bill 10 (SB 10). The 1969 measure that introduced Oregon's first statewide land-use planning legislation. The bill required local jurisdictions to adopt comprehensive plans, and it established ten statewide standards for such plans. It did not, however, provide for the effective monitoring or direction of such planning by any state agency, did not require coordination and did not give money to local governments to accomplish the required planning. SB 10 was brought before Oregon's voters by an initiative in 1970. By a margin of 3-2, they voted not to repeal it.

Septic tank. See *subsurface sewage disposal system.*

Series partition. See *partition.*

Service district. See *special district.*

Services. **1.** The public facilities and systems necessary to serve a subdivision or community.
2. The third in a three-part classification of economic activities. Primary activities are those that involve the growing, harvesting, or extraction of raw materials. Farming, logging, and mining fall into this category. Secondary activities involve processing of raw materials and manufacturing. Tertiary activities are those that do not fall into the first two categories—the white-collar jobs or services, in other words.

Servient tenement. See *easement.*

Setback. The placement of a building a specified distance away from a road, property line, or other structure. Most zoning ordinances require that buildings be set back a certain distance from any property line, well, septic tank drainfield, or road that adjoins the property. The words yard and setback are often synonymous. A typical zoning ordinance, for example, may require a 20-foot front yard and a 20-foot setback from the street for all buildings. The two requirements, however, can be different. Although the zoning ordinance might call for 20-foot front yards in all residential zones, for example, special ordinances might require larger setbacks from arterials or streams.

Sewage treatment. The processing of sewage so as to eliminate or reduce the harmful effects of household and industrial wastes on the environment and the community. Such processing may be done with individual systems, such as septic tanks for dwellings or package treatment plants for isolated industrial facilities. In urban areas, however, it is almost always done with a community system that comprises three main parts: a sewer system, the network of pipes that collects sewage and brings it to the treatment plant; the treatment facility; and a body of water to receive the treated effluent.

Sewage can be treated in several ways, but three stages are usually identified. Primary treatment uses mechanical processes to remove solid material that floats on or is suspended in the wastewater. Secondary treatment relies mainly on chemical and biological processes to remove or alter colloids or dissolved material. Tertiary treatment is a combination of mechanical, biological, and chemical processes that removes as many as 99 percent of some pollutants from the sewage. Not all municipal systems use all three stages.

Sewer system. A system of pipes and facilities to collect, transport, treat, and discharge sewage. Sewage enters the system through a 'house connection,' a pipe that connects the source to a 'lateral.' The lateral is linked to a larger 'main' or 'trunk.' This large pipe carries

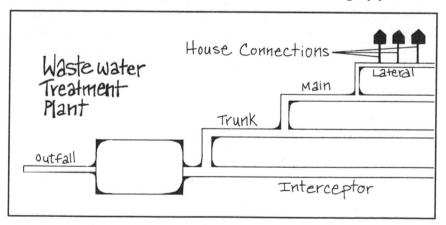

Figure 15. The branches of a sewer system. House connections are the smallest pipes. They connect individual buildings with the laterals, which in turn are linked with the larger mains, and so on. A typical lateral would have a diameter of 8 inches. An interceptor in a big-city sewerage system might be 10 or 20 feet in diameter.

sewage to the 'interceptor,' a pipe that moves wastewater to a sewage treatment plant. There are several different types of treatment plants. All require some body of water in which to discharge the treated effluent, and all generate sludge, which also must be disposed of. The pipe that carries the treated effluent to the river or sea where it is finally discharged is called an outfall.

Shallow-draft development estuaries. "Estuaries with maintained jetties and a main channel (not entrance channel) maintained by dredging at 22 feet or less. . ." OAR 660-17-010(3).

OAR 660-17-015(3) lists eight shallow-draft development estuaries: Tillamook Bay, Nehalem Bay, Depoe Bay, Siuslaw River, Umpqua River, Coquille River, Rogue River, and Chetco River. Oregon's other major estuaries are classified as deep-draft development, natural, or conservation.

Shoestring lot. See **ribbon lot.**

Shopping center. A group of stores designed as a unit and built together on the same property. Such retail centers provide economies of scale, greater convenience for shoppers, large parking areas, and certain amenities, such as central air conditioning. They are classified under a three-part system according to their floor area, number of stores, etc. The labels are widely agreed on, but the numerical standards are not. The numbers below are taken from So et al. 1979, pp. 248-255.

Type of center	Min. acreage of site	Total floor area (sq. ft.)	Population of trade area
Neighborhood	5-15	Up to 100,000	5,000-40,000
Community	15-30	150,000-300,000	At least 50,000
Regional	50	500,000-2,000,000	At least 150,000

The main unit (anchor) for a regional center is a large department store, one with a floor area of 100,000 square feet or more. The anchor (or 'key tenant') for a community center is typically a junior department store, such as a J. C. Penney or Montgomery Ward store. The main attraction in a neighborhood center is a supermarket, often accompanied by a variety store.

SIC. Standard industrial classification.

Sign.

Any sign, display, message, emblem, device, figure, painting, drawing, placard, poster, billboard or other thing that is designed, used or intended for advertising purposes or to inform or attract the attention of the public, and the term includes the sign structure, display surface and all other component parts of a sign; when dimensions of a sign are specified, the term includes panels and frames; and the term includes both sides of a sign of specified dimensions or area. (ORS 377.710(32))

This definition applies only to the statutes that regulate signs along state highways (i.e., ORS Chapter 377). It is not necessarily used in local land-use ordinances. Almost all such ordinances, however, do define and regulate this land use. Many jurisdictions have a special 'sign code.'

Similar uses. Many zoning ordinances have a section that bears this title. The purpose of the section is to explain how and where land uses omitted from the zoning ordinance may be permitted. Such provisions are needed because no matter how long or all-encompassing the lists of permitted and conditional uses in the ordinance are, there will always be at least one land use that was inadvertently left out or did not exist when the ordinance was drafted. The similar-use provisions enable the planning commission to compare the proposed use with the uses listed in various zones and determine which zones it would be most appropriate in.

Single-family dwelling. A residence designed for a single family or household, and sharing no wall with any other dwelling. Most ordinances distinguish conventional frame houses from modular homes, manufactured housing, and mobile homes, and do not classify the latter housing types as single-family dwellings. The most accurate rendering of this term would include the word 'detached,' in order to distinguish a free-standing dwelling from an attached dwelling, as in a rowhouse. The phrase 'single-family dwelling,' however, is usually understood to mean a detached single-family unit.

Site plan. A large-scale map of a proposed development site. Most zoning and subdivision ordinances require that a site plan accompany any application for a partition, variance, conditional use, zone change, or other quasi-judicial action. The standards for the drafting of such maps usually are not high, but each drawing should have a consistent scale (described on the plan), a north arrow, and a title or legend, and should show property lines, the locations of buildings, and the presence of roads, streams, and other major features of the landscape.

Slope. The angle of inclination of some surface—a building site, road, roof, etc.—with the horizontal. Also known as gradient, and, less commonly, grade. Slope can be expressed in several ways. The most common is as a percentage, i.e., the number of feet the surface rises for every 100 feet of distance horizontally. A 1-percent slope, then, is one that rises 1 foot over a horizonal distance of 100 feet.

Many commercial and industrial structures cannot be built efficiently on sites with slopes in excess of 5 percent. Dwellings can be built on steeper slopes—beyond 30 percent—but special design and construction techniques are required for slopes steeper than 15-20 percent. Costs increase rapidly, to the point that dwellings on steep slopes may cost more than twice as much as comparable structures built on level sites.

Slope is also an important consideration in building roads. The rule for freeways is a maximum slope of 6 percent. Local streets typically cannot exceed 12 percent. Driveways and other private roads sometimes have gradients higher than 20 percent, but they cannot be ascended by most vehicles if the surface is wet, muddy, or icy.

Slope is also expressed in degrees. Note that percentage and degrees are not the same. A surface that rises 100 feet over a horizontal distance of 100 feet is a 100-percent slope. Its angle, however, is only 45 degrees. Yes, it is possible to have a slope greater than 100 percent, but never one more than 90 degrees.

Builders often speak of the 'run' and the 'rise' of a sloping surface, such as a roof. The run is the horizontal distance; the rise is the vertical distance. 'Pitch' is a colloquial synonym for slope of a roof.

SMSA. Standard metropolitan statistical area.

Snob zoning. See ***exclusionary zoning.***

Social cost. See ***externality.***

Soil. The loose material at the surface of the earth in which plants grow. It is made up of disintegrated rock and organic material. The particles of rock in a soil are classified by their size. The largest are called sand, those of medium size are silt, and the smallest are called clay. Soils are often described in terms of their texture—the proportions of these three types of particles. A soil with a very high percentage of clay would be a clay soil. The term clay thus means both a type of particle and a soil. The same is true of the words silt and sand. Soils with a mixture of sand and silt but little clay are called loams.

There is a great variety of soil types and great variation in their suitability for agriculture, buildings, roads, septic tanks, and other land uses. Detailed information on such suitability is found in the OR-SOILS-1s (or, as they are called in more casual usage, the "OR-1s"). The OR-1s are soil interpretations prepared by the US Department of Agriculture's Soil Conservation Service (SCS). Each OR-1 has one to three pages of data on one of the many dozens of soil types in Oregon.

Most comprehensive plans contain maps of the different types of soils that occur in their planning areas. Such maps are often instrumental in determining what areas get planned and zoned for farming and forestry.

Soil and water conservation district (SWCD). A local improvement district organized under the provisions of ORS Chapter 568 for the purpose of reducing or controlling soil erosion and water pollution.

Soil capability class. A rating of a soil's suitability to grow field crops. This widely used system was established by the Soil Conservation Service (SCS) of the US Department of Agriculture. It uses eight broad categories designated by Roman numerals: Class I soils are the most suitable for farming and Class VIII soils are the least. The general classes are further divided into subclasses, indicated by one of four small letters: e (for erosion), w (wet), s (shallow or stony), or c (cold). "Class IIIw soil," for example, would describe a soil fairly suitable for farming but having problems of wetness that might require special drainage measures. Much of Oregon has been mapped by the SCS using this system. Goal 3 requires that agricultural lands be classified by soil capability class.

Solar access. The exposure of a building to the direct rays of the sun. Such access is necessary in order for solar heating devices to work. When structures are built that interfere with such access, conflict and litigation among neighbors may occur. Several cities in Oregon have passed solar-access ordinances to prevent that type of interference. The 1981 legislature amended ORS Chapter 227 to enable cities to pass such ordinances (ORS 227.190-227.195).

The sun's position varies with the time of the year and the latitude of the place from which it is observed. At noon on 21 December in Salem, for example, the sun will appear in the southern sky at an altitude of approximately 22 degrees. With such information one can calculate the directions from which solar radiation wil be received over the course of a year. Solar-access ordinances are designed to ensure that new construction will not block radiation to solar collection devices on neighboring buildings, particularly during those times of the year when the sun is low.

Solar heating hours. As defined in ORS 227.190(3)), " . . . those hours between three hours before and three hours after the sun is at its highest point above the horizon on December 21." The protection of solar access to the south face of buildings during solar heating hours is the main object of solar-access ordinances.

Solid-waste management. "Prevention or reduction of solid waste; management of the storage, collection, transportation, treatment, utilization, processing and final disposal of solid waste; or resource recovery from solid waste; and facilities necessary or convenient to such activities" (ORS 459.005(19)). See **resource recovery.**

Special assessment. A charge made by local government to certain property owners for the costs of installing capital improvements, such as streets, water systems, or sewers, in their neighborhood. Unlike property taxes, the special assessment is paid only by those who directly benefit from the improvements. The special assessment differs from a systems development charge in that the former occurs after development has already taken place, as when a neighborhood with failing septic tanks must have sewers installed. The systems development charge, on the other hand, is levied before development occurs in order to avoid future crises that would require special assessments.

Special district.

. . . any unit of local government, other than a city, county, metropolitan service district formed under ORS chapter 268 or an association of local governments performing land use planning functions under ORS 197.190 authorized and regulated by statute and includes, but is not limited to: Water control districts, domestic water associations and water cooperatives, irrigation districts, port districts, regional air quality control authorities, fire districts, school districts, hospital districts, mass transit districts and sanitary districts. (ORS 197.015(15))

The main characteristic of a special district (also known as a service district) is that it is a public agency established for only one purpose—to provide water, collect solid waste, administer schools, maintain cemeteries, provide fire protection, take care of sewage, etc. This is to be contrasted with the function of local 'general purpose' governments, which provide a full range of services. Special districts are funded by special tax levies, special assessments, or the sale of bonds. Their proliferation in the last two decades has caused political problems and encouraged sprawl in some areas. As a result, their creation or expansion has come to be more closely regulated.

General provisions regarding special districts are found in ORS Chapter 198. Other chapters in the statutes deal with specific types of districts. There is a great variety of types: ORS Chapter 198 lists more than two dozen. The term 'special district' is to be contrasted with the smaller 'local improvement district' (LID).

Spot zoning. The zoning of a single lot or small area for uses different from those permitted in the surrounding neighborhood. Zoning one lot commercial, for example, while zoning the remainder of the block residential would be considered spot zoning. Such zoning may or may not be valid. If it permits uses more intensive than those allowed on the neighboring properties, confers a special advantage on one landowner, and is not consistent with the comprehensive plan, then the spot zoning is not legitimate. It would be comparable to a traffic law that limits most cars to a speed of 55 miles per hour but allows Fords to do 70. But if the zoning of a single lot is done for some public purpose and is consistent with the community's comprehensive plan, the action may be perfectly valid. Despite that possibility, the term 'spot zoning' in popular usage almost always connotes something illegal or unethical.

Sprawl. The uncontrolled spread of development over rural or unde-veloped land. Although the term is widely used by planners to describe many of the ills that planning aims to lessen, it is not well defined. It usually connotes low densities, inefficient use of land, premature conversion of rural farm or forest land to urban uses, and the spread of development outward from cities in an amoeba-like manner. It is also called 'urban sprawl.' The definitive work on this topic is *The Costs Of Sprawl*, a 1974 study done by the Real Estate Research Corporation for several federal agencies.

Standard. A level or degree of quality that is proper and sufficient for some specific purpose. Suppose, for example, that a planning commis-sion gets a request to allow a mobile home as a conditional use in an R-1 zone. The local zoning ordinance will (or should) contain stan-dards against which such a request may be considered. The most obvious standard is that the request be for something that is consistent with the zoning ordinance. If a mobile home is not listed as a condi-tional use in the R-1 zone, the request will be denied because it fails to meet the first standard, consistency with the ordinance.

Many standards are not so precise. Some ordinances provide that a conditional use may be approved if the proposed use is "generally compatible with surrounding uses and does not harm the health, safety, or general welfare of the community." Such vague and discre-tionary statements really are not standards. They are so broad as to have no meaning to the planning commission, the applicant, or the neighbors. LCDC, in its housing policies, has ruled that such standards are not appropriate for the review of housing types needed in the community. The state now requires that the standards for approving such housing be "clear and objective." Similar requirements apply to some other types of land-use actions but not to all: vague and discre-tionary standards remain part and parcel of many ordinances.
ORS 215.416(6) requires counties to base permit decisions on:
> standards and criteria which shall be set forth in the zoning ordinance or other appropriate ordinance or regulation of the county and which shall relate approval or denial of a permit application to the zoning ordinance and comprehensive plan for the area in which the proposed use of land would occur and to the zoning ordinance and comprehensive plan for the county as a whole.

ORS 215.416(7) specifies that county permit decisions must be:
> based upon and accompanied by a brief statement that explains the criteria and standards considered relevant to the decision, states the facts relied upon in rendering the decision and explains the justification for the decision based on the criteria, standards and facts set forth.

Almost identical requirements for cities are found in ORS 227.173.

Standard industrial classification (SIC). A widely used system for classifying different types of industry using a numerical code. The system was developed by the federal Office of Management and Budget. Code numbers range from one to four digits, depending on the level of specificity that is needed. A different system has been developed to classify land use: see the entry immediately below.

Standard land-use code. A widely used system for classifying land uses with numbered codes. It begins with nine, generalized one-digit codes:

Code	Type of Land Use
1	Residential.
2 and 3	Manufacturing.
4	Transportation, communication, and utilities.
5	Trade.
6	Services.
7	Cultural, entertainment, and recreational.
8	Resource production and extraction.
9	Undeveloped land and water areas.

A higher level of detail can be provided by using up to four digits. In code '1221,' for example, the first digit indicates a residential use. The second digit indicates 'group quarters.' The third digit means 'membership lodgings.' The entire four-digit code distinguishes 'fraternity and sorority houses' from the dozens of other types of residential land uses.

The details of the coding system are set forth in US Department of Transportation 1977.

Standard metropolitan statistical area (SMSA). An area defined by the federal Census Bureau for statistical purposes as follows:

"Generally speaking an SMSA consists of a county or group of counties containing at least one city (or twin cities) having a population of 50,000 or more plus adjacent counties which are metropolitan in character and are economically and socially integrated with the central city" (Bureau of the Census 1970: Part 1, p. 83). The Census Bureau provides more detailed statistics for SMSAs than for nonmetropolitan counties. Oregon's three SMSAs are Portland, Salem, and Eugene.

Standing. The right to participate in or appeal a land-use action. Oregon's laws on this subject are quite liberal. That is, they extend such rights to a broad class of persons. The question of whether one has standing to appeal a certain action depends on several variables: the type of action being appealed, the tribunal to whom the appeal is to be made, etc. Generally, however, one can expect to have standing if he or she meets any of the following tests: *(1)* was required by law to get notice of the action being appealed; *(2)* has interests that would be "adversely affected" by the action; or *(3)* is "aggrieved" by the action. See ORS 197.830.

The statutes on LUBA appeals (ORS 197.830) describe "aggrieved" in broad terms. Those statutes and some recent court cases (*Warren v. Lane County* and *Jefferson Landfill Committee v. Marion County*) have, in effect, said to local government, "You may adopt ordinances that define and limit who shall have standing. But, if you lack such ordinances, we will assume that any person who takes the trouble to appeal a case can be considered aggrieved and thus has standing."

State agency coordination program. A program to ensure that the activities of state agencies, particularly those that regulate resources and land, are consistent with the statewide planning goals and acknowledged local comprehensive plans. ORS 197.180 sets forth the specifics of the program. OAR 660, Division 30, declares LCDC's policies and procedures for carrying it out. See **coordination.**

Statute. A law made by the state's legislature. Statutory law is to be distinguished from case law, which derives from the judgments of courts. Oregon's legislative laws, revised and codified, are known as the Oregon Revised Statutes (ORS). They are arranged in chapters ranging from 1 to 783. The chapters most pertinent to planning are numbers 92, "Subdivisions and Partitions"; 197, "Comprehensive Planning Coordination"; 215, "County Planning; Zoning; Housing Codes"; 227, "City Planning and Zoning."

Street. A public thoroughfare in a city, town, or village. The word usually connotes a paved roadway in an urban or suburban location. It may be used to refer to an entire right-of-way, including the paved roadway, curbs, sidewalks, and adjacent public land, or to the paved surface only. For a discussion of the different types of streets see *road.*

Street alignment. The arrangement of a community's streets in a safe and efficient pattern. Most cities do not have the opportunity to design and construct an entire network of streets in a single grand project. Rather, the streets are developed piecemeal, a few segments at a time, as subdivisions and other development occur. Without precise standards and effective regulations to control alignment a city soon finds its street system beset with problems: 'jog intersections,' acute-angle intersections, long stub streets that cannot be extended, etc.

Street furniture. The fixtures and devices placed on streets and sidewalks for the sake of providing a more pleasing appearance and comfort and shelter for pedestrians. The term includes benches, lights, planters, kiosks, and bus shelters. It is to be contrasted with the less aesthetic but more functional 'street hardware.'

Street hardware. The equipment located along streets and sidewalks and necessary to sustain the safe passage of cars and pedestrians or to support public utilities and services. Most of us have become so used to this hardware that we no longer see it as we walk or drive, but there is a huge amount of it. Along a typical street we find telephone poles and wires, electrical power lines and transformers, street lights and light poles, signs, traffic signals, fire hydrants, mailboxes, and parking meters. Strangely, many zoning ordinances have no provisions for these essential structures. They are (technically at least) illegal land uses in many places!

Streetplug. See *reserve strip.*

Strip development. A linear pattern of commercial development along a major street or highway. Location along such a thoroughfare has several advantages to the individual business: large volumes of traffic and potential customers; high visibility; proximity to other businesses that may attract customers to the area; and good access. Strip development brings several disadvantages to the community, however.

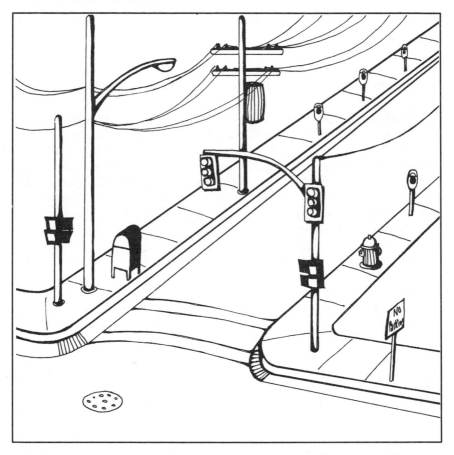

Figure 16. These pieces and fixtures of street hardware, combined with an unseen network of underground pipes, lines, and cables, make up the complex system that provides our urban services.

They include high costs to extend sewer, water, and other utilities over a long distance; higher fuel consumption for longer vehicle trips along the extended commercial area; isolation of land behind the strip; traffic problems resulting from the uncontrolled entrance and exit of many vehicles to and from a multitude of driveways; and the aesthetic costs of 'visual pollution' from neon signs, bright storefronts, parked cars, etc. Strip development generally is regarded by planners as being among the three 'cardinal sins' in land-use planning, along with urban sprawl and incompatibility.

Structure. "Anything constructed or installed or portable, the use of which requires a location on a parcel of land" (LCDC Goals). "That which is built or constructed, an edifice or building of any kind, or any piece of work artificially built up or composed of parts joined together in some definite manner" (State Structural Code, Section 420). 'Building' and 'structure' are not interchangeable terms. A building is a particular type of structure—one that shelters humans, animals, or activities. A telephone pole is a structure but it is not a building.

Stub street. A dead-end street that is intended to be developed and extended as a through street at some future time. The term is to be contrasted with 'cul-de-sac,' which is not intended for any further extension.

Studio apartment. A dwelling unit made up of one main room, a kitchen or kitchenette, and a bathroom. See *efficiency dwelling unit.*

Subdivide. "To divide land into four or more lots within a calendar year" (ORS 92.010(13)).

Subdivision. The act of dividing land into separate lots for future sale and development; a tract of land that has been so divided. Subdivisions are closely regulated by local governments throughout Oregon. The standards for regulating them are set forth in ORS Chapter 92. Typically, the subdivider must file an application accompanied by a tentative (or preliminary) plan. That plan is reviewed by the local planning department and commission to see that it meets the subdivision ordinance's standards for lot size and shape, street layout, and the design and installation of improvements, such as water lines, sewers, street lights, fire hydrants, etc. If the local government approves the tentative plan, the subdivider then proceeds with surveying and the making of a final plat.

The final plat is a carefully drafted map that shows the precise locations and dimensions of all proposed lots, blocks, streets, and easements. All of them are numbered or named so that the plat provides a legal description of each lot in the subdivision.

The review and approval of the tentative plan is a quasi-judicial action, typically with a public hearing by the planning commission. Approval of the tentative plan constitutes a promise by the local government to the subdivider: if the final plat is consistent with the approved tentative plan, then the plat will be given final approval. Approval of the final plat is a ministerial act. Technicians will check the details of the plat to see whether they are accurate and consistent with the tentative plan. Only if the subdivider turns in a final plat that is significantly different from the tentative plan or that is technically flawed will the final plat be denied.

Subdivision ordinances are often regarded by the subdivider as unnecessarily complex restrictions that exact large costs in both time and money. The review process may take many months. The local government often requires that the subdivider give land or money for the development of parks, schools, streets, and other public facilities. And the subdivider must complete the application process, incur major costs in surveying and drafting, and install streets, sidewalks, and other expensive improvements, all before a single lot can be sold.

Local governments, on the other hand, have learned from harsh experience how costly uncontrolled division of land can be. Some of the costs may be minor. If the subdivider chooses to name one of the new streets with the same title that graces another street on the far side of town, the result may be only confusion and irritation for mail carriers and motorists. But if the subdivider fails to match the streets with the city system and does not install sidewalks or sewers, the community may be faced with large bills and legal problems for many years to come—long after the subdivider has sold the lots and gone. It is an important characteristic of land use in the United States that the division and developing of land are two distinct processes. A typical tract of land is divided by one party and sold to another (or many others), only to be developed later. If the dividing is not controlled and carefully planned, the subsequent development may be far more expensive and inefficient than it need be. Some tracts are divided long before they can be served with public services or are needed for development. These are aptly described by Charles Abrams as 'premature subdivisions.' A second type, described by Abrams as 'abortive subdivisions,' comprises those tracts that are so badly designed or located that they can never be developed (Abrams 1971).

The word 'subdivision' does not encompass all types of land division. The simplest division—cutting a piece of land into two or three units—is known as a 'partition.' The resulting units of land are called 'parcels.' Only if four or more units of land are created is the act called a subdivision. The new units of land are then called 'lots.'

Although local ordinances will vary in their provisions, the statutory definition of subdivide and the basic standards of ORS Chapter 92 apply statewide. Note that since the definition is based on the number of pieces created per year, one can use the partition process to make a large number of divisions without having to go through the much more cumbersome subdivision procedures. For example, Mr. Smith owns a 90-acre tract. In 1980 he divides it into three parcels, and sells one each to Ms. Jones and Mr. Brown. In 1981, Smith, Jones, and Brown each partition their 30-acre holdings into three 10-acre parcels. Subsequent owners continue this process, within the limits of the partition ordinance and other regulations, until a *de facto* subdivision eventually occurs. This sort of end-run around the subdivision ordinance can cause significant problems. The resulting quasi-subdivisions often have poor access, inadequate services, and inefficient designs. See *partition.*

Subdivisions are regulated by the state, as well as by local governments, but the state's role is limited largely to protecting the consumer against deceptive sales practices. Except for a few exemptions, subdivisions and series partitions must be reported to the Oregon Real Estate Division. It is important to note that the statutes use a different definition of subdivision in specifying what types of land division must be reported. For the purpose of reporting, subdivision means "improved or unimproved land or lands divided, or created into interests or sold under an agreement to be subsequently divided or created into interests, for the purpose of sale or lease whether immediate or future, into 11 or more undivided interests or four or more other interests" (ORS 92.305(12)). Setting aside all the references to interests, the main difference between this definition and that of ORS 92.010 (12)) is in the matter of time. The Real Estate Division definition does not mention 'calendar year.' It simply specifies that if one party divides a tract into four pieces over any period, it constitutes a subdivision. Because of this difference the progressive partitioning of three parcels per year would have to be reported to the Real Estate Division even though it would not be considered to be a subdivision under local regulations.

Some subdivisions are also subject to federal regulation. The Interstate Land Sales Full Disclosure Act requires that certain types of subdivision be registered with the US Office of Interstate Land Sales Registration (OILSR). Generally, land division involving 25 or more lots and interstate sales and promotion is subject to some or all of these federal laws. The word 'lot' includes units in a condominium. Cemetery lots and several other types of land unit and division are exempted.

Submerged lands. Lands that are generally underwater even during low tide, as opposed to 'submersible lands,' which are exposed at such times. The statutes define submerged lands to be those "lying below the line of ordinary low water of all navigable waters within the boundaries of this state as heretofore or hereafter established, whether such waters are tidal or nontidal" (ORS 274.005(7)).

Submersible lands.

Lands lying between the line of ordinary high water and the line of ordinary low water of all navigable waters and all islands, shore lands or other such lands held by or granted to this state by virtue of her sovereignty, wherever applicable, within the boundaries of this state as heretofore or hereafter established, whether such waters or lands are tidal or nontidal. (ORS 274.005(8))

Subsurface sewage disposal system. "A cesspool or the combination of a septic tank or other treatment unit and effluent sewer and absorption facility" (ORS 454.605(14)). Cesspools are no longer used much, but septic tanks are widely used throughout rural areas, where sanitary sewers are not usually available. Approximately one-third of Oregon's residents were served by subsurface systems in 1980 (Department of Environmental Quality, Water Quality Division 1981, p. 38).

A septic tank system comprises four main parts: *(1)* a 'building sewer' that carries sewage into a septic tank; *(2)* the tank; *(3)* an 'effluent sewer,' which conveys treated sewage out of the septic tank; and *(4)* an 'absorption facility,' the drainfield that distributes treated sewage into the soil. The septic tank itself is "a watertight receptacle which receives the discharge of sewage from a sanitary drainage system and which is so designed and constructed as to separate solids from liquids, digest organic matter during a period of detention and allow the liquids to discharge into the soil outside of the tank through an absorption facility" (ORS 454.605(11)).

The installation, repair, alteration, or extension of a subsurface sewage disposal system requires a permit (ORS 454.655). Permits are issued in accordance with standards set by the state's Department of Environmental Quality (DEQ), but they are commonly administered by county officials known as sanitarians.

On receiving an application for a permit, a sanitarian will visit and evaluate the proposed site of the subsurface system. On larger parcels at least one suitable site usually can be found. On smaller parcels or parcels with poor soils, a suitable site may not be found, in which case no permit can be issued. With the advent of new technology and new standards for 'alternative systems,' however, that problem has come to be less common. Evaluation and issuance of a permit for a septic tank system takes at least several days and may take several weeks during the peak periods just before the construction season.

Septic tank drainfields must be set back prescribed distances from property lines, bodies of water, and wells. No structures or paving can be placed over a septic tank or its drainfield. A typical drainfield requires an area of approximately 5,000 square feet. An additional 'repair area' of equal size must be set aside in case a new drainfield is needed in the future.

Surety bond. A bond to guarantee that a certain specified act will be carried out as agreed. See **performance bond.**

Survey. 1. To determine and measure the boundaries, shape, location, and extent of a tract of land.
2. The act of determining and measuring the boundaries, shape, location, and extent of a tract of land.
3. The diagram, map, or description that results from such an operation.

Most local partition and subdivision ordinances require that a survey be completed of any property that is to be divided. The State Structural Code, Section 305, also provides that the building official may require a survey of some lots "to verify that the structure is located in accordance with approved [building] plans." The costs of a survey vary greatly, depending on the size of the property to be surveyed and the presence of monuments from earlier surveys. The costs of a rural survey frequently run into the thousands of dollars.

Systems development charge (SDC). Also called a systems charge or impact fee. A fee charged by a local government to a developer in order to recoup some of the city's general capital costs for sewer, water, or street systems. An SDC differs from a connection charge: the latter is simply a fee (typically $200-$300) to cover the city's costs of connecting a new dwelling to sewer and water lines. The SDC, on the other hand, is a broader source of revenue for capital improvements throughout the city. That distinction is blurred by the fact that some connection charges are higher than the actual cost to the city of making the connection. Such 'connection charges' have a hidden systems charge.

Systems development charges are used in many Oregon cities. Charges of $500 to $1,000 for single-family dwellings are typical (Bureau of Governmental Research and Service 1976: p. 19).

Proponents of systems charges argue that connection charges alone do not adequately defray a city's costs in serving new development. New dwellings, particularly in low densities at the city's edge, have disproportionate effects on city services, so special charges are warranted. Without systems charges, the inner-city residents are in effect subsidizing the new suburbanites and encouraging sprawl.

Opponents of SDCs declare that such large 'front-end costs' stifle development and are just one more obstacle to obtaining needed housing. Given the recent demise of many federal programs to assist cities to develop their service systems, it seems likely that the proponents of the SDC will win the debate. See **exactions.**

T

Taking. The confiscation of private property. Government has a right to take (condemn) land through its powers of eminent domain, but if it does, it must pay "just compensation." The quoted phrase is from what is called the taking clause, the last line of the Fifth Amendment to the United States Constitution: " . . . nor shall private property be taken for public use, without just compensation." A similar clause appears in Oregon's Constitution, Article I, Bill of Rights, Section 18.

Some governmental actions may have the effect of confiscating land, even though the government does not physically take the land or acquire title to it. The legal remedy for the owner of such property may be an "inverse condemnation" action. The owner of a dwelling, for example, might be unable to use that house if the government built an airport next door. If the court found that the situation constituted inverse condemnation, the court could order the government to compensate the landowner.

There are other remedies to governmental action that impinge on private property, however. If the offending activity is something that can be stopped or altered, an injunction—an order telling the government to stop—may be the appropriate remedy. The government does not always have to buy the land which it has impaired.

The framers of the Constitution probably were thinking of matters such as the king's soldiers seizing crops and homes when they wrote of 'taking.' Twentieth century case law, however, also has evolved the notion of a 'regulatory taking': when a government regulates private property so stringently that the owner loses all use of the land, then it may be considered a taking, for which the owner should be given appropriate remedy—compensation, injunction, etc.

The question of just what constitutes a regulatory taking has been a knotty problem ever since local governments began to zone. Opponents of zoning declared that zoning deprived land owners of their rights to use and develop their property fully, that such restriction was a taking, and that compensation was required. The advocates of zoning replied that such restriction was a proper exercise of a government's general regulatory powers, that the mere act of restricting some of the uses of property was not a taking, and that no compensation needed to be paid. Federal and state courts have debated the issue through most of this century. The resulting case law has not yielded clear or consistent criteria with which to define a taking, but a general pattern can be discerned.

First, some restriction, inconvenience, or loss of value to landowners as a result of zoning or planning is not a taking; the government can regulate the use of land without buying it.

Second, the extreme regulation of private land, to a point where the owner is denied all reasonable use of it, does constitute a 'compensable taking,' and the government must pay or provide some other relief. An ordinance that forbade the building of any structure in a floodplain and a regulation that prohibited any filling (and hence any development) in a marsh provide two examples of governmental actions that were found by the courts to be takings.

Third, the range of actions that the courts have come to see as takings is quite narrow. That is, a property can be closely regulated and its value greatly reduced—by half, three-quarters, or more—before a court will determine that a compensable taking has occurred. As Oregon's Court of Appeals stated in the 1972 case of *Multnomah County v. Howell,* 9 Or App 374, 496 P2d 235, "When a property owner can make a substantial beneficial use of his property notwithstanding a zone change, the change does not constitute a taking of private property. . . ."

Tax lot. A unit of land defined by the county tax assessor for the purpose of assessing and taxing real property. One should not infer that each tax lot is a separate legally created lot or parcel. Suppose, for instance, that Sam Slick offers to sell you 2 acres of suburban land. He hands to you the tax assessor's map of the property, which clearly shows two adjoining 1-acre lots numbered 101 and 102. And he declares, "You can buy the 2 acres, and then sell off one of those lots to help you pay for building your house." The existence of two separate tax lots should not be taken as proof that Sam is right. It may only indicate that half the property lies in one school district, and half in another. Whether the property has been legally divided—or can be—cannot be necessarily determined from the tax assessor's maps. Check with your local planning department.

TDR. *Transfer of development rights.*

Tenancy. The manner in which one possesses or exercises rights in real property. Leasing an office is one example of what is known as periodic tenancy. Other categories include joint tenancy, tenancy by entirety, and tenancy in common. See **estate.**

Tentative plan; tentative application. A preliminary proposal from a developer to a city or county to subdivide or partition land. Although the words 'tentative' and 'preliminary' might suggest that such proposals can be sketchy or conceptual, that is not the case. Most subdivision ordinances require that detailed data, maps, and descriptions accompany a tentative plan. See **subdivision.**

Tenure. The holding or possessing of real property. This is a broad word, often used in reference to a system of land ownership, as in the phrases 'feudal tenure,' or 'the Latin American system of land tenure.' It should not be confused with the more precise legal term, 'tenancy.' See also **estate.**

Tertiary sector. See **services.**

Thermal resistance. The ability of a material to resist the passage of heat; represented by the symbol 'R.' The State Structural Code (Section 5302) defines 'R' as follows: "the measure of the resistance of a material or building component to the passage of heat." Insulation, for example, is given an R-value, which indicates its effectiveness in keeping heat in a room. The higher the R-value, the greater is the insulative quality. The State Structural Code, Section 5303(c), specifies the following minimum values for insulation in new residential buildings in Oregon:

	Ceilings	Walls	Floors
Residences with high-efficiency heating	R-30	R-11	R-19
Other residences	R-39	R-19	R-19

Threatened species. "Any species which is likely to become an endangered species within the foreseeable future throughout all or a significant portion of its range" (Federal Endangered Species Act of 1973). See **endangered species.**

3008 conflict. See *Forest Practices Act.*

Through lot. A lot that extends through a block, thus having frontage on two streets. Also called a 'double-frontage lot.' Such lots are considered to be an inefficient use of land and roads in residential areas. Through lots may be useful and efficient in commercial and industrial areas.

Tillamook case. See *Forest Practices Act.*

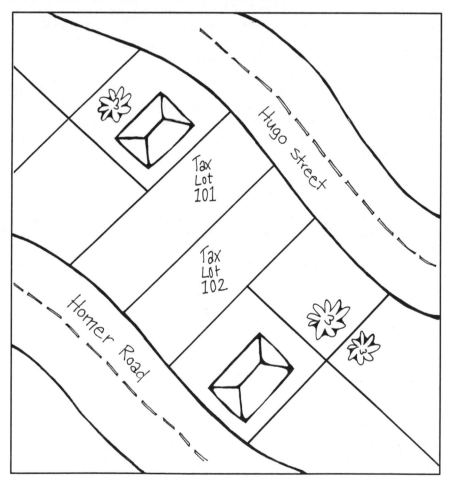

Figure 17. Tax lots 101 and 102 are 'through' or 'double-frontage' lots.

Time sharing. A system of ownership under which several parties share in the title to one unit in a condominium. It is most commonly used for recreational housing. For example, 26 couples may pay $4,000 per couple to purchase a $104,000 unit in a condominium on Maui. Each couple then is entitled to use the unit two weeks (one twenty-sixth) of every year. As a relatively new system, time sharing was not covered by many of Oregon's statutes on more conventional types of real property ownership. The 1983 legislature changed that situation with House Bill 2573. That bill, now codified as ORS 94.803-94.945, sets forth detailed requirements for timeshare development as defined in that statute.

Time zoning. See ***amortize.***

Title. 1. The right to or ownership of real property.
2. Proof or evidence of ownership or of rights to real property.
     A 'clouded' or 'cloudy' title is one that might prove to be invalid or improperly encumbered in the light of one or more claims that could be made against it. A 'defective' title is one against which a valid claim has been made. See ORS 105.605.

Topography. The relief features and characteristics of the land. Topography is an important consideration in planning land use, but it is a difficult quality to convey in two-dimensional documents and maps. The most common technique is the ***contour map,*** which uses lines of equal elevation to show topography. Such a map is also called a topographic, or 'topo,' map.

Townhouse. An attached, single-family dwelling, usually with two or more stories, living and dining areas on the first floor, and bedrooms on the upper floors.

Township. A square tract of land 6 miles on a side. See ***township-and-range survey system.***

Township-and-range survey system. A system used to classify and describe land. Thomas Jefferson receives the credit for devising it. His invention was immortalized through the US Public Lands Survey, which began in 1785 and eventually placed Jefferson's gridiron pattern on many western states, including Oregon.

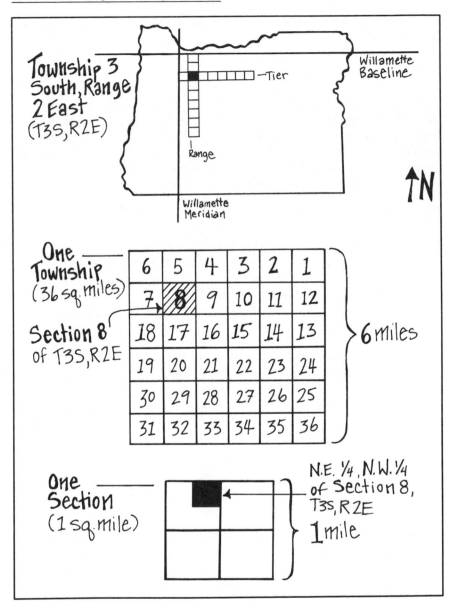

Township 3 South, Range 2 East (T3S, R2E)

Tier

Range

Willamette Baseline

Willamette Meridian

N

One Township (36 sq. miles)

Section 8 of T3S, R2E

6	5	4	3	2	1
7	8	9	10	11	12
18	17	16	15	14	13
19	20	21	22	23	24
30	29	28	27	26	25
31	32	33	34	35	36

6 miles

One Section (1 sq. mile)

N.E. ¼, N.W. ¼ of Section 8, T3S, R2E

1 mile

Figure 18. An example of the township-and-range system applied to a 40-acre parcel in Oregon.

The foundation of the system is a set of imaginary straight lines on the earth's surface. Those running east to west are called baselines (also known as parallels). Those running north to south are meridians. In Oregon the main east-west reference line is the Willamette Baseline, which extends across the northern part of the state, along the Columbia River Gorge. The main north-south reference is the Willamette Principal Meridian. It runs from Portland due south, through the Willamette Valley. It is more commonly called the Willamette Meridian or simply abbreviated WM. The two lines intersect in the west hills of Portland.

The Willamette Meridian and Baseline provide the initial lines for a series of squares known as townships (abbreviated T or Twp). A township contains 36 square miles, and is 6 miles on a side. A row of townships parallel to a baseline is called a tier. All of Oregon's townships can be described by their location in a certain tier north or south of the Willamette Baseline. 'T3S,' for example, means a township in the third tier south of the Willamette Baseline.

A column of townships east or west of the Willamette Meridian is called a range. 'R2E of the WM,' for example, means a township in the second range east of the Willamette Meridian. A combination of tiers and ranges can be used to describe a single, unique township— 'T3S, R2E of the WM,' for example.

But a 36-square-mile block is not a very precise unit with which to survey land, so townships are broken into successively smaller units. The first is the section, a square 1 mile on a side and containing 640 acres. The sections in each township are always numbered beginning in the northeast corner. The numbers grow larger moving across the section until 6 is reached in the northwest corner. Section 7 lies below 6; one then moves back to the east, counting across to section 12, and so on, until section 36 is reached in the southeast corner of the township.

A section is broken into quarter sections, which also are divided into quarters. The result is a description such as this: 'NE ¼ NW ¼ of Sec. 8, T3S, R2E of the WM.' The translation is 'the northeast quarter of the northwest quarter of section 8 of township 3 south, range 2 east of the Willamette Meridian.' This is the example shown in Figure 18.

Traffic flow (traffic volume). The number of vehicles that pass a certain point on a road during some specified period; the number of pedestrians that pass a certain point, usually in a shopping district, during a specified period. Such flows are often described graphically with a traffic-flow diagram, which depicts the volumes of traffic on various routes by drawing the lines for those routes with different thicknesses—perhaps a sixteenth of an inch per thousand vehicles. Traffic flows very widely. A rural lane may have only a few dozen vehicles pass over it each day. On arterials, the numbers range from 2,000 to 25,000 vehicles per day, and freeways may have as many as 2,200 vehicles per lane per hour (Goodman and Freund 1968, p. 149).

Trailer, trailer house, trailer home. See *mobile home.*

Transfer of development rights (TDR). The transfer from one property to another of certain legal rights granted by the zoning ordinance. Perhaps the best way to explain what development rights are and why anyone would want to transfer them is with an example.

Suppose that a certain rural neighborhood has ten vacant 1-acre lots. In the unlikely event that all of those lots were zoned so as to prohibit all forms of development or land use, they would have no development rights and little monetary value. But our hypothetical neighborhood is zoned rural residential, and allows the development of one single-family dwelling on each acre. These lots have a market value of $15,000 each. Land zoned exclusive farm use in the same area is selling for around $2,000 an acre, so the value of the development rights conferred by residential zoning certainly seems to be significant— perhaps as much as $13,000 per lot.

Now let's assume that one of our ten lots is found to be the home of an extremely rare, valuable, and endangered plant that everyone agrees must be protected from development. The county's officials are faced with a formidable task: to protect the plant and to protect the rights of the lot's owner. If the county simply downzones the lot to ban all development, the lot's owner might successfully sue the county for a 'taking.' If the county condemns the land, it must come up with $15,000 and go through litigation. This is a case where TDR offers a better alternative.

The county adopts an ordinance that allows the owner of the troublesome lot to transfer her development rights—to sell the right to build one dwelling—to a neighbor. The neighbor who buys that right (presumably for around $13,000) then can build two dwellings on his 1-acre lot. He gets some extra rights for his money. The owner of the lot with the rare plant on it gets compensated for her loss of development rights. The neighborhood retains the same average density: one house per acre. And the county protects the rare plant without having to downzone the lot, buy it, or face litigation. Nobody loses. It's a 'win-win' situation.

Although the theory behind TDR sounds attractive, the device itself is rarely used. It is a complex process, and the difficulty of writing the ordinances that define the development rights to be transferred is more difficult than my simplistic example may convey. TDR has been used most in urban settings, particularly to preserve historical buildings that might otherwise succumb to the development pressures generated by commercial zoning.

Transition zone. A temporary zone applied to an area in which the general pattern of land uses is changing rapidly, as in an urban neighborhood where old dwellings are being converted to or replaced by commercial buildings.

Transportation disadvantaged. "Those individuals who have difficulty in obtaining transportation because of their age, income, physical or mental disability" (LCDC Goal 12). This term is often used in comprehensive plans as if it were a synonym for the physically and mentally handicapped. It is not. It does include those persons who have difficulty in getting transportation because of physical or mental handicaps, but it also encompasses those who cannot afford to own a private automobile, elderly persons who are unable to drive, etc.

Tribunal. A body of officials that renders a judgment, as in a quasi-judicial hearing. In the case of a rezoning that begins with a hearings officer and then is appealed to a planning commission, city council, LUBA, the Court of Appeals, and the Supreme Court, the hearings officer and all the subsequent reviewing bodies are tribunals.

Trip. A movement from one point (the origin) to another (the destination); the basic unit for measuring traffic flows. As used by transportation planners and engineers, the word always means one-way. The journey from home to the work place and home again, for instance, is considered to be two trips.

Although this word is quite common in writings on planning, it often is used without enough consideration of its dual meaning. It can mean a trip by one person or a trip by one vehicle. An automobile with four carpoolers in it makes two vehicle-trips in its daily run to and from the office, but eight person-trips are made on the same journey. When the word is used without any modifier, it usually can be taken to mean a vehicle-trip.

Trip generation (traffic generation). The tendency of a land use to cause movement of persons and vehicles. A regional shopping center, for example, draws traffic in very large numbers from an area of many square miles. Transportation planners can predict the number of trips that land uses generate, and use this information to design roads and guide the location of development. Households, as well as commercial uses, generate trips. The number varies according to the type of home and its location. Small apartments generate less traffic than suburban houses, which may contain families with several vehicles and drivers.

Homes in sprawling western cities generate more trips than those in denser eastern cities. A common rule of thumb for low-density development in western towns is that each single-family dwelling generates ten vehicle trips per day. If this number sounds higher than you expected, remember that a trip is defined as a one-way journey. And remember that the average may be raised by families with several vehicles and drivers, all of whom drive to work, to school, to the store, etc.

Using numbers such as this, one can calculate the effects of a proposed development on the local street system. Suppose a developer proposes a two-hundred-lot subdivision at the end of Mulberry Lane. That project can be expected to increase the volume of traffic on the lane by 2,000 vehicles daily. If Mulberry Lane is a narrow local street, or if it is already carrying traffic near or beyond its design capacity, the proposed subdivision is sure to cause a need for a street widening or for a new collector.

True cash value. See *market value.*

Turning bulb. See *cul-de-sac.*

U

UBC. *Uniform Building Code.*

UGB. *Urban growth boundary.*

UMTA. Urban Mass Transit Administration (federal).

Undeveloped subdivision. A subdivision that has been platted for many years but that has not been developed, served with public facilities, or had its lots sold. ORS 92.205-92.245 provides that local governments can review such subdivisions and, if necessary, require that they be replatted or vacated.

Uniform Building Code (UBC). A book containing standards and regulations pertaining to the construction of buildings. Originally published in 1927 by the International Conference of Building Officials (ICBO), the UBC is revised each year by that organization.

Oregon has adopted the UBC, with modifications, as the state's *Structural Specialty Code and Fire and Life Safety Regulations* (Building Codes Division 1986). Although the UBC is often referred to as 'the code,' there are several other codes published by the ICBO (e.g., Uniform Mechanical Code, Uniform Housing Code, ICBO Plumbing Code). See **building code** and Chapter 2, section on building permits.

Upzone. To change the zoning on a property to allow more intensive development. A change of commercial zoning to industrial zoning, for example, is an upzoning. A change from one residential zone to another that permits higher densities would also constitute an upzoning. Upzoning usually increases the value of the property involved in the zone change. It thus is far more often the subject of individual requests for zone changes than is downzoning.

Urban facilities and services.

Key facilities and . . . appropriate types and levels of at least the following: police protection; fire protection; sanitary facilities; storm drainage facilities; planning, zoning and subdivision control; health services; recreation facilities and services; energy and communication services; and community government services. (Goal 11)

Key facilities are defined in the statewide goals to include public schools, transportation, water supply, sewage and solid waste disposal.

Urban fringe.

Generally, the developed and densely settled areas that surround a city. The federal Bureau of the Census defines the term to include the following types of areas adjoining a city: *(1)* incorporated places with 2,500 inhabitants or more; *(2)* incorporated places with fewer than 2,500 inhabitants but having a closely settled area of 100 dwelling units or more; and *(3)* enumeration districts in unincorporated areas with a density of 1,000 inhabitants or more per square mile.

Urban growth area.

Planning jargon for land that is inside a city's urban growth boundary but outside the city's corporate limits. The term is not used by all planners, and it has not been legitimized by use in the goals, statutes, or administrative rules of the state. *See also* **urbanizable land.** One also may encounter the term 'unincorporated urban growth boundary.' That's an unfortunate usage: a boundary, unincorporated or otherwise, cannot be the same thing as the land it bounds. See **urban planning area.**

Urban growth boundary (UGB).

A line that indicates the outermost limit of a city's planned expansion. It is strange that this highly significant term has not been defined in the goals, the statutes, or the administrative rules, even though every city is required to have one. In spite of that lack, however, several characteristics of the UGB are certain.

First, its location must be described precisely, either by a legal description or a map. The map should be of large enough scale and sufficient accuracy to determine whether a particular piece of property is within the boundary. To use the planners' current vogue phrase, the boundary must be 'site specific.'

Second, the boundary must be adopted by the city it surrounds and by the county in which the city is located.

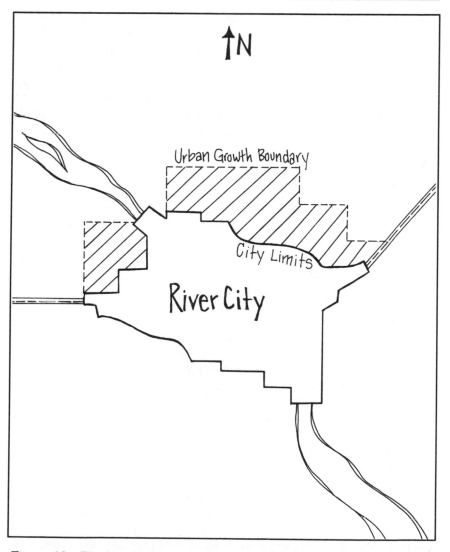

Figure 19. The hatched area is River City's urban growth area. It is the land that the city expects to annex as it grows over the next 15 to 25 years. Sewers, water lines, streets, and other urban services will be directed toward that area. They will not be extended into the rural areas south and east of the present city limits. The urban growth area is subject to River City's comprehensive plan, but it remains under the county's jurisdiction until the area becomes officially annexed to River City.

Third, the boundary is designed to indicate the planned extent of a city's growth over a certain period of time—to the year 2000, for example. If the UGB remained fixed until that time, the city's corporate limits and the UGB would, in theory, become one and the same. The UGBs for most cities, however, will not remain static. Each city's plan contains provisions for the review of the UGB every few years. As new information on population growth, need for land, and other significant factors become available, the UGB will be modified accordingly.

Urban growth management agreement. A written agreement between a city and the county in which it is located that specifies how the unincorporated area within the jointly adopted urban growth boundary is to be managed. Such an agreement spells out whose comprehensive plan (the city's or the county's) will govern the area, whose zoning will apply to it, how permits will be administered there, and by what process the urban growth boundary may be amended. Almost all jurisdictions in Oregon have such agreements.

Urbanizable land.
Urbanizable lands are those lands within the urban growth boundary and which are identified and *(a)* Determined to be necessary and suitable for future urban areas *(b)* Can be served by urban services and facilities *(c)* Are needed for the expansion of an urban area. (LCDC Goals)
Contrast this definition with the term 'urban growth area.' 'Urbanizable land' includes both the vacant, developable land within a city's present corporate limits and the land outside those limits but within the urban growth boundary. 'Urban growth area' refers only to the latter type of land. 'Urbanizable land' also differs from 'urban land.' The latter encompasses land within cities, in urban growth areas, and in some of the larger unincorporated rural centers.

Urbanization. An imprecise word with at least four different meanings. First, it is sometimes used simply as a synonym for increased development. Second, geographers often use the term to describe the percentage of the total population of a country, state, or region that resides in cities. This is usually referred to as the 'level of urbanization.' Third, the same geographers also use the word to describe the process in which the proportion of urban population is increasing. Finally, the term is used to describe the physical expansion of a city. This last usage is probably the most common.

Urbanized area. A term used by the federal Bureau of the Census to describe the area encompassed by a large city and its associated suburbs and developed fringe. The Bureau of the Census defines such areas quite precisely in accordance with several detailed criteria. An urbanized area often is smaller than the standard metropolitan statistical area (SMSA) of which it is a part. The latter term includes all of the county or counties in which a central city is located. The former refers only to the urban parts of those counties.

Urban land.
   Urban areas are those places which must have an incorporated city. Such areas may include lands adjacent to and outside the incorporated city and may also; *(a)* Have concentrations of persons who generally reside and work in the area *(b)* Have supporting public facilities and services. (LCDC Goals)
   This definition encompasses land in an incorporated city, in an urban growth area, or in an unincorporated rural center large enough to have such a "concentration of persons" and "supporting public facilities and services."

Urban place. As defined by the federal Bureau of the Census, any incorporated or unincorporated place of 2,500 persons or more.

Urban planning. The planning and regulation of land use in urban areas, as contrasted with regional planning, which involves multiple jurisdictions and larger areas, and county planning. Some authorities make a distinction between 'city planning,' which involves only the planning of areas within a city's corporate limits, and 'urban planning,' which involves the city and its unincorporated fringe. That distinction may be useful, but it is not widely maintained. For most intents and purposes, the two terms are synonyms.

Urban planning area. " . . .a geographical area within an urban growth boundary" (OAR 660-03-005(6)). This includes both the urban growth area and the land within the corporate limits of the city.

Urban plant. The system of public facilities needed to sustain a city; the structures and buildings in a city's infrastructure, as opposed to the services. See *public facilities and services.*

Urban population. As defined by the US Bureau of the Census, the population comprising all persons who reside in the following three types of areas: *(1)* incorporated cities and towns with populations of 2,500 persons or more; *(2)* densely settled fringes of urbanized areas; and *(3)* unincorporated places with 2,500 or more inhabitants.

Urban renewal. Generally, any program to restore or improve urban areas by replacing dilapidated structures, rehabilitating deteriorating buildings, installing wider streets, creating pedestrian malls, and so on. The term commonly refers specifically to the federally subsidized system in which a local public renewal agency condemns urban land, compensates its owners from federal grants and local matching grants, and sells the land to developers at a discounted price.

The theory of urban renewal is that the decline of certain urban areas can be halted or reversed by extensive (and expensive) rebuilding or new development. The theory overlooks the fact that unpainted storefronts, broken windows, and crumbling foundations may be only the physical signs of economic and social problems or of some inexorable cycle of decline in one part of the city as new areas prosper. Bright new buildings alone cannot solve social, economic, or geographic problems. The program's detractors are quick to note these flaws in the theory, and suggest that the enormous sums for urban renewal might better be spent in other ways. Supporters point with pride at new shopping malls and proclaim a victory against blight.

Urban reserve zone. A 'holding zone' placed on land that is within an urban growth boundary but not yet served by urban facilities or developed at urban densities. Such zones usually have requirements for large minimum lot sizes (10 acres or more) or redivision plans or both. The purpose of such measures is to keep urbanizable land from being divided or developed in a way that would preclude efficient urban development in the future. See **redivision plan.**

Use. See **land use.**

Use district. A section of a city or county that has been zoned so as to permit some uses and exclude others; a zone. See **district.**

User value. The value of a building to one who built it or is using it. In some cases user value may be much higher than market value. This is often true of unusual buildings, particularly public edifices, such as schools, armories, city halls, etc. An old but well-built brick school house in an urban area may be worth a million dollars to the school district that owns it. But if declining enrollments force the school district to sell that school, its market value may be far less than a million— perhaps only the value of the land minus the cost of demolishing the school.

Use variance. A variance (often improper) of a zoning ordinance's provisions regarding permitted and conditional uses, as opposed to a bulk variance. See *variance.*

US public land survey. The survey of the public domain in the western territories begun by the federal government in 1785. See *township-and-range survey system.*

Utility. **1.** A private business enterprise that performs an essential public service, that is granted an exclusive franchise by government, and that is closely regulated by government; a public utility, such as a natural gas, telephone, electricity, or cable television firm.
2. Any public service or system, such as busses, sewers, garbage pickup, etc.
3. From economics, the usefulness, satisfaction, or value from some good or service.

V

Vacancy rate. The ratio of vacant dwelling units to total dwellings in a community. This ratio is an indicator of availability of housing. If it is very high, it suggests that the community is 'overbuilt,' or at least that some economic or demographic effect is slowing growth or causing out-migration. If the vacancy rate is very low, it indicates a demand for housing that is not being met. Regarding the recommended range, Richard Ragatz, in the DLCD publication *Housing Planning in Oregon,* states, "Rules of thumb for vacancy rates range from 1.75 to 2.0 percent for owner occupied units and from 5.0 to 6.5 percent for renter occupied units" (Ragatz 1979, p. 60).

Vacant land. Land that is largely undeveloped and available for development or that can be expected to become available in the near future. Several points about vacant land should be noted. First, 'vacant land' and 'open space' are not synonyms; open space is not available for development. Second, not all vacant land can be developed: some of it is too steep, lacks services, has a poor location, or is not zoned for development. Third, vacant land often makes up a large part of a city's total land area: figures of 10-30 percent are common.

Vacate. 1. To make vacant by moving out; to give up occupancy or possession.
2. To set aside or declare void. A local government, for example, may vacate an old subdivision that has been platted but never developed. Similarly, it may vacate a right-of-way that is not needed or that cannot be used for a street or other public use.

Value. The relative worth, merit, or importance of something, usually as measured by the price it will command in a free market. The word is used in many specialized terms, such as 'assessed value,' 'market value,' and 'true cash value.' Abrams (1971) describes fifteen such variations. See *market value* and *user value.*

Variance. A quasi-judicial decision to lessen or otherwise modify the requirements of a land-use ordinance—allowing a home to be built 5 feet from a side lot line where the ordinance normally would require at least 10 feet, for example.

In order for a variance to be granted (under most ordinances), three conditions must exist. First, there must be some special circumstance that justifies a little bending of the law. That circumstance must not be one created by any action of the owner, and it must pertain to the property involved, not to the owner's health, bank account, domestic relations, etc.

Second, it must be shown that a strict application of the ordinance requirements would cause some hardship or practical difficulty. Note that a variance is one of the few types of land-use cases in which the deciding body can use hardship as partial justification for approving the requested action.

Third, the variance must not have a harmful effect on adjoining properties or neighbors. One of the primary purposes of a zoning ordinance is to protect properties from conflicting land uses. That purpose cannot be ignored, even if there is some unique circumstance and hardship that might otherwise warrant a variance.

A decade or two ago variances were frequently sought and almost as frequently granted. They were so common that some persons came to think that any land-use action was a variance. They applied that label even to partitions, zone changes, and conditional uses. All that has changed. The courts and local governments have come to insist that a variance be granted only if all of the required conditions exist.

There are two types of variances: bulk and use. A bulk variance is a modifying of the dimensional standards of a zoning ordinance— those involving setbacks, yards, lot area, and building heights. A use variance is one which allows the applicant to put the property to some use not generally permitted in the zone where it is located—starting a grocery store in a residential zone, for example. Use variances are far more difficult to justify to a hearing body and are frowned on by the courts. Some ordinances have special provisions for minor variances called 'adjustments.'

Vested right. The right to continue to build a structure that does not conform with regulations imposed upon it after its construction was begun. Consider, for example, the case of a landowner who wishes to build a grocery store on a lot zoned for commercial uses. He or she obtains a building permit, takes out a loan, and pours the foundation for the new store, but the property then is downzoned to a residential district that does not permit grocery stores. Under Oregon case law, the builder probably would have a vested right in the project and therefore could proceed. The builder might not retain such a right if he or she had obtained the building permit illegally or erected the store in violation of other regulations. The decision on whether a vested right does exist usually must be made by a circuit court.

Possession of a building permit alone usually is *not* sufficient to guarantee a vesting of rights; some construction or other expenditures must have been undertaken. The factors that a court considers in making such decisions are set forth in *Clackamas County v. Holmes,* 265 Or 193, 508 P2d 190 (1973). The Oregon Bar's *Land Use* (Oregon State Bar 1982: p. 30-38) summarizes the *Holmes'* factors as follows:

• "the ratio of expenditures incurred to the total cost of the project";

• "the good faith of the landowner";

• "whether or not he had notice of any proposed zoning or amendatory zoning before starting his improvements";

• "whether the expenditures have any relation to the completed project or could apply to various other uses of the land";

• "the kind of project, the location and ultimate cost"; and

• whether "the acts of the landowner . . . rise beyond mere contemplated use or preparation, such as leveling of land, boring test holes, or preliminary negotiations with contractors or architects."

See **grandfathered** and **nonconforming use.**

Vision clearance. Also called a vision triangle or a corner cutback. A triangular area that must be kept free of obstructions so that a driver's vision of pedestrians or oncoming vehicles will not be blocked. Almost all land-use ordinances require such triangles at the four corners of each intersection. Some require that smaller triangles be maintained where driveways and alleys intersect streets. Fences, foliage, branches, etc., may be permitted in the triangle so long as the area from 2 feet to 6 feet above the ground is kept clear. The horizontal dimensions of the clearance area vary with the type of intersection. A larger triangle is required where two arterials meet, for example, than is required where two local streets intersect.

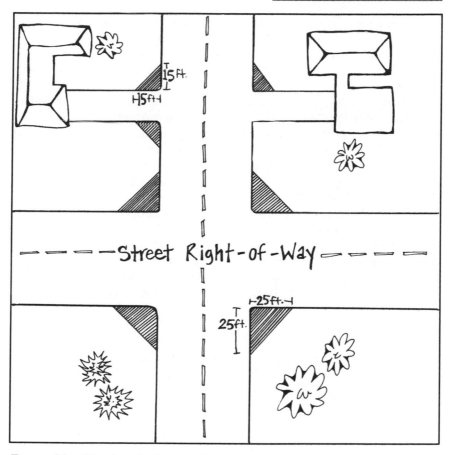

Figure 20. The hatched triangles are the vision clearance areas for a local street. Property owners must ensure that plants, fences, and other objects in those triangles do not project into the crucial area 2 to 6 feet above the ground. The horizontal and vertical dimensions required for such areas vary from city to city and with the type of street (collector, arterial, etc).

Voluntary association of governments. An association of city, county, and special-district governments formed for the purpose of planning and coordinating more effective governmental services; a council of governments (COG). Although such agencies are sometimes referred to as 'regional governments,' such phrasing is not really correct: they do not have the power to tax or make law.

These associations are significant in planning for three main reasons. First, they provide useful means to coordinate the plans of several different governments that have adjoining or overlapping jurisdictions. They often carry out the coordination activities called for in ORS 197.190.

Second, they frequently are responsible for obtaining, administering, and coordinating grants to local governments. Indeed, ORS 197.015(16) defines 'voluntary association of governments' largely in terms of this 'clearing-house' function: 'a regional planning agency in this state officially designated by the Governor pursuant to the federal Office of Management and Budget Circular A-95 as a regional clearinghouse." See *A-95 review.*

Third, these regional planning agencies provide technical assistance to local planners. For example, a COG may prepare computerized projections of population growth for a county and several cities that do not have ready access to computers or demographic experts. COG activities are not limited to those involving land use. COGs also coordinate various social services, such as criminal justice planning.

W

Wall. A vertical structure having a length much greater than its thickness, and a continuous surface except where pierced by doors, windows, etc.; used to provide protection, shelter, or privacy, or to support floors, roofs, and other walls. A bearing wall is one that supports overlying structural members and that is necessary to help a building stand. A nonbearing or curtain wall is one used mainly to divide interior spaces; it could be removed without weakening the building. Exterior walls for most structures are required by state codes to be fire resistant. The requirements vary with the type of building. Fire resistance is measured by the rate at which the wall will burn under certain specified conditions. That rate is usually expressed in hours, hence the term "one-hour wall." The code requirements range from one-hour walls for dwellings to four-hour walls for industrial plants that use combustible materials. See *common wall.*

Water-dependent. "A use or activity which can be carried out only on, in or adjacent to water areas because the use requires access to the water body for water-borne transportation, recreation, energy production, or source of water" (LCDC Goals). Compare this term with *water-related.*

Water-oriented. "A use whose attraction to the public is enhanced by a view of or access to coastal water" (LCDC Goals).

Water-related.
Uses which are not directly dependent upon access to a water body, but which provide goods or services that are directly associated with water-dependent land or waterway use, and which, if not located adjacent to water, would result in a public loss of quality in the goods or services offered. Except as necessary for water-dependent or water-related uses or facilities, residences, parking lots, spoil and dump sites, roads and

243

highways, restaurants, businesses, factories, and trailer parks are not generally considered dependent on or related to water location needs. (LCDC Goals)
Compare with *water-dependent.*

Water Resources Commission. The seven-member commission that oversees Oregon's programs for water resources as specified in ORS Title 45. The commission superseded the Water Policy Review Board under the provisions of the 1985 legislature's Senate Bill 287. That bill provided for many changes in the state's laws on water resources.

Water Resources Department. The administrative arm of the state's Water Resources Commission. The department's offices are in Salem at 3850 Portland Road NE.

Water right. The legal right to take water from an aquifer or body of surface water. Oregon's statutes specify that "All water within the state from all sources of water belongs to the public" (ORS 537.110).

The state regulates water use in accordance with some eighteen chapters of statutes in ORS Title 45. Permits from the state Water Resources Commission are required for many types of 'appropriation' (taking of water for irrigation, municipal water supply, industrial processing, etc.). Some small-scale appropriation of water is exempted from the permit process. ORS 537.545, for example, exempts six activities, including industrial and commercial operations that consume no more than 5,000 gallons of ground water a day; domestic consumption "not exceeding 15,000 gallons a day"; and the watering of livestock, small schoolyards, and noncommercial lawns and gardens of half an acre or less.

Typical consumption of water for domestic purposes ranges from 150 to 250 gallons per person per day. A family of four, then, could be expected to consume 1,000 gallons per day. That figure leaves it well within the exemption standards quoted above.

Water system. "A system for the provision of piped water for human consumption" (ORS 448.115(11)). That definition encompasses everything from a well serving one dwelling to municipal treatment, distribution, and storage facilities serving thousands of persons. Generally, any system that serves four or more dwelling units or a public or commercial development is regulated by the state Health Division under the provisions of ORS Chapter 448. See *well.*

Way of necessity. A right to travel across a neighbor's land in order to gain access to a landlocked parcel. Such an easement can be forced upon the owner of neighboring property only by the official action of a court or county governing body. The term is defined in Oregon's statutes as "a road established under ORS 376.150 to 376.200 to provide motor vehicle access from a public road to land that would otherwise have no motor vehicle access" (ORS 376.150). It is also known as an easement of necessity.

Well. A hole or shaft sunk into the earth to tap an underground supply of water; the most common form of water supply for rural residences. The state does not require permits for wells that serve one to three dwellings. The state's Water Resources Department, however, does set standards for the construction of wells. The location of a well may be subject to local siting requirements by the state Water Resources Department, Health Division, or Department of Environmental Quality. Administrative rules from the Water Resources Department, for example, specify that wells should not be sited within 50 feet of a septic tank or within 100 feet of a septic tank drainfield. See ***water system.***

The flow from a well is measured in gallons per minute (g.p.m.). The minimum flow needed to serve a single residence is subject to some debate, but 5 g.p.m. is a figure commonly used. Some lending institutions will not make loans for residential construction unless at least that much flow can be obtained at the homesite. If intermediate storage is provided, however, wells with smaller flows may suffice: 1 or 2 gallons per minute may be adequate.

The level of water in a well when no pumping is occurring is called the static level. The lower level that exists during pumping is called the pumping level. The difference between the static and pumping levels is referred to as drawdown. Some lowering of the water level occurs beyond the well during pumping, creating a 'cone of depression' in the aquifer. When the cone of depression from one well overlaps with another, 'interference' is said to occur. Widespread interference that causes a sustained lowering of the water table is described as 'overdraft.'

Wetlands.

Land areas where excess water is the dominant factor determining the nature of soil development and the types of plant and animal communities living at the soil surface. Wetland

soils retain sufficient moisture to support aquatic or semi-aquatic plant life. In marine and estuarine areas, wetlands are bounded at the lower extreme by extreme low water; in fresh-water areas, by a depth of 6 feet. The areas below wetlands are submerged lands. (LCDC Goals)
The term includes bogs, marshes, and swamps.

The federal Clean Water Act defines wetlands to be "areas that are inundated or saturated by surface or ground water at a frequency and duration sufficient to support, and that under normal circumstances do support, a prevalence of vegetation typically adapted for life in saturated soil conditions." Section 404 of that act specifies that placing fill material in such wetlands (and in all waters of the United States) requires a permit from the US Army Corps of Engineers.

Oregon's Division of State Lands (DSL) uses the same definition in its administrative rule on fill and removal (OAR 141-85-010). The fill or removal of 50 cubic yards or more in any "waters of this state" (including wetlands) is regulated by DSL.

Why are governmental agencies so involved in regulating swamps? The answer is that wetlands are complex ecosystems that are vital to fish and wildlife—and often to humans. A 1978 federal interagency report called *Our Nation's Wetlands* (Horwitz 1978) describes (on page 2) their importance in these words:

We do know that wetlands are vital fish and wildlife habitats. Two-thirds of the commercially important fish and shellfish harvested along the Atlantic and in the Gulf of Mexico depend on coastal estuaries and their wetlands for food sources, for spawning grounds, for nurseries for the young or for all these critical purposes; for the Pacific coast, the figure is almost one-half. Wetlands provide essential resting, wintering, and nesting grounds for many species of migratory waterfowl, other waterbirds, and many songbirds. They are among the most productive ecosystems in the world. They are important in maintenance of ground water supplies and water purification. Marshes and swamps along coasts, rivers, and lakes protect shorelines and banks from erosion. Wetlands also have the capacity to store floodwaters temporarily and in some instances to reduce the volume and severity of floods.

Wild and Scenic Rivers Act of 1968. Federal legislation to protect "certain selected rivers of the Nation which, with their immediate environments, possess outstandingly remarkable scenic, recreational, geologic, fish and wildlife, historic, cultural, or other similar values" (quoted in Natural Resources Defense Council 1977: p. 133). The act encompasses three different types of rivers or sections of rivers: wild, scenic, and recreational.

Wilderness areas. Oregon's Goal 5 defines this term as follows:
. . . areas where the earth and its community of life are untrammeled by man, where man himself is a visitor who does not remain. It is an area of undeveloped land retaining its primeval character and influence, without permanent improvement or human habitation, which is protected and managed so as to preserve its natural conditions and which *(1)* generally appears to have been affected primarily by the forces of nature, with the imprint of man's work substantially unnoticeable; *(2)* has outstanding opportunities for solitude or a primitive and unconfined type of recreation; *(3)* may also contain ecological, geological, or other features of scientific, educational, scenic or historic value.

This definition is almost identical to that provided in the federal Wilderness Act of 1964.

Windfall. An unexpected gain or profit. In planning, the word means a sudden increase in the value of real property as the result of a rezoning or the extension of some public facility, such as a road or sewer, to the property. Planning actions of course can also cause unexpected losses, or 'wipeouts.' Since neither windfalls nor wipeouts result from the individual actions of landowners, some planning theorists argue that the former should be taxed heavily (up to 100 percent) and the latter compensated. An entire book has been written on the subject. Its title, appropriately enough, is *Windfalls for Wipeouts* (Hagman and Misczynski 1978).

Windshield survey. A survey of land use, housing conditions, etc., conducted from a vehicle. Typically, one member of the surveying team drives the car slowly through a neighborhood while the partner observes and records data on a map or survey form. Windshield surveys of land uses can be done fairly accurately; on the other hand windshield surveys of housing conditions are relatively superficial because only a few indicators of a dwelling's quality can be observed from its exterior.

Wipeout. See the discussion of *windfall.*

Woodlot. A tract of land that is part of a farm and on which trees grow. The term often is used more narrowly to specify a tract on which the trees are managed and harvested for commercial purposes. Oregon's statutes on exclusive farm use zoning (ORS Chapter 215) use the word in that sense. But woodlot also is sometimes used to mean a small parcel of forest land managed by an individual or family, who often reside on the property. That usage distinguishes small, private forest holdings from larger industrial or corporate forest lands and forest land in public ownership.

Writ of review. An action taken by the circuit court to affirm, modify, reverse, or annul a decision made by some lower court, officer, or tribunal. Formerly this was the most common remedy for quasi-judicial land-use decisions by local governments. Amendments to Oregon's statutes, however, have directed most land-use cases to LUBA, thus freeing the circuit court from involvement in most planning litigation. Writ of review is described in ORS Chapter 34.

Y

Yard. The State Structural Code (Section 426) defines it this way: "an open, unoccupied space, other than a court, unobstructed from the ground to the sky, except where specifically provided by this code, on the lot on which a building is situated." In other words, a yard is an open area within which one is prohibited from placing or constructing a building.

Note that the planner's use of this word differs from popular usage. A homeowner whose house is 50 feet from the rear property line typically would say that his or her backyard is 50 feet deep. A planner looking at the same lot would consider the rear yard to be that smaller area along the rear property line in which building is not permitted.

Most zoning ordinances regulate the size of yards. Zones for single-family dwellings, for example, typically specify a front yard of 15-20 feet, sideyards of 5-10 feet, and a rear yard of 15-20 feet.

The term 'yard' also may apply to an open area required between two buildings on the same lot. Zoning ordinances, for example, often require that the buildings in an apartment complex be separated from each other by certain distances. The state's structural code has requirements of the same type. It is not entirely unusual for the two ordinances to conflict.

Z

Zero lot-line provision. A zoning ordinance provision that allows the placement of a dwelling directly against one or both of its side lot lines. The provision is, in effect, a reduction of the conventional requirement for two sideyards of 5 to 15 feet to a requirement for only one sideyard or none at all. The zero lot-line provision is in vogue now: it allows for more efficient use of small lots. See *common wall.*

Zone. **1.** A district or section of a city or county in which certain land uses are permitted and others are prohibited by ordinance; a use district.
2. A set of regulations governing the use of land in a particular district or section of a city or county. See *district.*
3. To divide a city or county into such zones.
    Zoning is the most common means of regulating land use in the United States. It is almost exclusively an instrument of local control; there is no federal zoning, and only a few states (e.g., Hawaii) have what might be described as state zoning. All privately owned lands in Oregon are subject to city or county zoning. Local zoning ordinances are reviewed by the state's Land Conservation and Development Commission (LCDC) to ensure that they comply with nineteen general statewide standards known as goals.
    The long history and widespread use of zoning has led to many variations of a once-simple concept. Different types of zones or zoning include the following: airport, cumulative, Euclidean, exclusionary, exclusive, exclusive farm use, fiscal, floating, holding, inclusionary, large-lot, performance, spot, and time zoning. Entries for all of those terms can be found in this glossary.

Zone change. An action taken by a city or county governing body to change the type of zoning on one or more pieces of land; a rezoning, as from R-1, "single-family residential," to R-2, "medium-density residential." A zone change may be sought by an individual property owner, in which case the request is usually considered to be a quasi-judicial action. Or it may be initiated by a planning commission or governing body, in which case the action is usually a legislative matter.

The term does not apply to an amendment of the general text of a zoning ordinance. It refers only to a change of the zoning on specific properties, and thus always requires an amendment of the zoning map. Some types of zone changes may also require an amendment of the comprehensive plan map.

Zoning ordinance. A set of land-use regulations enacted by a city or county to create districts within which the type, location, density, bulk, height, and lot coverage of land uses are restricted.

Bibliography

Abrams, Charles. *The Language of Cities*. New York: The Viking Press, 1971.

Aeronautics Division, Oregon Department of Transportation. *Airport Compatibility Guidelines*. Salem: 1981.

Building Codes Division, Oregon Department of Commerce. *Structural Specialty Code and Fire and Life Safety Regulations*, 1986 Edition.

Bureau of the Census, Department of Commerce. *Census User's Guide*, Part 1. 1970.

Bureau of Governmental Research and Service. *The Impact of Systems Charges*. Eugene: University of Oregon, 1976.

Bureau of Governmental Research and Service. *Case Studies*. Eugene: University of Oregon, 1984.

Bureau of Governmental Research and Service. *Guide to Local Planning and Development*. Eugene: University of Oregon, 1984.

Bureau of Governmental Research and Service. *Local Planning Digest*. Eugene: University of Oregon, 1984.

Bureau of Governmental Research and Service. *Land Use Procedures and Practices in Oregon*. Eugene: University of Oregon, 1985.

Bureau of Land Management, US Department of the Interior. *Public Land Statistics 1980*. Washington, D.C.:US Government Printing Office, 1981.

Cortright, Joseph. *Economic Planning in Oregon*, Vol. I, Final Report. Salem: Oregon Land Conservation and Development Commission and Oregon Economic Development Commission, 1977.

Department of Environmental Quality, Water Quality Division (State of Oregon). *Water Quality in Oregon 1980*. Portland: 1981.

Department of Forestry (State of Oregon). *Forestry Program for Oregon (Phase 1)*. 1977.

DeGrove, John M. *Land, Growth and Politics*. Washington, D.C.: APA Planners Press, 1984.

Executive Department, State of Oregon. *Adopted Budgets*. Salem: Oregon State Printer, 1975, 1977, 1979, 1981, 1983.

252

Federal Highway Administration, US Department of Transportation. *Standard Land Use Coding Manual*. Washington, D.C.: US Government Printing Office, 1977.

Goodman, William I., and Eric C. Freund, editors. *Principles and Practices of Urban Planning*. Washington, D.C.: International City Managers' Association, 1968.

Hagman, Donald G. *Urban Planning and Land Development Control Law*. St. Paul: West Publishing Co., 1971.

Hagman, Donald G., and Dean Misczynski, editors. *Windfalls for Wipeouts: Land Value Capture and Compensation*. Chicago: American Society of Planning Officials, 1978.

Horwitz, Elinor Lander. *Our Nation's Wetlands: An Interagency Task Force Report*. Washington, D.C.: US Government Printing Office, 1978.

Intergovernmental Relations Division, Executive Department, State of Oregon. *Handbook of State Programs for Local Governments*, 1984.

League of Oregon Cities. *League of Oregon Cities*.

Leonard, H. Jeffrey. *Managing Oregon's Growth*. Washington, D.C.: The Conservation Foundation, 1983.

Loy, William G., Stuart Allen, Clyde P. Patton, and Robert D. Plank. *Atlas of Oregon*. Eugene: University of Oregon Books, 1976.

Lynch, Kevin. *Site Planning*, Second Edition. Cambridge: The MIT Press, 1971.

National Association of Home Builders. *Land Development Manual*. Washington, D.C., 1972.

Natural Resources Defense Council. *Land Use Controls in the United States*, edited by Elaine Moss. New York: The Dial Press, 1977.

Northwest Interagency Fire Prevention Group. *Fire Safety Considerations for Developments in Forested Areas: A Guide for Planners and Developers*. Oregon State Department of Forestry, 1978.

Oregon State Bar Committee on Continuing Legal Education. *Land Use*. 1976.

Oregon State Bar Committee on Continuing Legal Education. *Local Government*. Portland: Durham & Downey, 1979.

Oregon State Bar Committee on Continuing Legal Education. *Land Use*, 1982 revision, Volumes I and II.

Oregon State Bar Committee on Continuing Legal Education. *Real Property*. 1985 revision, Volumes I-III.

Ragatz, Richard L., Associates, Inc. *Housing Planning in Oregon*. Salem: Department of Land Conservation and Development, 1979.

Real Estate Research Corporation. *The Costs of Sprawl (Executive Summary)*. Washington, D.C.: US Government Printing Office, 1974.

Sherton, Corinne C. *Recent Developments in Oregon Land Use Planning Law*. Salem: Department of Land Conservation and Development, 1979.

Schick, Jordis, editor. *Oregon Blue Book, 1985-1986.* Salem: Secretary of State's Office, 1985.

So, Frank S., et. al., editors. *The Practice of Local Government Planning.* Washington, D.C.: International City Management Association, 1979.

Thompson, Ken, and Dale Snow. *Fish and Wildlife Resources, Oregon Coastal Zone.* Portland: Oregon Coastal Conservation and Development Commission, 1974.

Unger, Maurice A. *Real Estate Principles and Practices,* Fourth Edition. Cincinnati: South-Western Publishing Co., 1969.

United States Department of Agriculture and the Council on Environmental Quality. *National Agricultural Lands Study, Final Report, 1981.* Washington, D.C.: US Government Printing Office, 1981.

US Department of Transportation, Federal Highway Administration. *Standard Land Use Coding Manual.* Washington, D.C.: 1977.

Oregon's Statewide Planning Goals

In 1973, Oregon's legislature created the Land Conservation and Development Commission (LCDC) and charged it with the task of developing statewide standards for planning. The LCDC ultimately adopted nineteen statewide planning goals. The first fourteen were adopted by the commission on 27 December 1974. Goal 15, the Willamette Greenway goal, was adopted 6 December 1975. The remaining four, the coastal goals, were adopted on 18 December 1976. Goals 2, 3, and 4 were amended late in 1983. Goals 8 and 16-19 were amended in 1984.

The goals are general standards for land-use planning. Planning remains the responsibility of city and county governments, but it must be done in accordance with these statewide standards.

The goals are mandatory. To say that they are state law is not technically correct: they are adopted as administrative rules (OAR 660-15-000, 005, and 010), not as statutes. Administrative rules are regulations that implement, interpret, or prescribe law or policy, or that describe the procedures or practices of a state agency (ORS 183.310(8)). Local comprehensive plans and land-use regulations are required by statute (ORS 197.250) to comply with the goals.

All of Oregon's statewide goals except number 15, "Willamette River Greenway," are accompanied by "guidelines." In contrast to the goals, the guidelines are not mandatory. They are merely suggestions about how a local government might comply with state standards. Because they are not mandatory, the guidelines have had little effect on state and local planning.

The following pages reproduce all nineteen of the statewide planning goals from the 1985 tabloid published by LCDC. The guidelines, however, have been omitted altogether. A free tabloid containing the complete goals and guidelines is available from:

> Department of Land Conservation and Development
> 1175 Court Street NE
> Salem, Oregon 97310

Goal 1: Citizen Involvement

Goal: To develop a citizen involvement program that insures the opportunity for citizens to be involved in all phases of the planning process.

The governing body charged with preparing and adopting a comprehensive plan shall adopt and publicize a program for citizen involvement that clearly defines the procedures by which the general public will be involved in the on-going land-use planning process.

The citizen involvement program shall be appropriate to the scale of the planning effort. The program shall provide for continuity of citizen participation and of information that enables citizens to identify and comprehend the issues.

Federal, state and regional agencies, and special-purpose districts shall coordinate their planning efforts with the affected governing bodies and make use of existing local citizen involvement programs established by counties and cities.

The citizen involvement program shall incorporate the following components:

1. Citizen Involvement—To provide for widespread citizen involvement.

The citizen involvement program shall involve a cross-section of affected citizens in all phases of the planning process. As a component, the program for citizen involvement shall include an officially recognized citizen advisory committee or committees broadly representative of geographic areas and interests related to land use and land-use decisions. Citizen advisory committee members shall be selected by an open, well-publicized public process.

The citizen advisory committee shall be responsible for assisting the governing body with the development of a program that promotes and enhances citizen involvement in land-use planning, assisting in the implementation of the citizen involvement program, and evaluating the process being used for citizen involvement.

If the governing body wishes to assume the responsibility for development as well as adoption and implementation of the citizen involvement program or to assign such responsibilities to a planning commission, a letter shall be submitted to the Land Conservation and Development Commission for the state Citizen Involvement Advisory Committee's review and recommendation stating the rationale for selecting this option, as well as indicating the mechanism to be used for an evaluation of the citizen involvement program. If the planning commission is used, its members shall be selected by an open, well-publicized public process.

2. Communication—To assure effective two-way communication with citizens.

Mechanisms shall be established which provide for effective communication between citizens and elected and appointed officials.

3. Citizen Influence—To provide the opportunity for citizens to be involved in all phases of the planning process.

Citizens shall have the opportunity to be involved in the phases of the planning process as set forth and defined in the goals and guidelines for Land-Use Planning, including *Preparation of Plans and Implementation Measures, Plan Content, Plan Adoption, Minor Changes and Major Revisions in the Plan, and Implementation Measures.*

4. Technical Information—To assure that technical information is available in an understandable form.

Information necessary to reach policy decisions shall be available in a simplified, understandable form. Assistance shall be provided to interpret and effectively use technical information. A copy of all technical information shall be available at a local public library or other location open to the public.

5. Feedback Mechanisms—To assure that citizens will receive a response from policymakers.

Recommendations resulting from the citizen involvement program shall be retained and made available for public assessment. Citizens who have participated in this program shall receive a response from policymakers. The rationale used to reach land-use policy decisions shall be available in the form of a written record.

6. Financial Support—To insure funding for the citizen involvement program.

Adequate human, financial, and informational resources shall be allocated for the citizen involvement program. These allocations shall be an integral component of the planning budget. The governing body shall be responsible for obtaining and providing these resources.

Goal 2: Land Use Planning
Goal: Part I—Planning.

To establish a land use planning process and policy framework as a basis for all decisions and actions related to use of land and to assure an adequate factual base for such decisions and actions.

City, county, state and federal agency and special district plans and actions related to land use shall be consistent with the comprehensive plans of cities and counties and regional plans adopted under ORS 197.705 through 197.795.

All land use plans shall include identification of issues and problems, inventories and other factual information for each applicable statewide planning goal, evaluation of alternative courses of action and ultimate policy choices, taking into consideration social, economic, energy and environmental needs. The required information shall be contained in the plan document or in supporting documents. The plans, supporting documents and implementation ordinances shall be filed in a public office or other place easily accessible to the public. The plans shall be the basis for specific implementation measures. These measures shall be consistent with and adequate to carry out the plans. Each plan and related implementation measure shall be coordinated with the plans of affected governmental units.

All land-use plans and implementation ordinances shall be adopted by the governing body after public hearing and shall be reviewed and, as needed, revised on a periodic cycle to take into account changing public policies and circumstances, in accord with a schedule set forth in the plan. Opportunities shall be provided for review and comment by citizens and affected governmental units during preparation, review and revision of plans and implementation ordinances.

Affected Governmental Units—are those local governments, state and federal agencies and special districts which have programs, land ownerships, or responsibilities within the area included in the plan.

Comprehensive Plan—as defined in ORS 197.015(5).

Coordinated—as defined in ORS 197.015(5). Note: It is included in the definition of comprehensive plan.

Implementation Measures—are the means used to carry out the plan. These are of two general types: *(1)* management implementation measures such as ordinances, regulations or project plans, and *(2)* site or area specific implementation measures such as permits and grants for construction, construction of public facilities or provision of services.

Plans—as used here encompass all plans which guide land-use decisions, including both comprehensive and single-purpose plans of cities, counties, state and federal agencies and special districts.

Part II—Exceptions

A local government may adopt an exception to a goal when:

(a) The land subject to the exception is physically developed to the extent that it is no longer available for uses allowed by the applicable goal;

(b) The land subject to the exception is irrevocably committed to uses not allowed by the applicable goal because existing adjacent uses and other relevant factors make uses allowed by the applicable goal impracticable; or

(c) The following standards are met:

  (1) Reasons justify why the state policy embodied in the applicable goals should not apply;

  (2) Areas which do not require a new exception cannot reasonably accommodate the use;

  (3) The long-term environmental, economic, social and energy consequences resulting from the use at the proposed site with measures designed to reduce adverse impacts are not significantly more adverse than would typically result from the same proposal being located in areas requiring a goal exception other than the proposed site; and

  (4) The proposed uses are compatible with other adjacent uses or will be so rendered through measures designed to reduce adverse impacts.

Compatible, as used in subparagraph *(4),* is not intended as an absolute term meaning no interference or adverse impacts of any type with adjacent uses.

A local government approving or denying a proposed exception shall set forth findings of fact and a statement of reasons which demonstrate that the standards for an exception have or have not been met.

Each notice of a public hearing on a proposed exception shall specifically note that a goal exception is proposed and shall summarize the issues in an understandable manner.

Upon review of a decision approving or denying an exception:

(a) The commission shall be bound by any finding of fact for which there is substantial evidence in the record of the local government proceedings resulting in approval or denial of the exception;

(b) The commission shall determine whether the local government's findings and reasons demonstrate that the standards for an exception have or have not been met; and

(c) The commission shall adopt a clear statement of reasons which sets forth the basis for the determination that the standards for an exception have or have not been met.

Exception means a comprehensive plan provision, including an amendment to an acknowledged comprehensive plan, that:

(a) Is applicable to specific properties or situations and does not establish a planning or zoning policy of general applicability;

(b) Does not comply with some or all goal requirements applicable to the subject properties or situations; and

(c) Complies with standards for an exception.

Part III—Use of Guidelines

Governmental units shall review the guidelines set forth for the goals and either utilize the guidelines or develop alternative means that will achieve the goals. All land-use plans shall state how the guidelines or alternative means utilized achieve the goals.

Guidelines—are suggested directions that would aid local governments in activating the mandated goals. They are intended to be instructive, directional and positive, not limiting local government to a single course of action when some other course would achieve the same result. Above all, guidelines are not intended to be a grant of power to the state to carry out zoning from the state level under the guise of guidelines. (Guidelines or the alternative means selected by governmental bodies will be part of the Land Conservation and Development Commission's process of evaluating plans for compliance with goals.)

Goal 3: Agricultural Lands
Goal: To preserve and maintain agricultural lands.

Agricultural lands shall be preserved and maintained for farm use, consistent with existing and future needs for agricultural products, forest and open space. These lands shall be inventoried and preserved by adopting exclusive farm use zones pursuant to ORS Chapter 215. Such minimum lot sizes as are utilized for any farm use zones shall be appropriate for the continuation of the existing commercial agricultural enterprise within the area.

Conversion of rural agricultural land to urbanizable land shall be based upon consideration of the following factors: *(1)* environmental, energy, social and economic consequences; *(2)* demonstrated need consistent with LCDC goals; *(3)* unavailability of an alternative suitable location for the requested use; *(4)* compatibility of the proposed use with related agricultural land; and *(5)* the retention of Class I, II, III and IV soils in farm use. A governing body proposing to convert rural agricultural land to urbanizable land shall follow the procedures and requirements set forth in the Land Use Planning goal (Goal 2) for goal exceptions.

Counties may designate agricultural land as marginal land and allow those uses and land divisions on the designated marginal land as allowed by ORS 197.247.

Agricultural Land—in western Oregon is land of predominantly Class I, II, III and IV soils and in eastern Oregon is land of predominantly Class I, II, III, IV, V and VI soils as identified in the Soil Capability Classification System of the United States Soil Conservation Service, and other lands which are suitable for farm use taking into consideration soil fertility, suitability for grazing, climatic conditions, existing and future availability of water for farm irrigation purposes, existing land use patterns, technological and energy inputs required, or accepted farming practices. Lands in other classes which are necessary to permit farm practices to be undertaken on adjacent or nearby lands, shall be included as agricultural land in any event.

More detailed soil data to define agricultural land may be utilized by local governments if such data permits achievement of this goal.

Farm Use—is as set forth in ORS 215.203 and includes the non-farm uses authorized by ORS 215.213.

Goal 4: Forest Lands

Goal: To conserve forest lands for forest uses.

Forest land shall be retained for the production of wood fibre and other forest uses. Lands suitable for forest uses shall be inventoried and designated as forest lands. Existing forest land uses shall be protected unless proposed changes are in conformance with the comprehensive plan.

In the process of designating forest lands, comprehensive plans shall include the determination and mapping of forest site classes according to the United States Forest Service manual "Field Instructions for Integrated Forest Survey and Timber Management Inventories—Oregon, Washington and California, 1974."

Counties may designate forest land as marginal land and allow those uses and land divisions on the designated marginal land as allowed by ORS 197.247.

Forest lands—are *(1)* lands composed of existing and potential forest lands which are suitable for commercial forest uses; *(2)* other forested lands needed for watershed protection, wildlife and fisheries habitat and recreation; *(3)* lands where extreme conditions of climate, soil and topography require the maintenance of vegetative cover irrespective of use; *(4)* other forested lands in urban and agricultural areas which provide urban buffers, wind breaks, wildlife and fisheries habitat, livestock habitat, scenic corridors, and recreational use.

Forest uses—are *(1)* the production of trees and the processing of forest products; *(2)* open space, buffers from noise, and visual separation of conflicting uses; *(3)* watershed protection and wildlife and fisheries habitat; *(4)* soil protection from wind and water; *(5)* maintenance of clean air and water; *(6)* outdoor recreational activities and related support services and wilderness values compatible with these uses; and *(7)* grazing land for livestock.

Goal 5: Open Spaces, Scenic and Historic Areas, and Natural Resources

Goal: To conserve open space and protect natural and scenic resources.

Programs shall be provided that will *(1)* insure open space, *(2)* protect scenic and historic areas and natural resources for future generations, and *(3)* promote healthy and visually attractive environments in harmony with the natural landscape character. The location, quality and quantity of the following resources shall be inventoried:

(a) Land needed or desirable for open space;
(b) Mineral and aggregate resources;
(c) Energy sources;
(d) Fish and wildlife areas and habitats;
(e) Ecologically and scientifically significant natural areas, including desert areas;
(f) Outstanding scenic views and sites;
(g) Water areas, wetlands, watersheds and groundwater resources;
(h) Wilderness areas;
(i) Historic areas, sites, structures and objects;
(j) Cultural areas;
(k) Potential and approved Oregon recreation trails;
(l) Potential and approved federal wild and scenic waterways and state scenic waterways.

Where no conflicting uses for such resources have been identified, such resources shall be managed so as to preserve their original character. Where conflicting uses have been identified the economic, social, environmental and energy consequences of the conflicting uses shall be determined and programs developed to achieve the goal.

Cultural Area—refers to an area characterized by evidence of an ethnic, religious or social group with distinctive traits, beliefs and social forms.

Historic Areas—are lands with sites, structures and objects that have local, regional, statewide or national historical significance.

Natural Area—includes land and water that has substantially retained its natural character and land and water that, although altered in character, is important as habitats for plant, animal or marine life, for the study of its natural historical, scientific or paleontological features, or for the appreciation of its natural features.

Open Space—consists of lands used for agricultural or forest uses, and any land area that would, if preserved and continued in its present use:

(a) Conserve and enhance natural or scenic resources;
(b) Protect air or streams or water supply;
(c) Promote conservation of soils, wetlands, beaches or tidal marshes;
(d) Conserve landscaped areas, such as public or private golf courses, that reduce air pollution and enhance the value of abutting or neighboring property;
(e) Enhance the value to the public of abutting or neighboring parks, forests, wildlife preserves, nature reservations or sanctuaries or other open space;
(f) Enhance recreation opportunities;
(g) Preserve historic sites;
(h) Promote orderly urban development.

Scenic Areas—are lands that are valued for their aesthetic appearance.

Wilderness Areas—are areas where the earth and its community of life are untrammeled by man, where man himself is a visitor who does not remain. It is an area of undeveloped land retaining its primeval character and influence, without permanent improvement or human habitation, which is protected and managed so as to preserve its natural conditions and which (1) generally appears to have been affected primarily by the forces of nature, with the imprint of man's work substantially unnoticeable; (2) has outstanding opportunities for solitude or a primitive and unconfined type of recreation; (3) may also contain ecological, geological, or other features of scientific, educational, scenic, or historic value.

Goal 6: Air, Water, and Land Resources Quality

Goal: To maintain and improve the quality of the air, water and land resources of the state.

All waste and process discharges from future development, when combined with such discharges from existing developments shall not threaten to violate, or violate applicable state or federal environmental quality statutes, rules and standards. With respect to the air, water and land resources of the applicable air sheds and river basins described or included in state environmental quality statutes, rules, standards and implementation plans, such discharges shall not (1) exceed the carrying capacity of such resources, considering long range needs; (2) degrade such resources; or (3) threaten the availability of such resources.

Waste and Process Discharges—refers to solid waste, thermal, noise, atmospheric or water pollutants, contaminants, or products therefrom. Included here also are indirect sources of air pollution which result in emissions of air contaminants for which the state has established standards.

Goal 7: Areas Subject to Natural Disasters and Hazards

Goal: To protect life and property from natural disasters and hazards.

Developments subject to damage or that could result in loss of life shall not be planned nor located in known areas of natural disasters and hazards without appropriate safeguards. Plans shall be based on an inventory of known areas of natural disaster and hazards.

Areas of Natural Disasters and Hazards — are areas that are subject to natural events that are known to result in death or endanger the works of man, such as stream flooding, ocean flooding, ground water, erosion and deposition, landslides, earthquakes, weak foundation soils and other hazards unique to local or regional areas.

Goal 8: Recreational Needs

Goal: To satisfy the recreational needs of the citizens of the state and visitors and, where appropriate, to provide for the siting of necessary recreational facilities including destination resorts.

Recreation Planning

The requirements for meeting such needs, now and in the future, shall be planned for by governmental agencies having responsibility for recreation areas, facilities and opportunities: *(1)* in coordination with private enterprise, *(2)* in appropriate proportions and *(3)* in such quantity, quality and location as is consistent with the availability of the resources to meet such requirements. State and federal agency recreation plans shall be coordinated with local and regional recreational needs and plans.

Destination Resort Siting

Comprehensive plans may provide for the siting of destination resorts on rural lands subject to the provisions of the Goal and without a Goal 2 exception to Goals 3, 4, 11, or 14.

1. To assure that resort development does not conflict with the objectives of other Statewide Planning Goals, destination resorts allowed by this Goal shall not be sited in the following areas:

(a) Within 30 air miles of an urban growth boundary with an existing population of 100,000 or more;

(b) On a site with 50 or more contiguous acres of unique or prime farm land identified and mapped by the Soil Conservation Service; or within three miles of farm land within a High-Value Crop Area.

(c) On predominantly Cubic Foot Site Class 1 or 2 forest lands which are not subject to an approved Goal exception;

(d) In the Columbia River Gorge (as defined by ORS 390.460);

(e) On areas protected as Goal 5 resource sites in acknowledged comprehensive plans protected in spite of identified conflicting uses ("3A" sites designated pursuant to OAR 660-16-010(1)).

(f) Especially sensitive to big game habitat as generally mapped by the Oregon Department of Fish and Wildlife in July 1984 and as further refined through development of comprehensive plans implementing this requirement.

2. Counties shall ensure that destination resorts are compatible with the site and adjacent land uses through the following measures:

(a) Important natural features, including habitat of threatened or endangered species, streams, rivers, and significant wetlands shall be maintained.

Riparian vegetation within 100 feet of streams, rivers, and significant wetlands shall be maintained. Alterations to important natural features, including placement of structures which maintain the overall values of the feature may be allowed.

(b) Improvements and activities shall be located and designed to avoid or minimize adverse effects of the resort on uses on surrounding lands, particularly effects on intensive farming operations in the area. At a minimum, measures to accomplish this shall include:

    (i) Establishment and maintenance of buffers between the resort and adjacent land uses, including natural vegetation and where appropriate, fences, berms, landscaped areas, and other similar types of buffers.

    (ii) Setbacks of structures and other improvements from adjacent land uses.

3. Comprehensive plans allowing for destination resorts shall include implementing measures which:

(a) Map areas where destination resorts are permitted by requirement (1) above.

(b) Limit uses and activities to those permitted by this Goal.

(c) Assure developed recreational facilities and key facilities intended to serve the entire development and visitor oriented accommodations are physically provided or are guaranteed through surety bonding or substantially equivalent financial assurances prior to closure of sale of individual lots or units. In phased developments, developed recreational facilities and other key facilities intended to serve a particular phase shall be constructed prior to sales in that phase or guaranteed through surety bonding.

Definitions

Destination Resort—a self-contained development providing visitor-oriented accommodations and developed recreational facilities in a setting with high natural amenities. To qualify as a destination resort under Goal 8, a proposed development must meet the following standards:

(1) The resort is located on a site of 160 acres or more except within two miles of the ocean shoreline and the site is 40 acres or more.

(2) At least 50 percent of the site is dedicated permanent open space excluding yards, streets, and parking areas.

(3) At least $2 million (in 1984 dollars) is spent on improvements for on-site developed recreational facilities and visitor-oriented accommodations exclusive of costs for land, sewer, and water facilities and roads. Not less than one-third of this amount shall be spent on developed recreational facilities.

(4) Visitor-oriented accommodations including meeting rooms, restaurants with seating for 100 persons, and 150 separate rentable units for overnight lodging are provided. Accommodations available for residential use shall not exceed two such units for each unit of overnight lodging.

(5) Commercial uses provided are limited to types and levels necessary to meet the needs of visitors to the development, and industrial uses are not permitted.

Developed Recreation Facilities—are improvements constructed for the purpose of recreation and may include but are not limited to golf courses, tennis courts, swimming pools, marinas, ski runs, and bicycle paths.

High Value Crop Area—an area in which there is a concentration of commercial farms capable of producing crops or products with a minimum gross value of $1000 per acre per year. These crops and products include field crops, small fruits, berries, tree fruits, nuts, or vegetables, dairying, livestock feedlots, or Christmas trees as these terms are used in the 1983 County and State Agricultural Estimates prepared by the Oregon State University Extension Service. The High Value Crop Area designation is used for the purpose of minimizing conflicting uses in resort siting and is not meant to revise the requirements of Goal 3 or administrative rules interpreting the Goal.

Overnight Lodgings—are permanent, separately rentable accommodations which are not available for residential use. Overnight lodgings include hotel or motel rooms, cabins, and time share units. Individually owned units may be considered overnight lodgings if they are available for overnight rental use by the general public for at least 48 weeks per calendar year through a central reservation and check-in service. Tent sites, recreational vehicle parks, mobile homes, dormitory rooms, and similar accommodations do not qualify as overnight lodgings for the purpose of this definition.

Recreation Areas, Facilities and Opportunities—provide for human development and enrichment, and include but are not limited to: open space and scenic landscapes; recreational lands; history, archaeology and natural science resources; scenic roads and travelways; sports and cultural events; camping, picnicking and recreational lodging; tourist facilities and accommodations; trails; waterway use facilities; hunting; angling; winter sports; mineral resources; active and passive games and activities.

Recreational Needs—refers to existing and future demand by citizens and visitors for recreation areas, facilities and opportunities.

Self-contained Development—means that community sewer, water, and recreational facilities are provided on-site and are limited to meet the needs of the resort.

Visitor-oriented Accommodations—are overnight lodging, restaurants, meeting facilities which are designed to and provide for the needs of visitors rather than year-round residents.

Goal 9: Economy of the State
Goal: To diversify and improve the economy of the state.

Both state and federal economic plans and policies shall be coordinated by the state with local and regional needs. Plans and policies shall contribute to a stable and healthy economy in all regions of the state. Plans shall be based on inventories of areas suitable for increased economic growth and activity after taking into consideration the health of the current economic base; materials and energy availability; labor market factors; transportation; current market forces: availability of renewable and non-renewable resources; availability of land; and pollution control requirements.

Economic growth and activity in accordance with such plans shall be encouraged in areas that have underutilized human and natural resource capabilities and want increased growth and activity. Alternative sites suitable for economic growth and expansion shall be designated in such plans.

Diversify—refers to increasing the variety, type, scale and location of business, industrial and commercial activities.

Improve the Economy of the State—refers to a beneficial change in those business, industrial and commercial activities which generate employment, products and services consistent with the availability of long term human and natural resources.

Areas Which Have Underutilized Human and Natural Resource Capabilities—refer to cities, counties, or regions which are characterized by chronic unemployment or a narrow economic base, but have the capacity and resources to support additional economic activity.

Goal 10: Housing
Goal: To provide for the housing needs of citizens of the state.

Buildable lands for residential use shall be inventoried and plans shall encourage the availability of adequate numbers of housing units at price ranges and rent levels which are commensurate with the financial capabilities of Oregon households and allow for flexibility of housing location, type and density.

Buildable Lands—refers to lands in urban and urbanizable areas that are suitable, available and necessary for residential use.

Household—refers to one or more persons occupying a single housing unit.

Goal 11: Public Facilities and Services
Goal: To plan and develop a timely, orderly and efficient arrangement of public facilities and services to serve as a framework for urban and rural development.

Urban and rural development shall be guided and supported by types and levels of urban and rural public facilities and services appropriate for, but limited to, the needs and requirements of the urban, urbanizable and rural areas to be served. A provision for key facilities shall be included in each plan. To meet current and long-range needs, a provision for solid waste disposal sites, including sites for inert waste, shall be included in each plan.

A Timely, Orderly and Efficient Arrangement—refers to a system or plan that coordinates the type, location and delivery of public facilities and services in a manner that best supports the existing and proposed land uses.

Rural Facilities and Services—refers to facilities and services which the governing body determines to be suitable and appropriate solely for the needs of rural use.

Urban Facilities and Services—refers to key facilities and to appropriate types and levels of at least the following: police protection; fire protection; sanitary facilities; storm drainage facilities; planning, zoning and subdivision control; health services; recreation facilities and services; energy and communication services; and community governmental services.

Goal 12: Transportation
Goal: To provide and encourage a safe, convenient and economic transportation system.

A transportation plan shall (1) consider all modes of transportation including mass transit, air, water, pipeline, rail, highway, bicycle and pedestrian; (2) be based upon an inventory of local, regional and state transportation needs; (3) consider the differences in social consequences that would result from utilizing differing combinations of transportation modes; (4) avoid principal reliance upon any one mode of transportation; (5) minimize adverse social, economic and environmental impacts and costs; (6) conserve energy; (7) meet the needs of the transportation disadvantaged by improving transportation services, (8) facilitate the flow of goods and services so as to strengthen the local and regional economy; and (9) conform with local and regional comprehensive land use plans. Each plan shall include a provision for transportation as a key facility.

Transportation—refers to the movement of people and goods.

Transportation Facility—refers to any physical facility that moves or assists in the movement of people and goods excluding electricity, sewage and water.

Transportation System—refers to one or more transportation facilities that are planned, developed, operated and maintained in a coordinated manner to supply continuity of movement between modes, and within and between geographic and jurisdictional areas.

Mass Transit—refers to any form of passenger transportation which carries members of the public on a regular and continuing basis.

Transportation Disadvantaged—refers to those individuals who have difficulty in obtaining transportation because of their age, income, physical or mental disability.

Goal 13: Energy Conservation
Goal: To conserve energy.

Land and uses developed on the land shall be managed and controlled so as to maximize the conservation of all forms of energy, based upon sound economic principles.

Goal 14: Urbanization
Goal: To provide for an orderly and efficient transition from rural to urban land use.

Urban growth boundaries shall be established to identify and separate urbanizable land from rural land.

Establishment and change of the boundaries shall be based upon considerations of the following factors:

(1) Demonstrated need to accommodate long-range urban population growth requirements consistent with LCDC goals;

(2) Need for housing, employment opportunities, and livability;

(3) Orderly and economic provision for public facilities and services;

(4) Maximum efficiency of land uses within and on the fringe of the existing urban area;

(5) Environmental, energy, economic and social consequences;

(6) Retention of agricultural land as defined, with Class I being the highest priority for retention and Class VI the lowest priority; and,

(7) Compatibility of the proposed urban uses with nearby agricultural activities.

The results of the above considerations shall be included in the comprehensive plan. In the case of a change of a boundary, a governing body proposing such change in the boundary separating urbanizable land from rural land, shall follow the procedures and requirements as set forth in the Land Use Planning goal (Goal 2) for goal exceptions.

Any urban growth boundary established prior to January 1, 1975, which includes rural lands that have not been built upon shall be reviewed by the governing body, utilizing the same factors applicable to the establishment or change of urban growth boundaries.

Establishment and change of the boundaries shall be a cooperative process between a city and the county or counties that surround it.

Land within the boundaries separating urbanizable land from rural land shall be considered available over time for urban uses. Conversion of urbanizable land to urban uses shall be based on consideration of:

(1) Orderly, economic provision for public facilities and services;
(2) Availability of sufficient land for the various uses to insure choices in the market place;
(3) LCDC goals; and,
(4) Encouragement of development within urban areas before conversion of urbanizable areas.

Goal 15: Willamette River Greenway

The Willamette River Greenway presents a unique and unprecedented problem. The outlines of the problem are *(1)* a legislative policy directing development and maintenance of a natural, scenic, historical and recreational greenway along the Willamette River; *(2)* accomplishment of this purpose by the development and implementation of a "plan" *(3)* through the "cooperative efforts" of the state and local units of government (ORS 390.314 (1) and (2)(a)). Except for this broad directive, there is no specific legislative guidance as to how this undertaking is to be accomplished for what amounts to over 600 miles of riverbank. The legislature did direct the Oregon Department of Transportation (DOT) to prepare a plan "for the development and management of the Willamette River Greenway." (ORS 390.318(1)) However, the detail as to what was to go into the plan is sketchy. The legislature required the setting forth

of the boundaries of the Greenway, interests to be acquired by units of governments, the location of publicly owned property and the locations of aggregate deposits. (ORS 390.318(2) and (3)) The legislature also directed the Land Conservation and Development Commission (LCDC), following preparation of the Plan by DOT, to make such investigation and review of the plan "as it considers necessary" and to "revise the plan . . . itself or require such revision by the Department and units of local government." (ORS 390.322(1)) Again, however, the question of how the Greenway was to come about through the cooperative efforts of the various units of government was not spelled out.

The situation therefore calls for some overall management framework within which the various public agencies can act to accomplish the legislative intent.

Accordingly, the LCDC deems a statewide planning goal to be necessary not only to implement the policy of the Greenway Law, but also to provide the parameters within which the DOT plan can be formulated and carried out for the Greenway. Within those parameters local governments can formulate and implement (in a manner in harmony with the DOT plan), those Greenway portions of their comprehensive plans and implementing ordinances within their boundaries.

Goal: To protect, conserve, enhance and maintain the natural, scenic, historical, agricultural, economic and recreational qualities of lands along the Willamette River as the Willamette River Greenway.

A. General
1. The qualities of the Willamette River Greenway shall be protected, conserved, enhanced and maintained consistent with the lawful uses present on December 6, 1975. Intensification of uses, changes in

use or developments may be permitted after this date only when they are consistent with the Willamette Greenway Statute, this goal, the interim goals in ORS 215. 515(1) and the statewide planning goals, as the case may be, and when such changes have been approved as provided in the Preliminary Greenway Plan or similar provisions in the completed plan as appropriate.

2. The Willamette Greenway Program shall be composed of cooperative local and state government plans for the protection, conservation, enhancement and maintenance of the Greenway, and of implementation measures including management through ordinances, rules, regulations, permits, grants as well as acquisition and development of property, etc. It shall also become a part of all other local and state plans and programs within and near the Greenway.

3. The Greenway Program shall include:

(a) Boundaries within which special Greenway considerations shall be taken into account;
(b) Management of uses on lands within and near the Greenway to maintain the qualities of the Greenway;
(c) Acquisition of lands or interests in lands from a donor or willing seller or as otherwise provided by law in areas where the public's need can be met by public ownership.

B. Inventories and Data

Information and data shall be collected to determine the nature and extent of the resources, uses and rights associated directly with the Willamette River Greenway. These inventories are for the purpose of determining which lands are suitable or necessary for inclusion within the Willamette River Greenway boundaries and to develop the plans and management and acquisition programs.

Each of the following items shall be inventoried[1] as it relates to the Greenway objectives:

1. All agricultural lands as provided in Goal 3. This includes all land currently in farm use as defined in ORS Chapter 215.203(2);

2. All current aggregate excavation and processing sites, and all known extractable aggregate sources;

3. All current public recreation sites, including public access points to the river and hunting and fishing areas;

4. Historical and archaeological sites;

5. Timber resources;

6. Significant natural and scenic areas, and vegetative cover;

7. Fish and wildlife habitats;

8. Areas of annual flooding and flood plains;

9. Land currently committed to industrial, commercial and residential uses;

10. The ownership of property, including riparian rights;

11. Hydrological conditions;

12. Ecologically fragile areas;

13. Recreational needs as set forth in Goal 8;

14. Other uses of land and water in or near the Greenway;

15. Acquisition areas which include the identification of areas suitable for protection or preservation through public acquisition of lands or an interest in land. Such acquisition areas shall include the following:

[1] When information on such items is not available through previous studies, information will be maintained by the agencies for those portions of the plan for which they are responsible. This requirement shall not limit units of government from collecting information on other items.

(a) Areas which may suitably be protected by scenic easements;
(b) Scenic and recreational land for exclusive use of the public;
(c) Sites for the preservation and restoration of historic places;
(d) Public access corridors;
(e) Public parks;
(f) Ecologically fragile areas; and
(g) Other areas which are desirable for public acquisition may also be identified if the reasons for public acquisition for the Greenway are also identified.

C. Considerations and Requirements

The Oregon Department of Transportation (DOT) Greenway Plan, the portions of each city and county comprehensive plan within the Greenway, the portions of plans and programs and implementation measures of all special districts, state and federal agencies within the Greenway shall be based on the following factors:

1. *General Considerations and Requirements*

(a) Statutory requirements in ORS Chapter 390.010 to 390.220 and in ORS Chapter 390.310 to 390.368;
(b) City, county and regional comprehensive plans adopted pursuant to ORS Chapter 197 for jurisdictions along the river;
(c) Statewide planning goals and guidelines adopted pursuant to ORS Chapter 197 by LCDC;
(d) Interim goals set forth in ORS Chapter 215.515(1).

2. *Boundary Considerations and Requirements.*[2] The temporary and preliminary Greenway boundaries shall be reviewed as to their appropriateness and refined as needed based on the information contained in the inventories. The refined boundaries shall include such lands along the Willamette River as are necessary to carry out the purpose and intent

of the Willamette River Greenway through a coordinated management and acquisition program.

Within farm areas, consideration shall be given to the ability of agricultural land adjacent to the Willamette River Greenway to enhance and protect the Greenway.

3. *Use Management Considerations and Requirements.* Plans and implementation measures shall provide for the following:

(a) Agricultural lands—The agricultural lands identified in the inventory shall be preserved and maintained as provided in Goal 3 as an effective means to carry out the purposes of the Greenway including those agricultural lands near the Greenway. Lands devoted to farm use which are not located in an exclusive farm use zone shall be allowed to continue in such farm use without restriction as provided in ORS 390.314(2)(c), ORS 390.332(4) and ORS 390.334(2);

(b) Recreation—
 (1) Local, regional and state recreational needs shall be provided for consistent with the carrying capacity of the land;
 (2) Zoning provisions shall allow recreational uses on lands to the extent that such use would not substantially interfere with the long-term capacity of the land for farm use as defined in ORS 215.203;

---

[2] See ORS Chapter 390.318 (1) for specific statutory language . . . "There shall be included within the boundaries of the Willamette River Greenway all lands situated within 150 feet from the ordinary low water line on each side of each channel of the Willamette River and such other lands along the Willamette River as the department and units of local government consider necessary for the development of such Greenway; however, the total area included within the boundaries of such Greenway shall not exceed, on the average, 320 acres per river mile along the Willamette River; however, for the purpose of computing the maximum acreage of lands within such Greenway, the acreage of lands situated on such islands and within state parks and recreation areas shall be excluded."

(3) The possibility that public recreation use might disturb adjacent property shall be considered and minimized to the greatest extent practicable;

(4) The public parks established by section 8a of Chapter 558, 1973 Oregon Laws, shall be set forth on the appropriate comprehensive plans and zoning established which will permit their development, use and maintenance;

(c) Access—Adequate public access to the river shall be provided for, with emphasis on urban and urbanizable areas;

(d) Fish and wildlife habitat—Significant fish and wildlife habitats shall be protected;

(e) Scenic qualities and views—identified scenic qualities and viewpoints shall be preserved;

(f) Protection and safety—The Willamette River Greenway Program shall provide for the maintenance of public safety and protection of public and private property, especially from vandalism and trespass in both rural and urban areas to the maximum extent practicable;

(g) Vegetative fringe—The natural vegetative fringe along the River shall be enhanced and protected to the maximum extent practicable;

(h) Timber resource—The partial harvest of timber shall be permitted beyond the vegetative fringes in areas not covered by a scenic easement when the harvest is consistent with an approved plan under the Forest Practices Act, or, if not covered by the Forest Practices Act, then with an approved plan under the Greenway compatibility review provisions. Such plan shall insure that the natural scenic qualities of the Greenway will be maintained to the greatest extent practicable or restored within a brief period of time;

(i) Aggregate extraction—Extraction of known aggregate deposits may be permitted when compatible with the purposes of the Willamette River Greenway and when economically feasible, subject to compliance with ORS 541. 605 to 541.695; ORS 517.750 to 517.900 and subject to compliance with local regulations designed to minimize adverse effects on water quality, fish and wildlife, vegetation, bank stabilization, streamflow, visual quality, noise, safety and to guarantee necessary reclamation;

(j) Development away from river—Developments shall be directed away from the river to the greatest possible degree; provided, however, lands committed to urban uses within the Greenway shall be permitted to continue as urban uses, including port, industrial, commercial and residential uses pertaining to navigational requirements, water and land access needs and related facilities;

(k) Greenway setback—A setback line will be established to keep structures separated from the river in order to protect, maintain, preserve and enhance the natural, scenic, historic and recreational qualities of the Willamette River Greenway, as identified in the Greenway Inventories. The setback line shall not apply to water-related or water-dependent uses.

4. Areas to be Acquired—Considerations and Requirements
Areas to be acquired must:

(a) Have potential to serve the purposes of the Greenway;

(b) To the maximum extent practicable, be consistent with non-interference or non-interruption of farm uses as defined in ORS Chapter 215.203(2);

(c) Be suitable for permitting the enforcement of existing statutes relating to trespass and vandalism along the Greenway, and be suitable for allowing

maintenance of the lands or interests acquired.

D. DOT Greenway Plan

The DOT will prepare and keep current, through appropriate revisions, a Greenway Plan setting forth the state interests in the Greenway. The plan will show:

1. The boundaries of the Willamette River Greenway;

2. The boundaries of the areas in which interests in property may be acquired. These shall be depicted clearly on maps or photographs together with the nature of the acquisition such as fee title or scenic easement; the general public purposes of each such area, and the conditions under which such acquisition may occur.

3. Use Intensity Classifications for the areas acquired by the State for Greenway purposes; and

4. The locations of public access, either already existing or to be acquired.

The DOT plan or revision thereto will be reviewed by the Land Conservation and Development Commission (LCDC) as provided in ORS 390.322. When the Commission has determined that the revision is consistent with the statutes and this goal it shall approve the plan for recording.

E. Comprehensive Plans of Cities and Counties

Each city and county in which the Willamette River Greenway is located, shall incorporate the portions of the approved DOT Greenway Plan in its comprehensive plan and implementing ordinances and other implementation measures.

1. *Boundaries:* Boundaries of the approved Willamette River Greenway shall be shown on every comprehensive plan.

2. *Uses:* Each comprehensive plan shall designate the uses to be permitted for the rural and urban areas of each jurisdiction, which uses shall be consistent with the

approved DOT Greenway Plan, the Greenway Statutes and this Goal.

3. *Acquisition Areas:* Each comprehensive plan shall designate areas identified for possible public acquisition and the conditions under which such acquisition may occur as set forth in the approved DOT Willamette Greenway Plan and any other area which the city or county intends to acquire.

F. Implementation Measures

Implementation of the Greenway Program shall occur through the cooperative efforts of state and local units of government and shall be consistent with the approved DOT Greenway Plan and the city and county comprehensive plans, the goals and appropriate statutes.

1. *Boundaries:* Willamette River Greenway boundaries shall be shown on city and county zoning maps and referred to in the zoning ordinance and the subdivision ordinance.

2. *Uses:* Measures for managing uses within the Greenway shall include at least:

(a) Exclusive farm use zoning of all agricultural land within and adjacent to the Greenway;

(b) Flood plain zoning of all areas subject to flooding;

(c) Open space zoning (see ORS Chapter 308.740) of all open space areas; and

(d) Provisions for the use management considerations and requirements set forth in C 3 of this Goal.

3. *Greenway Compatibility Review:* Cities and counties shall establish provisions by ordinance for the review of intensifications, changes of use or developments to insure their compatibility with the Willamette River Greenway. Such ordinances shall include the matters in (a) through (e) below:

(a) The establishment of Greenway compatibility review boundaries adjacent to the river within which review of developments shall take place. Such boundaries in urban areas shall be not less than 150 feet from the ordinary low water line of the Willamette River; in rural areas such boundaries shall include all lands within the boundaries of the Willamette River Greenway;

(b) The review of intensification, changes of use and developments as authorized by the Comprehensive Plan and zoning ordinance to insure their compatibility with the Greenway statutes and to insure that the best possible appearance, landscaping and public access are provided. Such review shall include the following findings, that to the greatest possible degree:

(1) The intensification, change of use or development will provide the maximum possible landscaped area, open space or vegetation between the activity and the river;

(2) Necessary public access will be provided to and along the river by appropriate legal means;

(c) Provision is made for at least one public hearing on each application to allow any interested person an opportunity to speak;

(d) Provision is made for giving notice of such hearing at least to owners of record of contiguous property and to any individual or groups requesting notice; and

(e) Provision is made to allow the imposing of conditions on the permit to carry out the purpose and intent of the Willamette River Greenway Statutes.

(f) As an alternative to the review procedures in subparagraphs 3 (a) to 3 (e), a city or county governing body may prepare and adopt, after public hearing and notice thereof to DOT, a design plan and administrative review procedure for a portion of the Greenway. Such design plan must provide for findings equivalent to those required in subparagraphs 3 (b)(1) and (2) of paragraph F so as to insure compatibility with the Greenway of proposed intensification, changes of use or developments. If this alternative procedure is adopted and approved by DOT and LCDC, a hearing will not be required on each individual application.

G. Notice of Proposed Intensification, Change of Use or Development

Government agencies, including cities, counties, state agencies, federal agencies, special districts, etc., shall not authorize or allow intensification, change of use or development on lands within the boundaries of the Willamette River Greenway compatibility review area established by cities and counties as required by paragraph F 3.a without first giving written notice to the DOT by immediately forwarding a copy of any application by certified mail—return receipt requested. Notice of the action taken by federal, state, city, county, and special districts on an application shall be furnished to DOT.

H. Agency Jurisdiction

Nothing in this order is intended to interfere with the duties, powers and responsibilities vested by statute in agencies to control or regulate activities on lands or waters within the boundaries of the Greenway so long as the exercise of the authority is consistent with the legislative policy set forth in ORS 390.310 to 390.368 and the applicable statewide planning goal for the Willamette River Greenway, as the case may be. An agency receiving an application for a permit to conduct an activity on lands or waters within the Greenway shall immediately forward a copy of such request to the Department of Transportation.

I. DOT Scenic Easements

Nothing in this Goal is intended to alter the authority of DOT to acquire property or a scenic easement therein as set forth in ORS 390.310 to 390.368.

J. Trespass by Public

Nothing in this Goal is intended to authorize public use of private property. Public use of private property is a trespass unless appropriate easements and access have been acquired in allowance with law to authorize such use.

K. Definitions for Willamette River Greenway Goal

1. *Change of Use* means making a different use of the land or water than that which existed on December 6, 1975. It includes a change which requires construction, alterations of the land, water or other areas outside of existing buildings or structures and which substantially alters or affects the land or water. It does not include a change of use of a building or other structure which does not substantially alter or affect the land or water upon which it is situated. Change of use shall not include the completion of a structure for which a valid permit had been issued as of December 6, 1975 and under which permit substantial construction has been undertaken by July 1, 1976. The sale of property is not in itself considered to be a change of use. An existing open storage area shall be considered to be the same as a building.

Landscaping, construction of driveways, modifications of existing structures, or the construction or placement of such subsidiary structures or facilities as are usual and necessary to the use and enjoyment of existing improvements shall not be considered a change of use for the purpose of this Goal.

2. *Lands Committed to Urban Use* means those lands upon which the economic, developmental and locational factors have,

when considered together, made the use of the property for other than urban purposes inappropriate. Economic, developmental and locational factors include such matters as ports, industrial, commercial, residential or recreational uses of property; the effect these existing uses have on properties in their vicinity, previous public decisions regarding the land in question, as contained in ordinances and such plans as the Lower Willamette River Management Plan, the city or county comprehensive plans and similar public actions.

3. *Intensification* means any additions which increase or expand the area or amount of an existing use, or the level of activity. Remodeling of the exterior of a structure not excluded below is an intensification when it will substantially alter the appearance of the structure. Intensification shall not include the completion of a structure for which a valid permit was issued as of December 6, 1975 and under which permit substantial construction has been undertaken by July 1, 1976. Maintenance and repair usual and necessary for the continuance of an existing use is not an intensification of use. Reasonable emergency procedures necessary for the safety or the protection of property are not an intensification of use. Residential use of lands within the Greenway includes the practices and activities customarily related to the use and enjoyment of one's home. Landscaping, construction of driveways, modifications of existing structures or construction or placement of such subsidiary structures or facilities adjacent to the residence as are usual and necessary to such use and enjoyment shall not be considered an intensification for the purposes of this Goal. Seasonal increases in gravel operations shall not be considered an intensification of use.

Goal 16: Estuarine Resources

Goal: To recognize and protect the unique environmental, economic, and social values of each estuary and associated wetlands; and

To protect, maintain, where appropriate develop, and where appropriate restore the long-term environmental, economic, and social values, diversity and benefits of Oregon's estuaries.

Comprehensive management programs to achieve these objectives shall be developed by appropriate local, state, and federal agencies for all estuaries.

To assure diversity among the estuaries of the State, by June 15, 1977, LCDC with the cooperation and participation of local governments, special districts, and state and federal agencies shall classify the Oregon estuaries to specify the most intensive level of development or alteration which may be allowed to occur within each estuary. After completion for all estuaries of the inventories and initial planning efforts, including identification of needs and potential conflicts among needs and goals and upon request of any coastal jurisdiction, the Commission will review the overall Oregon Estuary Classification.

Comprehensive plans and activities for each estuary shall provide for appropriate uses (including preservation) with as much diversity as is consistent with the overall Oregon Estuary Classification, as well as with the biological, economic, recreational, and aesthetic benefits of the estuary. Estuary plans and activities shall protect the estuarine ecosystem, including its natural biological productivity, habitat, diversity, unique features and water quality.

The general priorities (from highest to lowest) for management and use of estuarine resources as implemented through the management unit designation and permissible use requirements listed below shall be:

1. Uses which maintain the integrity of the estuarine ecosystem;
2. Water-dependent uses requiring estuarine location, as consistent with the overall Oregon Estuary Classification;
3. Water-related uses which do not degrade or reduce the natural estuarine resources and values;
4. Nondependent, nonrelated uses which do not alter, reduce or degrade estuarine resources and values.

Inventory Requirements

Inventories shall be conducted to provide information necessary for designating estuary uses and policies. These inventories shall provide information on the nature, location, and extent of physical, biological, social, and economic resources in sufficient detail to establish a sound basis for estuarine management and to enable the identification of areas for preservation and areas of exceptional potential for development.

State and federal agencies shall assist in the inventories of estuarine resources. The Department of Land Conservation and Development, with assistance from local government, state and federal agencies, shall establish common inventory standards and techniques, so that inventory data collected by different agencies or units of government, or data between estuaries, will be comparable.

Comprehensive Plan Requirements

Based upon inventories, the limits imposed by the overall Oregon Estuary Classification, and needs identified in the planning process, comprehensive plans for coastal areas shall:

1. Identify each estuarine area:
2. Describe and maintain the diversity of important and unique environmental, economic and social features within the estuary;

3. Classify the estuary into management units; and

4. Establish policies and use priorities for each management unit using the standards and procedures set forth below.

5. Consider and describe in the plan the potential cumulative impacts of the alterations and development activities envisioned. Such a description may be general but shall be based on the best available information and projections.

Management Units

Diverse resources, values, and benefits shall be maintained by classifying the estuary into distinct water use management units. When classifying estuarine areas into management units, the following shall be considered in addition to the inventories:

1. Adjacent upland characteristics and existing land uses;

2. Compatibility with adjacent uses.

3. Energy costs and benefits; and

4. The extent to which the limited water surface area of the estuary shall be committed to different surface uses.

As a minimum, the following kinds of management units shall be established:

1. *Natural*—In all estuaries, areas shall be designated to assure the protection of significant fish and wildlife habitats, of continued biological productivity within the estuary, and of scientific, research, and educational needs. These shall be managed to preserve the natural resources in recognition of dynamic, natural, geological, and evolutionary processes. Such areas shall include, at a minimum, all major tracts of salt marsh, tideflats, and seagrass and algae beds.

Permissible uses in natural management units shall include the following:

(a) undeveloped low-intensity, water-dependent recreation;

(b) research and educational observations;

(c) navigation aids, such as beacons and buoys;

(d) protection of habitat, nutrient, fish, wildlife and aesthetic resources;

(e) passive restoration measures;

(f) dredging necessary for on-site maintenance of existing functional tidegates and associated drainage channels and bridge crossing support structures;

(g) riprap for protection of uses existing as of October 7, 1977, unique natural resources, historical and archeological values; and public facilities; and

(h) bridge crossings.

Where consistent with the resource capabilities of the area and the purposes of this management unit the following uses may be allowed:

(a) aquaculture which does not involve dredge or fill or other estuarine alteration other than incidental dredging for harvest of benthic species or removable in-water structures such as stakes or racks;

(b) communication facilities;

(c) active restoration of fish and wildlife habitat or water quality and estuarine enhancement;

(d) boat ramps for public use where no dredging or fill for navigational access is needed; and,

(e) pipelines, cables and utility crossings, including incidental dredging necessary for their installation.

(f) installation of tidegates in existing functional dikes.

(g) temporary alterations.

(h) bridge crossing support structures and dredging necessary for their installation.

A use or activity is consistent with the resource capabilities of the area when either the impacts of the use on estuarine species, habitats, biological productivity and water quality are not significant or that the resources of the area are able to assimilate the use and activity and their effects and continue to function in a manner to protect significant wildlife habitats, natural biological productivity, and values for scientific research and education.

2. *Conservation*—In all estuaries, except those in the overall Oregon Estuary Classification which are classed for preservation, areas shall be designated for long-term uses of renewable resources that do not require major alteration of the estuary, except for the purpose of restoration. These areas shall be managed to conserve the natural resources and benefits. These shall include areas needed for maintenance and enhancement of biological productivity, recreational and aesthetic uses, and aquaculture. They shall include tracts of significant habitat smaller or of less biological importance than those in (1) above, and recreational or commercial oyster and clam beds not included in (1) above. Areas that are partially altered and adjacent to existing development of moderate intensity which do not possess the resource characteristics of natural or development units shall also be included in this classification.

Permissible uses in conservation management units shall be all uses listed in (1) above except temporary alterations.

Where consistent with the resource capabilities of the area and the purposes of this management unit the following uses may be allowed:

(a) high-intensity water-dependent recreation, including boat ramps, marinas and new dredging for boat ramps and marinas;
(b) minor navigational improvements;
(c) mining and mineral extraction, including dredging necessary for mineral extraction;
(d) other water dependent uses requiring occupation of water surface area by means other than dredge or fill;
(e) aquaculture requiring dredge or fill or other alteration of the estuary;

(f) active restoration for purposes other than those listed in 1(d).
(g) temporary alterations.

A use or activity is consistent with the resource capabilities of the area when either the impacts of the use on estuarine species, habitats, biological productivity, and water quality are not significant or that the resources of the area are able to assimilate the use and activity and their effects and continue to function in a manner which conserves long-term renewable resources, natural biologic productivity, recreational and aesthetic values and aquaculture.

3. *Development*—In estuaries classified in the overall Oregon Estuary Classification for more intense development or alteration, areas shall be designated to provide for navigation and other identified needs for public, commercial, and industrial water-dependent uses, consistent with the level of development or alteration allowed by the overall Oregon Estuary Classification. Such areas shall include deep-water areas adjacent or in proximity to the shoreline, navigation channels, subtidal areas for in-water disposal of dredged material and areas of minimal biological significance needed for uses requiring alteration of the estuary not included in (1) and (2) above.

Permissible uses in areas managed for water-dependent activities shall be navigation and water-dependent commercial and industrial uses.

As appropriate the following uses shall also be permissible in development management units:

(a) dredge or fill, as allowed elsewhere in the goal;
(b) navigation and water-dependent commercial enterprises and activities;
(c) water transport channels where dredging may be necessary;
(d) flow-lane disposal of dredged material monitored to assure that estuarine

sedimentation is consistent with the resource capabilities and purposes of affected natural and conservation management units.

(e) water storage areas where needed for products used in or resulting from industry, commerce, and recreation;

(f) marinas.

Where consistent with the purposes of this management unit and adjacent shorelands designated especially suited for water-dependent uses or designated for waterfront redevelopment, water-related and nondependent, nonrelated uses not requiring dredge or fill; mining and mineral extraction; and activities identified in (1) and (2) above shall also be appropriate.

In designating areas for these uses, local governments shall consider the potential for using upland sites to reduce or limit the commitment of the estuarine surface area for surface uses.

Implementation Requirements
1. Unless fully addressed during the development and adoption of comprehensive plans, actions which would potentially alter the estuarine ecosystem shall be preceded by a clear presentation of the impacts of the proposed alteration. Such activities include dredging, fill, in-water structures, riprap, log storage, application of pesticides and herbicides, water intake or withdrawal and effluent discharge, flow-lane disposal of dredged material, and other activities which could affect the estuary's physical processes or biological resources.

The impact assessment need not be lengthy or complex, but it should enable reviewers to gain a clear understanding of the impacts to be expected. It shall include information on:

(a) The type and extent of alterations expected;

(b) The type of resource(s) affected;

(c) The expected extent of impacts of the proposed alteration on water quality

and other physical characteristics of the estuary, living resources, recreation and aesthetic use, navigation and other existing and potential uses of the estuary; and

(d) The methods which could be employed to avoid or minimize adverse impacts.

2. Dredging and/or filling shall be allowed only:

(a) If required for navigation or other water-dependent uses that require an estuarine location or if specifically allowed by the applicable management unit requirements of this goal; and,

(b) if a need (i.e., a substantial public benefit) is demonstrated and the use or alteration does not unreasonably interfere with public trust rights; and

(c) if no feasible alternative upland locations exist; and,

(d) if adverse impacts are minimized.

Other uses and activities which could alter the estuary shall only be allowed if the requirements in (b), (c), and (d) are met. All or portions of these requirements may be applied at the time of plan development for actions identified in the plan. Otherwise, they shall be applied at the time of permit review.

3. State and federal agencies shall review, revise, and implement their plans, actions, and management authorities to maintain water quality and minimize man-induced sedimentation in estuaries. Local government shall recognize these authorities in managing lands rather than developing new or duplicatory management techniques or controls.

Existing programs which shall be utilized include:

(a) The Oregon Forest Practices Act and Administrative Rules, for forest lands as defined in ORS 527.610-527.730 and 527.990 and the Forest Lands Goal;

(b) The programs of the Soil and Water Conservation Commission and local districts and the Soil Conservation Service, for Agricultural Lands Goal;

(c) The nonpoint source discharge water quality program administered by the Department of Environmental Quality under Section 208 of the Federal Water Quality Act as amended in 1972 (PL 92-500); and

(d) The Fill and Removal Permit Program administered by the Division of State Lands under ORS 541.605-541.665.

4. The State Water Policy Review Board, assisted by the staff of the Oregon Department of Water Resources, and the Oregon Department of Fish and Wildlife, the Oregon Department of Environmental Quality, the Division of State Lands, and the U.S. Geological Survey, shall consider establishing minimum fresh-water flow rates and standards so that resources and uses of the estuary, including navigation, fish and wildlife characteristics, and recreation, will be maintained.

5. When dredge or fill activities are permitted in intertidal or tidal marsh areas, their effects shall be mitigated by creation, restoration or enhancement of another area to ensure that the integrity of the estuarine ecosystem is maintained. Comprehensive plans shall designate and protect specific sites for mitigation which generally correspond to the types and quantity of intertidal area proposed for dredging or filling, or make findings demonstrating that it is not possible to do so.

6. Local government and state and federal agencies shall develop comprehensive programs, including specific sites and procedures for disposal and stockpiling of dredged materials. These programs shall encourage the disposal of dredged material in uplands or ocean waters, and shall permit disposal in estuary waters only where such disposal will clearly be consistent with the objectives of this goal and state and federal law. Dredged material shall not be disposed in intertidal or tidal marsh estuarine areas unless part of an approved fill project.

7. Local government and state and federal agencies shall act to restrict the proliferation of individual single-purpose docks and piers by encouraging community facilities common to several uses and interests. The size and shape of a dock or pier shall be limited to that required for the intended use. Alternatives to docks and piers, such as mooring buoys, dryland storage, and launching ramps shall be investigated and considered.

8. State and federal agencies shall assist local government in identifying areas for restoration. Restoration is appropriate in areas where activities have adversely affected some aspect of the estuarine system, and where it would contribute to a greater achievement of the objective of this goal. Appropriate sites include areas of heavy erosion or sedimentation, degraded fish and wildlife habitat, anadromous fish spawning areas, abandoned diked estuarine marsh areas, and areas where water quality restricts the use of estuarine waters for fish and shellfish harvest and production, or for human recreation.

9. State agencies with planning, permit, or review authorities affected by this goal shall review their procedures and standards to assure that the objectives and requirements of the goal are fully addressed. In estuarine areas the following authorities are of special concern:

Division of State Lands
Fill and Removal Law	ORS 541.605 -ORS 541.665
Mineral Resources	ORS 273.551; ORS 273.775-273.780

Submersible and
Submerged Lands   ORS 274.005
-274.940

Economic Development Department
Ports Planning   ORS 777.835

Water Resources Department
Appropriation of   ORS 537.010-
Water   537.990
ORS 543.010-543.620

Department of Geology and Mineral Industries
Mineral Extraction   ORS 520.005
Oil and Gas Drilling   -520.095

Department of Forestry
Forest Practices Act   ORS 527.610
-527.730

Department of Energy
Regulation of Thermal
Power and Nuclear   ORS 469.300
Installation   -469.570

Department of Environmental Quality
Water Quality   ORS 468.700
-468.775

Sewage Treatment   ORS 454.010
and Disposal   -454.755
Systems

Goal 17: Coastal Shorelands

Goal: To conserve, protect, where appropriate, develop and where appropriate restore the resources and benefits of all coastal shorelands, recognizing their value for protection and maintenance of water quality, fish and wildlife habitat, water-dependent uses, economic resources and recreation and aesthetics. The management of these shoreland areas shall be compatible

with the characteristics of the adjacent coastal waters; and

To reduce the hazard to human life and property, and the adverse effects upon water quality and fish and wildlife habitat, resulting from the use and enjoyment of Oregon's coastal shorelands.

Programs to achieve these objectives shall be developed by local, state, and federal agencies having jurisdiction over coastal shorelands.

Land use plans, implementing actions and permit reviews shall include consideration of the critical relationships between coastal shorelands and resources of coastal waters, and of the geologic and hydrologic hazards associated with coastal shorelands. Local, state and federal agencies shall within the limit of their authorities maintain the diverse environmental, economic, and social values of coastal shorelands and water quality in coastal waters. Within those limits, they shall also minimize man-induced sedimentation in estuaries, nearshore ocean waters, and coastal lakes.

General priorities for the overall use of coastal shorelands (from highest to lowest) shall be to:

1. Promote uses which maintain the integrity of estuaries and coastal waters;
2. Provide for water-dependent uses;
3. Provide for water-related uses;
4. Provide for nondependent, nonrelated uses which retain flexibility of future use and do not prematurely or inalterably commit shorelands to more intensive uses;
5. Provide for development, including nondependent, nonrelated uses, in urban areas compatible with existing or committed uses;
6. Permit nondependent, nonrelated uses which cause a permanent or long-term change in the features of coastal shorelands only upon a demonstration of public need.

Inventory Requirements

Inventories shall be conducted to provide information necessary for identifying coastal shorelands and designating uses and policies. These inventories shall provide information on the nature, location, and extent of geologic and hydrologic hazards and shoreland values, including fish and wildlife habitat, water-dependent uses, economic resources, recreational uses, and aesthetics in sufficient detail to establish a sound basis for land and water use management.

The inventory requirements shall be applied within an area known as a coastal shorelands planning area. This planning area is not an area within which development or use is prohibited. It is an area for inventory, study, and initial planning for development and use to meet the Coastal Shorelands Goal.

The planning area shall be defined by the following:

1. All lands west of the Oregon Coast Highway as described in ORS 366.235, except that:

(a) In Tillamook County, only the lands west of a line formed by connecting the western boundaries of the following described roadways: Brooten Road (County Road 887) northerly from its junction with the Oregon Coast Highway to Pacific City, Mc-Phillips Drive (County Road 915) northerly from Pacific City to its junction with Sandlake Road (County Road 871), Sandlake-Cape Lookout Road, (County Road 871) northerly to its junction with Cape Lookout Park, Netarts Bay Drive (County Road 665) northerly from its junction with the Sandlake-Cape Lookout Road (County Road 871) to its junction at Netarts with State Highway 131, and northerly along State Highway 131 to its junction with the Oregon Coast Highway near Tillamook.

(b) In Coos County, only the lands west of a line formed by connecting the western boundaries of the following described roadways: Oregon State 240, Cape Arago Secondary (FAS 263) southerly from its junction with the Oregon Coast Highway to Charleston; Seven Devils Road (County Road 33) southerly from its junction with Oregon State 240 (FAS 263) to its junction with the Oregon Coast Highway, near Bandon;

and

2. All lands within an area defined by a line measured horizontally

(a) 1000 feet from the shoreline of estuaries; and

(b) 500 feet from the shoreline of coastal lakes.

Comprehensive Plan Requirements

Based upon inventories, comprehensive plans for coastal areas adjacent to the ocean, estuaries, or coastal lakes shall:

1. Identify coastal shorelands;
2. Establish policies and uses of coastal shorelands in accordance with standards set forth below:

Identification of Coastal Shorelands

Lands contiguous with the ocean, estuaries, and coastal lakes shall be identified as coastal shorelands. The extent of shorelands shall include at least:

1. Areas subject to ocean flooding and lands within 100 feet of the ocean shore or within 50 feet of an estuary or a coastal lake;
2. Adjacent areas of geologic instability where the geologic instability is related to or will impact a coastal water body;
3. Natural or man-made riparian resources, especially vegetation necessary to stabilize the shoreline and to maintain water quality and temperature necessary for the maintenance of fish habitat and spawning areas;

4. Areas of significant shoreland and wetland biological habitats whose habitat quality is primarily derived from or related to the association with coastal water areas;

5. Areas necessary for water-dependent and water-related uses, including areas of recreational importance which utilize coastal water or riparian resources, areas appropriate for navigation and port facilities, dredge material disposal and mitigation sites, and areas having characteristics suitable for aquaculture;

6. Areas of exceptional aesthetic or scenic quality, where the quality is primarily derived from or related to the association with coastal water areas; and

7. Coastal headlands.

Coastal Shoreland Uses

1. Major marshes, significant wildlife habitat, coastal headlands, and exceptional aesthetic resources inventoried in the Identification Section, shall be protected. Uses in these areas shall be consistent with protection of natural values. Such uses may include propagation and selective harvesting of forest products consistent with the Oregon Forest Practices Act, grazing, harvesting, wild crops, and low intensity water-dependent recreation.

2. Shorelands in urban and urbanizable areas and in rural areas built upon or irrevocably committed to non-resource use especially suited for water-dependent uses shall be protected for water-dependent recreational, commercial and industrial uses. Some factors which contribute to this special suitability are:

(a) deep water close to shore with supporting land transport facilities suitable for ship and barge facilities;
(b) potential for aquaculture;
(c) protected areas subject to scour which would require little dredging for use as marinas; and
(d) potential for recreational utilization of coastal water or riparian resources.

Other uses which may be permitted in these areas are temporary uses which involve minimal capital investment and no permanent structures, or a use in conjunction with and incidental to a water-dependent use.

3. Local governments shall determine whether there are any existing, developed commercial/industrial waterfront areas which are suitable for redevelopment which are not designated as especially suited for water-dependent uses. Plans shall be prepared for these areas which allow for a mix of water-dependent, water-related, and water oriented nondependent uses and shall provide for public access to the shoreline.

4. Shorelands in rural areas other than those built upon or irrevocably committed to nonresource use and those designated in (1) above shall be used as appropriate for:

(a) farm uses as provided in ORS Chapter 215;
(b) propagation and harvesting of forest products consistent with the Oregon Forest Practices Act;
(c) private and public water-dependent recreation developments;
(d) aquaculture;
(e) water-dependent, commercial and industrial uses, water-related uses and other uses only upon a finding by the county that such uses satisfy a need which cannot be accommodated on uplands or in urban and urbanizable areas or in rural areas built upon or irrevocably committed to non-resource use.

Implementation Requirements

1. The Oregon Department of Forestry shall recognize the unique and special values provided by coastal shorelands when developing standards and policies to regulate uses of forest lands within

coastal shorelands. With other state and federal agencies, the Department of Forestry shall develop forest management practices and policies including, where necessary, amendments to the FPA rules and programs which protect and maintain the special shoreland values and forest uses especially for natural shorelands and riparian vegetation.

2. Local government, with assistance from state and federal agencies, shall identify coastal shoreland areas which may be used to fulfill the mitigation requirement of the Estuarine Resources Goal. These areas shall be protected from new uses and activities which would prevent their ultimate restoration or addition to the estuarine ecosystem.

3. Coastal shorelands identified under the Estuarine Resources Goal for dredged material disposal shall be protected from new uses and activities which would prevent their ultimate use for dredged material disposal.

4. Because of the importance of the vegetative fringe adjacent to coastal waters to water quality, fish and wildlife habitat, recreational use and aesthetic resources, riparian vegetation shall be maintained; and where appropriate, restored and enhanced, consistent with water-dependent uses.

5. Land-use management practices and nonstructural solutions to problems or erosion and flooding shall be preferred to structural solutions. Where shown to be necessary, water and erosion control structures, such as jetties, bulkheads, seawalls, and similar protective structures; and fill, whether located in the waterways or on shorelands above ordinary high water mark, shall be designed to minimize adverse impacts on water currents, erosion, and accretion patterns.

6. Local government in coordination with the Parks and Recreation Division shall develop and implement a program to provide increased public access. Existing public ownerships, rights of way, and similar public easements in coastal shorelands which provide access to or along coastal waters shall be retained or replaced if sold, exchanged or transferred. Rights of way may be vacated to permit redevelopment of shoreland areas provided public access across the affected site is retained.

Goal 18: Beaches and Dunes

Goal: To conserve, protect, where appropriate develop, and where appropriate restore the resources and benefits of coastal beach and dune areas; and

To reduce the hazard to human life and property from natural or man-induced actions associated with these areas.

Coastal comprehensive plans and implementing actions shall provide for diverse and appropriate use of beach and dune areas consistent with their ecological, recreational, aesthetic, water resource, and economic values, and consistent with the natural limitations of beaches, dunes, and dune vegetation for development.

Inventory Requirements

Inventories shall be conducted to provide information necessary for identifying and designating beach and dune uses and policies. Inventories shall describe the stability, movement, groundwater resource, hazards and values of the beach and dune areas in sufficient detail to establish a sound basis for planning and management. For beach and dune areas adjacent to coastal waters, inventories shall also address the inventory requirements of the Coastal Shorelands Goal.

Comprehensive Plan Requirements

Based upon the inventory, comprehensive plans for coastal areas shall:

1. Identify beach and dune areas; and

2. Establish policies and uses for these areas consistent with the provisions of this goal.

Identification of Beaches and Dunes

Coastal areas subject to this goal shall include beaches, active dune forms, recently stabilized dune forms, older stabilized dune forms and interdune forms.

Uses

Uses shall be based on the capabilities and limitations of beach and dune areas to sustain different levels of use or development, and the need to protect areas of critical environmental concern, areas having scenic, scientific, or biological importance, and significant wildlife habitat as identified through application of Goals 5 and 17.

Implementation Requirements

1. Local governments and state and federal agencies shall base decisions on plans, ordinances and land use actions in beach and dune areas, other than older stabilized dunes, on specific findings that shall include at least:

   (a) The type of use proposed and the adverse effects it might have on the site and adjacent areas;

   (b) Temporary and permanent stabilization programs and the planned maintenance of new and existing vegetation;

   (c) Methods for protecting the surrounding area from any adverse effects of the development; and

   (d) Hazards to life, public and private property, and the natural environment which may be caused by the proposed use.

2. Local governments and state and federal agencies shall prohibit residential developments and commercial and industrial buildings on beaches, active foredunes, on other foredunes which are conditionally stable and that are subject to ocean undercutting or wave overtopping, and on interdune areas (deflation plains) that are subject to ocean flooding. Other development in these areas shall be permitted only if the findings required in *(1)* above are presented and it is demonstrated that the proposed development:

   (a) Is adequately protected from any geologic hazards, wind erosion, undercutting, ocean flooding and storm waves; or is of minimal value; and

   b) Is designed to minimize adverse environmental effects.

3. Local governments and state and federal agencies shall regulate actions in beach and dune areas to minimize the resulting erosion. Such actions include, but are not limited to, the destruction of desirable vegetation (including inadvertent destruction by moisture loss or root damage), the exposure of stable and conditionally stable areas to erosion, and construction of shore structures which modify current or wave patterns leading to beach erosion.

4. Local, state and federal plans, implementing actions and permit reviews shall protect the groundwater from drawdown which would lead to loss of stabilizing vegetation, loss of water quality, or intrusion of salt water into water supplies. Building permits for single family dwellings are exempt from this requirement if appropriate findings are provided in the comprehensive plan or at the time of subdivision approval.

5. Permits for beachfront protective structures shall be issued only where development existed on January 1, 1977. Local comprehensive plans shall identify areas where development existed on January 1, 1977. For the purposes of this requirement and Implementation Requirement

7 "development" means houses, commercial and industrial buildings, and vacant subdivision lots which are physically improved through construction of streets and provision of utilities to the lot and includes areas where an exception to *(2)* above has been approved.

The criteria for review of all shore and beachfront protective structures shall provide that:

(a) visual impacts are minimized;
(b) necessary access to the beach is maintained;
(c) negative impacts on adjacent property are minimized; and
(d) long-term or recurring costs to the public are avoided.

6. Foredunes shall be breached only to replenish sand supply in interdune areas, or on a temporary basis in an emergency (e.g., fire control, cleaning up oil spills, draining farm lands, and alleviating flood hazards), and only if the breaching and restoration after breaching is consistent with sound principles of conservation.

7. Grading or sand movement necessary to maintain views or to prevent sand inundation may be allowed for structures in foredune areas only if the area is committed to development and only as part of an overall plan for managing foredune grading. A foredune grading plan shall include the following elements based on consideration of factors affecting the stability of the shoreline to be managed including sources of sand, ocean flooding, and patterns of accretion and erosion (including wind erosion), and effects of beachfront protective structures and jetties. The plan shall:

(a) Cover an entire beach and foredune area subject to an accretion problem, including adjacent areas potentially affected by changes in flooding, erosion, or accretion as a result of dune grading;

(b) Specify minimum dune height and width requirements to be maintained for protection from flooding and erosion. The minimum height for flood protection is 4 feet above the 100 year flood elevation;
(c) Identify and set priorities for low and narrow dune areas which need to be built up;
(d) Prescribe standards for redistribution of sand and temporary and permanent stabilization measures including the timing of these activities; and
(e) Prohibit removal of sand from the beach-foredune system.

The Commission shall, by January 1, 1987, evaluate plans and actions which implement this requirement and determine whether or not they have interfered with maintaining the integrity of beach and dune areas and minimize flooding and erosion problems. If the Commission determines that these measures have interfered it shall initiate Goal amendment proceedings to revise or repeal these requirements.

Goal 19: Ocean Resources
Goal: To conserve the long-term values, benefits, and natural resources of the nearshore ocean and the continental shelf.

All local, state, and federal plans, policies, projects, and activities which affect the territorial sea shall be developed, managed and conducted to maintain, and where appropriate, enhance and restore, the long-term benefits derived from the nearshore oceanic resources of Oregon. Since renewable ocean re-

sources and uses, such as food production, water quality, navigation, recreation, and aesthetic enjoyment, will provide greater long-term benefits than will nonrenewable resources, such plans and activities shall give clear priority to the proper management and protection of renewable resources.

Inventory Requirements

As state and federal agencies develop and implement plans or carry out actions, projects, or activities related to or affecting ocean resources, they shall develop inventory information necessary to understand the impacts and relationship of the proposed activity to continental shelf and nearshore ocean resources. As specific actions are proposed, inventory information shall be gathered by the unit of government considering the action with assistance from those agencies and governments which use or manage the resources. The inventory shall be sufficient to describe the long-term impacts of the proposed action on resources and uses of the continental shelf and nearshore ocean.

Implementation Requirements

1. State and federal agencies with planning, permit, or review authorities affected by the Ocean Resources Goal shall review their procedures and standards to assure that the objectives and requirements of the goal are fully addressed. The following authorities are of special concern:

Division of State Lands
Fill and Removal Law   ORS 541.605
                        -541.665
Mineral Resources   ORS 273.775
                        -273.780
Submersible and   ORS 274.005
  Submerged Lands   -274.940
Kelp Law   ORS 274.885
                        -274.895

Economic Development Department
Ports Planning   ORS 777.835

Department of Geology & Mineral Industries
Mineral Extraction and ORS 520.005
  Oil & Gas Drilling   -520.095

Department of Energy
Regulation of Thermal
  Power & Nuclear   ORS 469.300
  Installation   -469.570

Department of Environmental Quality
Water Quality Permits   ORS 468.700
                        -468.775
Oil Spillage Regulation ORS 468.780
                        -468.815

Department of Fish and Wildlife
Fisheries Regulation   ORS Chapter 506

2. Each state and federal agency, special district, city and county within the limits of its jurisdiction and as necessary to:

   i.   determine the impact of proposed projects or actions; and
   ii. for the sound conservation of ocean resources; shall:

a. *Fishery Resources*
   i.   Develop scientific information on the stocks and life histories of commercially, recreationally, and ecologically important species of fish, shellfish, marine mammals and other marine fauna.
   ii. Designate and enforce fishing regulations to maintain the optimum sustainable yield (OSY) while protecting the natural marine ecosystem.
   iii. Develop and encourage improved fishing practices and equipment to achieve the OSY while protecting the natural marine ecosystem.
   iv. Develop scientific understanding of the effects of man's activities, including navigation, mineral

extraction, recreation, and waste discharge, on the marine ecosystem.

b. *Biological Habitat*
  i. Identify and protect areas of important biological habitat, including kelp and other algae beds, seagrass beds, rock reef areas and areas of important fish, shellfish and invertebrate concentration.
  ii. Identify and protect important feeding areas; spawning areas; nurseries; migration routes; and other biologically important areas of marine mammals, marine birds, and commercially and recreationally important fish and shellfish.
  iii. Determine and protect the integrity of the marine ecosystem, including its natural biological productivity and diversity.

c. *Navigation and Ports*
  i. Determine for the state as a whole, the navigation needs for the coast of Oregon. Such needs will reflect, in part, the capability of each port to handle differing types of ship traffic, consistent with other state-wide planning goals.
  ii. Maintain appropriate navigation lanes and facilities free from interference by other uses to provide safe transportation along and to the Oregon Coast.

d. *Aesthetic Use*—Maintain the aesthetic enjoyment and experiences provided by ocean resources.

e. *Recreation*—Identify, maintain, and enhance the diversity, quality, and quantity of recreational opportunities on and over the Oregon continental shelf, as consistent with the Beaches and Dunes Goal and Estuarine Resources Goal.

f. *Waste Discharge and Mineral Extraction*—Provide that extraction of materials from or discharge of waste products into or affecting the Oregon territorial sea do not substantially interfere with or detract from the use of the continental shelf for fishing, navigation, recreation, or aesthetic purposes, or from the long-term protection of renewable resources.

g. *Dredged Material Disposal*—Provide for suitable sites and practices for the open sea discharge of dredged materials, which do not substantially interfere with or detract from the use of the continental shelf for fishing, navigation, or recreation, or from the long-term protection of renewable resources.

h. *Archaeological Sites*—Identify and protect, whenever possible, significant underwater archaeological sites of the continental shelf.

3. *Contingency Plans*
  Before issuing permits for development on the Oregon continental shelf, state and federal agencies, in coordination with the permittee, shall establish contingency plans and emergency procedures to be followed in the event that the operation results in conditions which threaten to damage the environment.

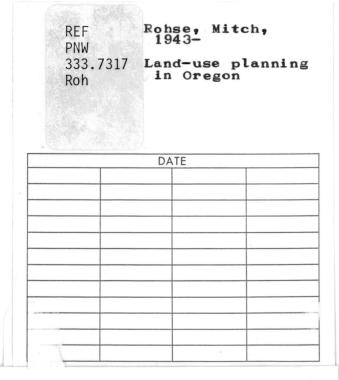

DATE			